ALBERT EINSTEIN
In His Own Words

TWO COMPLETE BOOKS

Relativity
The Special and the General Theory

Out of My Later Years
The Scientist, Philosopher and Man
Portrayed Through His Own Words

PORTLAND HOUSE

This 2000 edition is published by Portland House, an imprint of Random House
Value Publishing, Inc., 201 East 50th Street, New York, N.Y. 10022
by arrangement with Allied Books Ltd.

This edition is to be sold only in the United States of America
and may not be sold anywhere in the British Empire.

Random House
New York • Toronto • London • Sydney • Auckland
http://www.randomhouse.com/

Publisher's Note for Out of My Later Years

The Einstein Estate has requested that we revise the 1950 edition by
replacing Chapter 12 with a complete translation. Chapter 12 in the
1950 edition entitled "Time, Space and Gravitation" (1948) is not complete.
The complete translation in this reprint edition was originally published
in the London Times (November 28, 1919).

Printed and bound in the United States of America

ISBN 0-517-20984-5

8 7 6 5 4 3 2 1

Albert Einstein: In His Own Words

Contents

Part I
The Special Theory of Relativity

Part II
The General Theory of Relativity

Part III
Considerations on the Universe as a Whole

Appendices

Convictions and Beliefs

Science

Physics and Reality (1936)

Public Affairs

Science and Life

Military Intrusion in Science (1947)

Personalities

My People

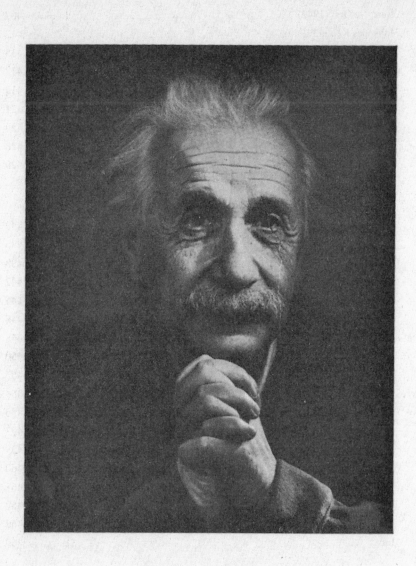

A. Einstein.

RELATIVITY

The Special and the General Theory

★

A Popular Exposition by

ALBERT EINSTEIN

Late Institute for Advanced Study, Princeton, New Jersey

★

Authorised Translation by

ROBERT W. LAWSON
University of Sheffield

PORTLAND HOUSE

Preface

The present book is intended, as far as possible, to give an exact insight into the theory of Relativity to those readers who, from a general scientific and philosophical point of view, are interested in the theory, but who are not conversant with the mathematical apparatus of theoretical physics. The work presumes a standard of education corresponding to that of a university matriculation examination, and, despite the shortness of the book, a fair amount of patience and force of will on the part of the reader. The author has spared himself no pains in his endeavour to present the main ideas in the simplest and most intelligible form, and on the whole, in the sequence and connection in which they actually originated. In the interest of clearness, it appeared to me inevitable that I should repeat myself frequently, without paying the slightest attention to the elegance of the presentation. I adhered scrupulously to the precept of that brilliant theoretical physicist L. Boltzmann, according to whom matters of elegance ought to be left to the tailor and to the cobbler. I make no pretence of having withheld from the reader diffculties which are inherent to the subject. On the other hand, I have purposely treated the empirical physical foundations of the theory in a "step-motherly" fashion, so that readers unfamiliar with physics may not feel like the wanderer who was unable to see the forest for trees. May the book bring some one a few happy hours of suggestive thought!

December 1916   A. EINSTEIN

Note to
the Fifteenth Edition

In this edition I have added, as a fifth appendix, a presentaton of my views on the problem of space in general and on the gradual modifications of our ideas on space resulting from the influence of the relativistic view-point. I wished to show that space-time is not necessarily something to which one can ascribe a separate existence, independently of the actual objects of physical reality. Physical objects are not *in space*, but these objects are *spatially extended*. In this way the concept "empty space" loses its meaning.

A. EINSTEIN

June 9th, 1952

Contents

Part I
The Special Theory of Relativity

Part II
The General Theory of Relativity

Part III
Considerations on the Universe as a Whole

Appendices

Plates

THE AUTHOR, 1920

Drawn by Hermann Struck

Part I

The Special Theory of Relativity

ONE

Physical Meaning
of Geometrical Propositions

In your schooldays most of you who read this book made
acquaintance with the noble building of Euclid's geometry, and you remember—perhaps with more respect than
love—the magnificent structure, on the lofty staircase of which
you were chased about for uncounted hours by conscientious
teachers. By reason of your past experience, you would certainly regard everyone with disdain who should pronounce
even the most out-of-the-way proposition of this science to be
untrue. But perhaps this feeling of proud certainty would leave
you immediately if some one were to ask you: "What, then, do
you mean by the assertion that these propositions are true?"
Let us proceed to give this question a little consideration.

Geometry sets out from certain conceptions such as "plane,"
"point," and "straight line," with which we are able to associate more or less definite ideas, and from certain simple propositions (axioms) which, in virtue of these ideas, we are
inclined to accept as "true." Then, on the basis of a logical process, the justification of which we feel ourselves compelled to
admit, all remaining propositions are shown to follow from

those axioms, *i.e.* they are proven. A proposition is then correct ("true") when it has been derived in the recognised manner from the axioms. The question of the "truth" of the individual geometrical propositions is thus reduced to one of the "truth" of the axioms. Now it has long been known that the last question is not only unanswerable by the methods of geometry, but that it is in itself entirely without meaning. We cannot ask whether it is true that only one straight line goes through two points. We can only say that Euclidean geometry deals with things called "straight lines," to each of which is ascribed the property of being uniquely determined by two points situated on it. The concept "true" does not tally with the assertions of pure geometry, because by the word "true" we are eventually in the habit of designating always the correspondence with a "real" object; geometry, however, is not concerned with the relation of the ideas involved in it to objects of experience, but only with the logical connection of these ideas among themselves.

It is not difficult to understand why, in spite of this, we feel constrained to call the propositions of geometry "true." Geometrical ideas correspond to more or less exact objects in nature, and these last are undoubtedly the exclusive cause of the genesis of those ideas. Geometry ought to refrain from such a course, in order to give to its structure the largest possible logical unity. The practice, for example, of seeing in a "distance" two marked positions on a practically rigid body is something which is lodged deeply in our habit of thought. We are accustomed further to regard three points as being situated on a straight line, if their apparent positions can be made to coincide for observation with one eye, under suitable choice of our place of observation.

If, in pursuance of our habit of thought, we now supplement the propositions of Euclidean geometry by the single proposition that two points on a practically rigid body always correspond to the same distance (line-interval), independently of any changes in position to which we may subject the body, the propositions of Euclidean geometry then resolve themselves into propositions on the possible relative position of practically rigid bodies.[1] Geometry which has been supplemented in this way is then to be treated as a branch of physics. We can now legitimately ask as to the "truth" of geometrical propositions interpreted in this way, since we are justified in asking whether these propositions are satisfied for those real things we have associated with the geometrical ideas. In less exact terms we can express this by saying that by the "truth" of a geometrical proposition in this sense we understand its validity for a construction with ruler and compasses.

Of course the conviction of the "truth" of geometrical propositions in this sense is founded exclusively on rather incomplete experience. For the present we shall assume the "truth" of the geometrical propositions, then at a later stage (in the general theory of relativity) we shall see that this "truth" is limited, and we shall consider the extent of its limitation.

---

[1] It follows that a natural object is associated also with a straight line. Three points A, B and C on a rigid body thus lie in a straight line when, the points A and C being given, B is chosen such that the sum of the distances $A\,B$ and $B\,C$ is as short as possible. This incomplete suggestion will suffice for our present purpose.

TWO

The System of
Co-ordinates

On the basis of the physical interpretation of distance which has been indicated, we are also in a position to establish the distance between two points on a rigid body by means of measurements. For this purpose we require a "distance" (rod S) which is to be used once and for all, and which we employ as a standard measure. If, now, A and B are two points on a rigid body, we can construct the line joining them according to the rules of geometry; then, starting from A, we can mark off the distance S time after time until we reach B. The number of these operations required is the numerical measure of the distance $A\,B$. This is the basis of all measurement of length.[1]

Every description of the scene of an event or of the position of an object in space is based on the specification of the point on a rigid body (body of reference) with which that event or object coincides. This applies not only to scientific descrip-

---

[1] Here we have assumed that there is nothing left over, *i.e.* that the measurement gives a whole number. This difficulty is got over by the use of divided measuring-rods, the introduction of which does not demand any fundamentally new method.

tion, but also to everyday life. If I analyse the place specification "Trafalgar Square, London,"[1] I arrive at the following result. The earth is the rigid body to which the specification of place refers; "Trafalgar Square, London," is a well-defined point, to which a name has been assigned, and with which the event coincides in space.[2]

This primitive method of place specification deals only with places on the surface of rigid bodies, and is dependent on the existence of points on this surface which are distinguishable from each other. But we can free ourselves from both of these limitations without altering the nature of our specification of position. If, for instance, a cloud is hovering over Trafalgar Square, then we can determine its position relative to the surface of the earth by erecting a pole perpendicularly on the Square, so that it reaches the cloud. The length of the pole measured with the standard measuring-rod, combined with the specification of the position of the foot of the pole, supplies us with a complete place specification. On the basis of this illustration, we are able to see the manner in which a refinement of the conception of position has been developed.

(a) We imagine the rigid body, to which the place specification is referred, supplemented in such a manner that the object whose position we require is reached by the completed rigid body.

[1] I have chosen this as being more familiar to the English reader than the "Potsdamer Platz, Berlin," which is referred to in the original. (R. W. L.)

[2] It is not necessary here to investigate further the significance of the expression "coincidence in space." This conception is sufficiently obvious to ensure that differences of opinion are scarcely likely to arise as to its applicability in practice.

(b) In locating the position of the object, we make use of a number (here the length of the pole measured with the measuring-rod) instead of designated points of reference.

(c) We speak of the height of the cloud even when the pole which reaches the cloud has not been erected. By means of optical observations of the cloud from different positions on the ground, and taking into account the properties of the propagation of light, we determine the length of the pole we should have required in order to reach the cloud.

From this consideration we see that it will be advantageous if, in the description of position, it should be possible by means of numerical measures to make ourselves independent of the existence of marked positions (possessing names) on the rigid body of reference. In the physics of measurement this is attained by the application of the Cartesian system of co-ordinates.

This consists of three plane surfaces perpendicular to each other and rigidly attached to a rigid body. Referred to a system of co-ordinates, the scene of any event will be determined (for the main part) by the specification of the lengths of the three perpendiculars or co-ordinates (x, y, z) which can be dropped from the scene of the event to those three plane surfaces. The lengths of these three perpendiculars can be determined by a series of manipulations with rigid measuring-rods performed according to the rules and methods laid down by Euclidean geometry.

In practice, the rigid surfaces which constitute the system of co-ordinates are generally not available; furthermore, the magnitudes of the co-ordinates are not actually determined by constructions with rigid rods, but by indirect means. If the results of physics and astronomy are to maintain their clearness, the physical meaning of specifications of position must always be sought in accordance with the above considerations.[1]

We thus obtain the following result: Every description of events in space involves the use of a rigid body to which such events have to be referred. The resulting relationship takes for granted that the laws of Euclidean geometry hold for "distances," the "distance" being represented physically by means of the convention of two marks on a rigid body.

[1] A refinement and modification of these views does not become necessary until we come to deal with the general theory of relativity, treated in the second part of this book.

THREE

Space and Time in Classical Mechanics

The purpose of mechanics is to describe how bodies change their position in space with "time." I should load my conscience with grave sins against the sacred spirit of lucidity were I to formulate the aims of mechanics in this way, without serious reflection and detailed explanations. Let us proceed to disclose these sins.

It is not clear what is to be understood here by "position" and "space." I stand at the window of a railway carriage which is travelling uniformly, and drop a stone on the embankment, without throwing it. Then, disregarding the influence of the air resistance, I see the stone descend in a straight line. A pedestrian who observes the misdeed from the footpath notices that the stone falls to earth in a parabolic curve. I now ask: Do the "positions" traversed by the stone lie "in reality" on a straight line or on a parabola? Moreover, what is meant here by motion "in space"? From the considerations of the previous section the answer is self-evident. In the first place we entirely shun the vague word "space," of which, we must honestly acknowledge, we cannot form the slightest conception, and we replace it by "motion relative to a practically rigid body of reference." The positions relative to the body of reference (railway carriage or embankment) have already been defined in detail in the preceding section. If instead of "body of reference" we insert "system of co-ordinates," which is a useful idea for mathematical description, we are in a position to say: The stone traverses a straight line relative to a system of co-ordinates rigidly attached to the carriage, but relative to a system of co-ordinates rigidly attached to the ground (embankment) it describes a parabola. With the aid of this example it is clearly seen that there is no such thing as an independently existing trajectory (lit. "path-curve"[1]), but only a trajectory relative to a particular body of reference.

In order to have a *complete* description of the motion, we must specify how the body alters its position *with time*; *i.e.* for every point on the trajectory it must be stated at what time the body is situated there. These data must be supplemented by such a definition of time that, in virtue of this definition, these time-values can be regarded essentially as magnitudes (results of measurements) capable of observation. If we take our stand on the ground of classical mechanics, we can satisfy this requirement for our illustration in the following manner. We imagine two clocks of identical construction; the man at the railway-carriage window is holding one of them, and the man on the footpath the other. Each of the observers determines

---

[1] That is, a curve along which the body moves.

the position on his own reference-body occupied by the stone at each tick of the clock he is holding in his hand. In this connection we have not taken account of the inaccuracy involved by the finiteness of the velocity of propagation of light. With this and with a second difficulty prevailing here we shall have to deal in detail later.

FOUR

The Galileian System of
Co-ordinates

As is well known, the fundamental law of the mechanics of Galilei-Newton, which is known as the *law of inertia*, can be stated thus: A body removed sufficiently far from other bodies continues in a state of rest or of uniform motion in a straight line. This law not only says something about the motion of the bodies, but it also indicates the reference-bodies or systems of co-ordinates, permissible in mechanics, which can be used in mechanical description. The visible fixed stars are bodies for which the law of inertia certainly holds to a high degree of approximation. Now if we use a system of co-ordinates which is rigidly attached to the earth, then, relative to this system, every fixed star describes a circle of immense radius in the course of an astronomical day, a result which is opposed to the statement of the law of inertia. So that if we adhere to this law we must refer these motions only to systems of co-ordinates relative to which the fixed stars do not move in a circle. A system of co-ordinates of which the state of motion is such that the law of inertia holds relative to it is called a "Galileian system of co-ordinates." The laws of the mechanics of Galilei-Newton can be regarded as valid only for a Galileian system of co-ordinates.

FIVE

The Principle of Relativity (in the Restricted Sense)

In order to attain the greatest possible clearness, let us return to our example of the railway carriage supposed to be travelling uniformly. We call its motion a uniform translation ("uniform" because it is of constant velocity and direction, "translation" because although the carriage changes its position relative to the embankment yet it does not rotate in so doing). Let us imagine a raven flying through the air in such a manner that its motion, as observed from the embankment, is uniform and in a straight line. If we were to observe the flying raven from the moving railway carriage, we should find that the motion of the raven would be one of different velocity and direction, but that it would still be uniform and in a straight line. Expressed in an abstract manner we may say: If a mass m is moving uniformly in a straight line with respect to a co-ordinate system K, then it will also be moving uniformly and in a straight line relative to a second co-ordinate system K', provided that the latter is executing a uniform translatory motion with respect to K. In accordance with the discussion contained in the preceding section, it follows that:

If K is a Galileian co-ordinate system, then every other co-ordinate system K' is a Galileian one, when, in relation to K, it is in a condition of uniform motion of translation. Relative to K' the mechanical laws of Galilei-Newton hold good exactly as they do with respect to K.

We advance a step farther in our generalisation when we express the tenet thus: If, relative to K, K' is a uniformly moving co-ordinate system devoid of rotation, then natural phenomena run their course with respect to K' according to exactly the same general laws as with respect to K. This statement is called the *principle of relativity* (in the restricted sense).

As long as one was convinced that all natural phenomena were capable of representation with the help of classical mechanics, there was no need to doubt the validity of this principle of relativity. But in view of the more recent development of electrodynamics and optics it became more and more evident that classical mechanics affords an insufficient foundation for the physical description of all natural phenomena. At this juncture the question of the validity of the principle of relativity became ripe for discussion, and it did not appear impossible that the answer to this question might be in the negative.

Nevertheless, there are two general facts which at the outset speak very much in favour of the validity of the principle of relativity. Even though classical mechanics does not supply us with a sufficiently broad basis for the theoretical presentation of all physical phenomena, still we must grant it a considerable measure of "truth," since it supplies us with the actual motions of the heavenly bodies with a delicacy of detail little short of wonderful. The principle of relativity must therefore apply with great accuracy in the domain of *mechanics*. But that a principle of such broad generality should hold with such exactness in one domain of phenomena, and yet should be invalid for another, is *a priori* not very probable.

We now proceed to the second argument, to which, moreover, we shall return later. If the principle of relativity (in the restricted sense) does not hold, then the Galileian co-ordinate systems K, K', K'', etc., which are moving uniformly relative to each other, will not be *equivalent* for the description of natural phenomena. In this case we should be constrained to believe that natural laws are capable of being formulated in a particularly simple manner, and of course only on condition that, from amongst all possible Galileian co-ordinate systems, we should have chosen *one* (K_0) of a particular state of motion as our body of reference. We should then be justified (because of its merits for the description of natural phenomena) in calling this system "absolutely at rest," and all other Galileian systems K "in motion." If, for instance, our embankment were the system K_0, then our railway carriage would be a system K, relative to which less simple laws would hold than with respect to K_0. This diminished simplicity would be due to the fact that the carriage K would be in motion (*i.e.* "really") with respect to K_0. In the general laws of nature which have been formulated with reference to K, the magnitude and direction of the velocity of the carriage would necessarily play a part. We should expect, for instance, that the note emitted by an organ-pipe placed with its axis parallel to the direction of travel would be different from that emitted if the axis of the pipe were placed perpendicular to this direction. Now in virtue of its motion in an orbit round the sun, our earth is comparable with a railway carriage travelling with a velocity of about 30 kilometres per second. If the principle of relativity were not valid we should therefore expect that the direction of motion of the earth at any moment would enter into the laws of nature, and also that physical systems in their behaviour would be dependent on the orientation in space with respect to the earth. For owing to the alteration in direction of the velocity of revolution of the earth in the course of a year, the earth cannot be at rest relative to the hypothetical system K_0 throughout the whole year. However, the most careful observations have never revealed such anisotropic properties in terrestrial physical space, *i.e.* a physical non-equivalence of different directions. This is very powerful argument in favour of the principle of relativity.

SIX

The Theorem of
the Addition of Velocities Employed
in Classical Mechanics

Let us suppose our old friend the railway carriage to be travelling along the rails with a constant velocity v, and that a man traverses the length of the carriage in the direction of travel with a velocity w. How quickly or, in other words, with what velocity W does the man advance relative to the embankment during the process? The only possible answer seems to result from the following consideration: If the man were to stand still for a second, he would advance relative to the embankment through a distance v equal numerically to the velocity of the carriage. As a consequence of his walking, however, he traverses an additional distance w relative to the carriage, and hence also relative to the embankment, in this second, the distance w being numerically equal to the velocity with which he is walking. Thus in total he covers the distance $W = v + w$ relative to the embankment in the second considered. We shall see later that this result, which expresses the theorem of the addition of velocities employed in classical mechanics, cannot be maintained; in other words, the law that we have just written down does not hold in reality. For the time being, however, we shall assume its correctness.

SEVEN

The Apparent Incompatibility of the Law of Propagation of Light with the Principle of Relativity

There is hardly a simpler law in physics than that according to which light is propagated in empty space. Every child at school knows, or believes he knows, that this propagation takes place in straight lines with a velocity c = 300,000 km./sec. At all events we know with great exactness that this velocity is the same for all colours, because if this were not the case, the minimum of emission would not be observed simultaneously for different colours during the eclipse of a fixed star by its dark neighbour. By means of similar considerations based on observations of double stars, the Dutch astronomer De Sitter was also able to show that the velocity of propagation of light cannot depend on the velocity of motion of the body emitting the light. The assumption that this velocity of propagation is dependent on the direction "in space" is in itself improbable.

In short, let us assume that the simple law of the constancy of the velocity of light c (in vacuum) is justifiably believed by the child at school. Who would imagine that this simple law has plunged the conscientiously thoughtful physicist into the greatest intellectual difficulties? Let us consider how these difficulties arise.

Of course we must refer the process of the propagation of light (and indeed every other process) to a rigid reference-body (co-ordinate system). As such a system let us again choose our embankment. We shall imagine the air above it to have been removed. If a ray of light be sent along the embankment, we see from the above that the tip of the ray will be transmitted with the velocity c relative to the embankment. Now let us suppose that our railway carriage is again travelling along the railway lines with the velocity v, and that its direction is the same as that of the ray of light, but its velocity of course much less. Let us inquire about the velocity of propagation of the ray of light relative to the carriage. It is obvious that we can here apply the consideration of the previous section, since the ray of light plays the part of the man walking along relatively to the carriage. The velocity W of the man relative to the embankment is here replaced by the velocity of light relative to the embankment. w is the required velocity of light with respect to the carriage, and we have

$$w = c - v.$$

The velocity of propagation of a ray of light relative to the carriage thus comes out smaller than c.

But this result comes into conflict with the principle of relativity set forth in Section 5. For, like every other general law of nature, the law of the transmission of light *in vacuo* must, according to the principle of relativity, be the same for the railway carriage as reference-body as when the rails are the body of reference. But, from our above consideration, this would appear to be impossible. If every ray of light is propagated relative to the embankment with the velocity c, then for this reason it would appear that another law of propagation of light must necessarily hold with respect to the carriage—a result contradictory to the principle of relativity.

In view of this dilemma there appears to be nothing else for it than to abandon either the principle of relativity or the simple law of the propagation of light *in vacuo*. Those of you who have carefully followed the preceding discussion are almost sure to expect that we should retain the principle of relativity, which appeals so convincingly to the intellect because it is so natural and simple. The law of the propagation of light *in vacuo* would then have to be replaced by a more complicated law comformable to the principle of relativity. The development of theoretical physics shows, however, that we cannot pursue this course. The epoch-making theoretical investigations of H. A. Lorentz on the electrodynamical and optical phenomena connected with moving bodies show that experience in this domain leads conclusively to a theory of electromagnetic phenomena, of which the law of the constancy of the velocity of light *in vacuo* is a necessary consequence. Prominent theoretical physicists were therefore more inclined to reject the principle of relativity, in spite of the fact that no empirical data had been found which were contradictory to this principle.

At this juncture the theory of relativity entered the arena. As a result of an analysis of the physical conceptions of time and space, it became evident that *in reality there is not the least incompatibility between the principle of relativity and the law of propagation of light*, and that by systematically holding fast to both these laws a logically rigid theory could be arrived at. This theory has been called the *special theory of relativity* to distinguish it from the extended theory, with which we shall deal later. In the following pages we shall present the fundamental ideas of the special theory of relativity.

EIGHT

On the Idea of
Time in Physics

Lightning has struck the rails on our railway embankment at two places *A* and *B* far distant from each other.
I make the additional assertion that these two lightning flashes occurred simultaneously. If I ask you whether
there is sense in this statement, you will answer my question
with a decided "Yes." But if I now approach you with the
request to explain to me the sense of the statement more
precisely, you find after some consideration that the answer to
this question is not so easy as it appears at first sight.

After some time perhaps the following answer would occur
to you: "The significance of the statement is clear in itself and
needs no further explanation; of course it would require some
consideration if I were to be commissioned to determine by
observations whether in the actual case the two events took
place simultaneously or not." I cannot be satisfied with this
answer for the following reason. Supposing that as a result of
ingenious consideration an able meteorologist were to discover that the lightning must always strike the places *A* and *B*
simultaneously, then we should be faced with the task of

testing whether or not this theoretical result is in accordance with the reality. We encounter the same difficulty with all physical statements in which the conception "simultaneous" plays a part. The concept does not exist for the physicist until he has the possibility of discovering whether or not it is fulfilled in an actual case. We thus require a definition of simultaneity such that this definition supplies us with the method by means of which, in the present case, he can decide by experiment whether or not both the lightning strokes occurred simultaneously. As long as this requirement is not satisfied, I allow myself to be deceived as a physicist (and of course the same applies if I am not a physicist), when I imagine that I am able to attach a meaning to the statement of simultaneity. (I would ask the reader not to proceed farther until he is fully convinced on this point.)

After thinking the matter over for some time you then offer the following suggestion with which to test simultaneity. By measuring along the rails, the connecting line *AB* should be measured up and an observer placed at the mid-point *M* of the distance *AB*. This observer should be supplied with an arrangement (*e.g.* two mirrors inclined at 90°) which allows him visually to observe both places *A* and *B* at the same time. If the observer perceives the two flashes of lightning at the same time, then they are simultaneous.

I am very pleased with this suggestion, but for all that I cannot regard the matter as quite settled, because I feel constrained to raise the following objection: "Your definition would certainly be right, if only I knew that the light by means of which the observer at *M* perceives the lightning flashes travels along the length $A \longrightarrow M$ with the same velocity as along the length $B \longrightarrow M$. But an examination of this supposition would only be possible if we already had at our disposal the means of measuring time. It would thus appear as though we were moving here in a logical circle."

After further consideration you cast a somewhat disdainful glance at me—and rightly so—and you declare: "I maintain my previous definition nevertheless, because in reality it assumes absolutely nothing about light. There is only *one* demand to be made of the definition of simultaneity, namely, that in every real case it must supply us with an empirical decision as to whether or not the conception that has to be defined is fulfilled. That my definition satisfies this demand is indisputable. That light requires the same time to traverse the path $A \longrightarrow M$ as for the path $B \longrightarrow M$ is in reality neither a *supposition nor a hypothesis* about the physical nature of light, but a *stipulation* which I can make of my own freewill in order to arrive at a definition of simultaneity."

It is clear that this definition can be used to give an exact meaning not only to *two* events, but to as many events as we care to choose, and independently of the positions of the scenes of the events with respect to the body of reference[1] (here the railway embankment). We are thus led also to a definition of "time" in physics. For this purpose we suppose

---

[1] We suppose further, that, when three events A, B and C occur in different places in such a manner that A is simultaneous with B, and B is simultaneous with C (simultaneous in the sense of the above definition), then the criterion for the simultaneity of the pair of events A, C is also satisfied. This assumption is a physical hypothesis about the law of propagation of light; it must certainly be fulfilled if we are to maintain the law of the constancy of the velocity of light *in vacuo*.

that clocks of identical construction are placed at the points A, B and C of the railway line (co-ordinate system), and that they are set in such a manner that the positions of their pointers are simultaneously (in the above sense) the same. Under these conditions we understand by the "time" of an event the read- ing (position of the hands) of that one of these clocks which is in the immediate vicinity (in space) of the event. In this manner a time-value is associated with every event which is essentially capable of observation.

This stipulation contains a further physical hypothesis, the validity of which will hardly be doubted without empirical evidence to the contrary. It has been assumed that all these clocks go *at the same rate* if they are of identical construction. Stated more exactly: When two clocks arranged at rest in dif- ferent places of a reference-body are set in such a manner that a *particular* position of the pointers of the one clock is *simul- taneous* (in the above sense) with the *same* position of the pointers of the other clock, then identical "settings" are al- ways simultaneous (in the sense of the above definition).

NINE

The Relativity of
Simultaneity

U p to now our considerations have been referred to a
particular body of reference, which we have styled a
"railway embankment." We suppose a very long train
travelling along the rails with the constant velocity v and in
the direction indicated in Fig. 1. People travelling in this train

FIG. 1

will with advantage use the train as a rigid reference-body
(co-ordinate system); they regard all events in reference to the
train. Then every event which takes place along the line also
takes place at a particular point of the train. Also the definition
of simultaneity can be given relative to the train in exactly the
same way as with respect to the embankment. As a natural
consequence, however, the following question arises:

Are two events (*e.g.* the two strokes of lightning A and B)
which are simultaneous *with reference to the railway embankment*

also simultaneous *relatively to the train?* We shall show directly that the answer must be in the negative.

When we say that the lightning strokes A and B are simultaneous with respect to the embankment, we mean: the rays of light emitted at the places A and B, where the lightning occurs, meet each other at the mid-point M of the length $A \longrightarrow B$ of the embankment. But the events A and B also correspond to positions A and B on the train. Let M' be the mid-point of the distance $A \dashrightarrow B$ on the travelling train. Just when the flashes[1] of lightning occur, this point M' naturally coincides with the point M, but it moves towards the right in the diagram with the velocity v of the train. If an observer sitting in the position M' in the train did not possess this velocity, then he would remain permanently at M, and the light rays emitted by the flashes of lightning A and B would reach him simultaneously, *i.e.* they would meet just where he is situated. Now in reality (considered with reference to the railway embankment) he is hastening towards the beam of light coming from B, whilst he is riding on ahead of the beam of light coming from A. Hence the observer will see the beam of light emitted from B earlier than he will see that emitted from A. Observers who take the railway train as their reference-body must therefore come to the conclusion that the lightning flash B took place earlier than the lightning flash A. We thus arrive at the important result:

Events which are simultaneous with reference to the embankment are not simultaneous with respect to the train, and

---

[1] As judged from the embankment.

vice versa (relativity of simultaneity). Every reference-body (co-ordinate system) has its own particular time; unless we are told the reference-body to which the statement of time refers, there is no meaning in a statement of the time of an event.

Now before the advent of the theory of relativity it had always tacitly been assumed in physics that the statement of time had an absolute significance, *i.e.* that it is independent of the state of motion of the body of reference. But we have just seen that this assumption is incompatible with the most natural definition of simultaneity; if we discard this assumption, then the conflict between the law of the propagation of light *in vacuo* and the principle of relativity (developed in Section 7) disappears.

We were led to that conflict by the considerations of Section 6, which are now no longer tenable. In that section we concluded that the man in the carriage, who traverses the distance *w per second* relative to the carriage, traverses the same distance also with respect to the embankment *in each second* of time. But, according to the foregoing considerations, the time required by a particular occurrence with respect to the carriage must not be considered equal to the duration of the same occurrence as judged from the embankment (as reference-body). Hence it cannot be contended that the man in walking travels the distance *w* relative to the railway line in a time which is equal to one second as judged from the embankment.

Moreover, the considerations of Section 6 are based on yet a second assumption, which, in the light of a strict consideration, appears to be arbitrary, although it was always tacitly made even before the introduction of the theory of relativity.

TEN

On the Relativity
of the Conception
of Distance

Let us consider two particular points on the train[1] travelling along the embankment with the velocity v, and inquire as to their distance apart. We already know that it is necessary to have a body of reference for the measurement of a distance, with respect to which body the distance can be measured up. It is the simplest plan to use the train itself as reference-body (co-ordinate system). An observer in the train measures the interval by marking off his measuring-rod in a straight line (*e.g.* along the floor of the carriage) as many times as is necessary to take him from the one marked point to the other. Then the number which tells us how often the rod has to be laid down is the required distance.

It is a different matter when the distance has to be judged from the railway line. Here the following method suggests itself. If we call A' and B' the two points on the train whose distance apart is required, then both of these points are mov-

---

[1] *E.g.* the middle of the first and of the twentieth carriage.

ing with the velocity v along the embankment. In the first place we require to determine the points A and B of the embankment which are just being passed by the two points A' and B' at a particular time t—judged from the embankment. These points A and B of the embankment can be determined by applying the definition of time given in Section 8. The distance between these points A and B is then measured by repeated application of the measuring-rod along the embankment.

A priori it is by no means certain that this last measurement will supply us with the same result as the first. Thus the length of the train as measured from the embankment may be different from that obtained by measuring in the train itself. This circumstance leads us to a second objection which must be raised against the apparently obvious consideration of Section 6. Namely, if the man in the carriage covers the distance w in a unit of time—*measured from the train*—then this distance—*as measured from the embankment*—is not necessarily also equal to w.

ELEVEN

The Lorentz Transformation

The results of the last three sections show that the apparent incompatibility of the law of propagation of light with the principle of relativity (Section 7) has been derived by means of a consideration which borrowed two unjustifiable hypotheses from classical mechanics; these are as follows:

(1) The time-interval (time) between two events is independent of the condition of motion of the body of reference.

(2) The space-interval (distance) between two points of a rigid body is independent of the condition of motion of the body of reference.

If we drop these hypotheses, then the dilemma of Section 7 disappears, because the theorem of the addition of velocities derived in Section 6 becomes invalid. The possibility presents itself that the law of the propagation of light *in vacuo* may be compatible with the principle of relativity, and the question arises: How have we to modify the considerations of Section 6 in order to remove the apparent disagreement between these two fundamental results of experience? This question leads to a general one. In the discussion of Section 6 we have to do with places and times relative both to the train and to the embankment. How are we to find the place and time of an event in relation to the train, when we know the place and time of the event with respect to the railway embankment? Is there a thinkable answer to this question of such a nature that the law of transmission of light *in vacuo* does not contradict the principle of relativity? In other words: Can we conceive of a relation between place and time of the individual events relative to both reference-bodies, such that every ray of light possesses the velocity of transmission *c* relative to the embankment and relative to the train? This question leads to a quite definite positive answer, and to a perfectly definite transformation law for the space-time magnitudes of an event when changing over from one body of reference to another.

Before we deal with this, we shall introduce the following incidental consideration. Up to the present we have only considered events taking place along the embankment, which had mathematically to assume the function of a straight line. In the manner indicated in Section 2 we can imagine this reference-body supplemented laterally and in a vertical direction by means of a framework of rods, so that an event which takes place anywhere can be localised with reference to this framework. Similarly, we can imagine the train travelling with the velocity *v* to be continued across the whole of space, so that every event, no matter how far off it may be, could also be localised with respect to the second framework. Without committing any fundamental error, we can disregard the fact that in reality these frameworks would continually interfere with each other, owing to the impenetrability of solid bodies. In every such framework we imagine three surfaces perpendicular to each other marked out, and designated as "co-ordinate planes" ("co-ordinate system"). A co-ordinate system K then corresponds to the embankment, and a co-ordinate system K' to the train. An event, wherever it may have taken place, would be fixed in space with respect to K by the three perpendiculars x, y, z on the co-ordinate planes, and with regard to time by a time-value t. Relative to K', *the same event* would be fixed in respect of space and time by corresponding values x', y', z', t', which of course are not identical with x, y, z, t. It has already been set forth in detail how these magnitudes are to be regarded as results of physical measurements.

FIG. 2

Obviously our problem can be exactly formulated in the following manner. What are the values x', y', z', t', of an event with respect to K', when the magnitudes x, y, z, t, of the same event with respect to K are given? The relations must be so chosen that the law of the transmission of light *in vacuo* is satisfied for one and the same ray of light (and of course for every ray) with respect to K and K'. For the relative orientation in space of the co-ordinate systems indicated in the diagram (Fig. 2), this problem is solved by means of the equations:

$$x' = \frac{x - vt}{\sqrt{1 - \frac{v^2}{c^2}}}$$

$$y' = y$$

$$z' = z$$

$$t' = \frac{t - \frac{v}{c^2} \cdot x}{\sqrt{1 - \frac{v^2}{c^2}}}$$

This system of equations is known as the "Lorentz transformation."[1]

If in place of the law of transmission of light we had taken as our basis the tacit assumptions of the older mechanics as to the absolute character of times and lengths, then instead of the above we should have obtained the following equations:

$$x' = x - vt$$

$$y' = y$$

$$z' = z$$

$$t' = t.$$

[1] A simple derivation of the Lorentz transformation is given in Appendix 1.

This system of equations is often termed the "Galilei transformation." The Galilei transformation can be obtained from the Lorentz transformation by substituting an infinitely large value for the velocity of light c in the latter transformation.

Aided by the following illustration, we can readily see that, in accordance with the Lorentz transformation, the law of the transmission of light *in vacuo* is satisfied both for the reference-body K and for the reference-body K'. A light-signal is sent along the positive x-axis, and this light-stimulus advances in accordance with the equation.

$$x = ct,$$

i.e. with the velocity c. According to the equations of the Lorentz transformation, this simple relation between x and t involves a relation between x' and t'. In point of fact, if we substitute for x the value ct in the first and fourth equations of the Lorentz transformation, we obtain:

$$x' = \frac{(c - v)t}{\sqrt{1 - \dfrac{v^2}{c^2}}}$$

$$t' = \frac{\left(1 - \dfrac{v}{c}\right)t}{\sqrt{1 - \dfrac{v^2}{c^2}}},$$

from which, by division, the expression

$$x' = ct'$$

immediately follows. If referred to the system K', the propagation of light takes place according to this equation. We thus see that the velocity of transmission relative to the reference-body K' is also equal to c. The same result is obtained for rays of light advancing in any other direction whatsoever. Of course this is not surprising, since the equations of the Lorentz transformation were derived conformably to this point of view.

TWELVE

The Behaviour of Measuring-Rods and Clocks in Motion

I place a metre-rod in the x'-axis of K' in such a manner that one end (the beginning) coincides with the point $x' = 0$, whilst the other end (the end of the rod) coincides with the point $x' = 1$. What is the length of the metre-rod relatively to the system K? In order to learn this, we need only ask where the beginning of the rod and the end of the rod lie with respect to K at a particular time t of the system K. By means of the first equation of the Lorentz transformation the values of these two points at the time $t = 0$ can be shown to be

$$x_{(\text{beginning of rod})} = 0 \sqrt{1 - \frac{v^2}{c^2}}$$

$$x_{(\text{end of rod})} = 1.\sqrt{1 - \frac{v^2}{c^2}},$$

the distance between the points being $\sqrt{1 - \frac{v^2}{c^2}}$. But the metre-rod is moving with the velocity v relative to K. It therefore follows that the length of a rigid metre-rod moving in the direction of its length with a velocity v is $\sqrt{1 - v^2/c^2}$ of a metre. The rigid rod is thus shorter when in motion than when at rest, and the more quickly it is moving, the shorter is the rod. For the velocity $v = c$ we should have $\sqrt{1 - v^2/c^2} = 0$, and for still greater velocities the square-root becomes imaginary. From this we conclude that in the theory of relativity the velocity c plays the part of a limiting velocity, which can neither be reached nor exceeded by any real body.

Of course this feature of the velocity c as a limiting velocity also clearly follows from the equations of the Lorentz transformation, for these become meaningless if we choose values of v greater than c.

If, on the contrary, we had considered a metre-rod at rest in the x-axis with respect to K, then we should have found that the length of the rod as judged from K' would have been $\sqrt{1 - v^2/c^2}$; this is quite in accordance with the principle of relativity which forms the basis of our considerations.

A priori it is quite clear that we must be able to learn something about the physical behaviour of measuring-rods and clocks from the equations of transformation, for the magnitudes x, y, z, t, are nothing more nor less than the results of measurements obtainable by means of measuring-rods and clocks. If we had based our considerations on the Galileian transformation we should not have obtained a contraction of the rod as a consequence of its motion.

Let us now consider a seconds-clock which is permanently

situated at the origin ($x' = 0$) of K'. $t' = 0$ and $t' = 1$ are two successive ticks of this clock. The first and fourth equations of the Lorentz transformation give for these two ticks:

$$t = 0$$

and

$$t = \frac{1}{\sqrt{1 - \dfrac{v^2}{c^2}}}$$

As judged from K, the clock is moving with the velocity v; as judged from this reference-body, the time which elapses between two strokes of the clock is not one second, but $\dfrac{1}{\sqrt{1 - \dfrac{v^2}{c^2}}}$ seconds, *i.e.* a somewhat larger time. As a consequence of its motion the clock goes more slowly than when at rest. Here also the velocity c plays the part of an unattainable limiting velocity.

THIRTEEN

Theorem of the Addition of the Velocities. The Experiment of Fizeau

Now in practice we can move clocks and measuring-rods only with velocities that are small compared with the velocity of light; hence we shall hardly be able to compare the results of the previous section directly with the reality. But, on the other hand, these results must strike you as being very singular, and for that reason I shall now draw another conclusion from the theory, one which can easily be derived from the foregoing considerations, and which has been most elegantly confirmed by experiment.

In Section 6 we derived the theorem of the addition of velocities in one direction in the form which also results from the hypotheses of classical mechanics. This theorem can also be deduced readily from the Galilei transformation (Section 11). In place of the man walking inside the carriage, we introduce a point moving relatively to the co-ordinate system K' in accordance with the equation

$$x = wt'.$$

By means of the first and fourth equations of the Galilei transformation we can express x' and t' in terms of x and t, and we
then obtain

$$x = (v + w)t.$$

This equation expresses nothing else than the law of motion
of the point with reference to the system K (of the man with
reference to the embankment). We denote this velocity by
the symbol W, and we then obtain, as in Section 6,

$$W = v + w \qquad . \qquad . \qquad . \qquad \text{(A)}.$$

But we can carry out this consideration just as well on the
basis of the theory of relativity. In the equation

$$x' = wt'$$

we must then express x' and t' in terms of x and t, making use
of the first and fourth equations of the *Lorentz transformation*.
Instead of the equation (A) we then obtain the equation

$$W = \frac{v + w}{1 + \dfrac{vw}{c^2}} \qquad . \qquad . \qquad . \qquad \text{(B)},$$

which corresponds to the theorem of addition for velocities in
one direction according to the theory of relativity. The ques-

tion now arises as to which of these two theorems is the better in accord with experience. On this point we are enlightened by a most important experiment which the brilliant physicist Fizeau performed more than half a century ago, and which has been repeated since then by some of the best experimental physicists, so that there can be no doubt about its result. The experiment is concerned with the following question. Light travels in a motionless liquid with a particular velocity w. How quickly does it travel in the direction of the arrow in the tube T (see the accompanying diagram, Fig. 3) when the liquid above mentioned is flowing through the tube with a velocity v?

FIG. 3

In accordance with the principle of relativity we shall certainly have to take for granted that the propagation of light always takes place with the same velocity w *with respect to the liquid*, whether the latter is in motion with reference to other bodies or not. The velocity of light relative to the liquid and the velocity of the latter relative to the tube are thus known, and we require the velocity of light relative to the tube.

It is clear that we have the problem of Section 6 again before us. The tube plays the part of the railway embankment or of the co-ordinate system K, the liquid plays the part of the carriage or of the co-ordinate system K', and finally, the light plays the part of the man walking along the carriage, or of the moving point in the present section. If we denote the velocity of the light relative to the tube by W, then this is given by the equation (A) or (B), according as the Galilei transformation or the Lorentz transformation corresponds to the facts. Experiment[1] decides in favour of equation (B) derived from the theory of relativity, and the agreement is, indeed, very exact. According to recent and most excellent measurements by Zeeman, the influence of the velocity of flow v on the propagation of light is represented by formula (B) to within one per cent.

Nevertheless we must now draw attention to the fact that a theory of this phenomenon was given by H. A. Lorentz long before the statement of the theory of relativity. This theory was of a purely electrodynamical nature, and was obtained by the use of particular hypotheses as to the electromagnetic structure of matter. This circumstance, however, does not in the least diminish the conclusiveness of the experiment as a crucial test in favour of the theory of relativity, for the electrodynamics of Maxwell-Lorentz, on which the original theory was based, in no way opposes the theory of relativity. Rather has the latter been developed from electrodynamics as an astoundingly simple combination of generalisation of the hypotheses, formerly independent of each other, on which electrodynamics was built.

---

[1] Fizeau found $W = w + v \left(1 - \dfrac{1}{n^2} \right)$, where $n = \dfrac{c}{w}$ is the index of refraction of the liquid. On the other hand, owing to the smallness of $\dfrac{vw}{c^2}$ as compared with 1, we can replace (B) in the first place by $W = (w + v \left(1 - \dfrac{vw}{c^2} \right)$, or to the same order of approximation by $w + v \left(1 - \dfrac{1}{n^2} \right)$, which agrees with Fizeau's result.

FOURTEEN

The Heuristic Value of
the Theory of Relativity

Our train of thought in the foregoing pages can be epit-
omised in the following manner. Experience has led
to the conviction that, on the one hand, the principle
of relativity holds true and that on the other hand the velocity
of transmission of light *in vacuo* has to be considered equal to
a constant *c*. By uniting these two postulates we obtained the
law of transformation for the rectangular co-ordinates *x*, *y*, *z*
and the time *t* of the events which constitute the processes of
nature. In this connection we did not obtain the Galilei transformation, but, differing from classical mechanics, the *Lorentz
transformation*.

The law of transmission of light, the acceptance of which is
justified by our actual knowledge, played an important part in
this process of thought. Once in possession of the Lorentz
transformation, however, we can combine this with the principle of relativity, and sum up the theory thus:

Every general law of nature must be so constituted that it is
transformed into a law of exactly the same form when, instead
of the space-time variables *x*, *y*, *z*, *t* of the original co-ordinate

system K, we introduce new space-time variables x', y', z', t' of a co-ordinate system K'. In this connection the relation between the ordinary and the accented magnitudes is given by the Lorentz transformation. Or in brief: General laws of nature are co-variant with respect to Lorentz transformations.

This is a definite mathematical condition that the theory of relativity demands of a natural law, and in virtue of this, the theory becomes a valuable heuristic aid in the search for general laws of nature. If a general law of nature were to be found which did not satisfy this condition, then at least one of the two fundamental assumptions of the theory would have been disproved. Let us now examine what general results the latter theory has hitherto evinced.

FIFTEEN

General Results of
the Theory

I t is clear from our previous considerations that the (special) theory of relativity has grown out of electrodynamics
and optics. In these fields it has not appreciably altered
the predictions of theory, but it has considerably simplified
the theoretical structure, *i.e.* the derivation of laws, and—what
is incomparably more important—it has considerably reduced
the number of independent hypotheses forming the basis of
theory. The special theory of relativity has rendered the
Maxwell-Lorentz theory so plausible, that the latter would
have been generally accepted by physicists even if experiment had decided less unequivocally in its favour.

Classical mechanics required to be modified before it could
come into line with the demands of the special theory of
relativity. For the main part, however, this modification affects
only the laws for rapid motions, in which the velocities of
matter v are not very small as compared with the velocity of
light. We have experience of such rapid motions only in the
case of electrons and ions; for other motions the variations
from the laws of classical mechanics are too small to make

themselves evident in practice. We shall not consider the motion of stars until we come to speak of the general theory of relativity. In accordance with the theory of relativity the kinetic energy of a material point of mass m is no longer given by the well-known expression

$$m \frac{v^2}{2},$$

but by the expression

$$\frac{mc^2}{\sqrt{1 - \frac{v^2}{c^2}}}.$$

This expression approaches infinity as the velocity v approaches the velocity of light c. The velocity must therefore always remain less than c, however great may be the energies used to produce the acceleration. If we develop the expression for the kinetic energy in the form of a series, we obtain

$$mc^2 + m \frac{v^2}{2} = \frac{3}{8} m \frac{v^4}{c^2} + \ldots .$$

When $\frac{v^2}{c^2}$ is small compared with unity, the third of these terms is always small in comparison with the second, which last is alone considered in classical mechanics. The first term

mc^2 does not contain the velocity, and requires no consideration if we are only dealing with the question as to how the energy of a point-mass depends on the velocity. We shall speak of its essential significance later.

The most important result of a general character to which the special theory of relativity has led is concerned with the conception of mass. Before the advent of relativity, physics recognised two conservation laws of fundamental importance, namely, the law of the conservation of energy and the law of the conservation of mass; these two fundamental laws appeared to be quite independent of each other. By means of the theory of relativity they have been united into one law. We shall now briefly consider how this unification came about, and what meaning is to be attached to it.

The principle of relativity requires that the law of the conservation of energy should hold not only with reference to a co-ordinate system K, but also with respect to every co-ordinate system K' which is in a state of uniform motion of translation relative to K, or, briefly, relative to every "Galileian" system of co-ordinates. In contrast to classical mechanics, the Lorentz transformation is the deciding factor in the transition from one such system to another.

By means of comparatively simple considerations we are led to draw the following conclusion from these premises, in conjunction with the fundamental equations of the electrodynamics of Maxwell: A body moving with the velocity v, which absorbs[1] an amount of energy E_0 in the form of radiation

---

[1] E_0 is the energy taken up, as judged from a co-ordinate system moving with the body.

without suffering an alteration in velocity in the process, has, as a consequence, its energy increased by an amount

$$\frac{E_0}{\sqrt{1 - \dfrac{v^2}{c^2}}}.$$

In consideration of the expression given above for the kinetic energy of the body, the required energy of the body comes out to be

$$\frac{\left(m + \dfrac{E_0}{c^2}\right)c^2}{\sqrt{1 - \dfrac{v^2}{c^2}}}.$$

Thus the body has the same energy as a body of mass $\left(m + \dfrac{E_0}{c^2}\right)$ moving with the velocity v. Hence we can say: If a body takes up an amount of energy E_0, then its inertial mass increases by an amount $\dfrac{E_0}{c^2}$; the inertial mass of a body is not a constant, but varies according to the change in the energy of the body. The inertial mass of a system of bodies can even be regarded as a measure of its energy. The law of the conservation of the mass of a system becomes identical with the law of the conservation of energy, and is only valid provided that the system neither takes up nor sends out energy. Writing the expression for the energy in the form

$$\frac{mc^2 + E_0}{\sqrt{1 - \dfrac{v^2}{c^2}}},$$

we see that the term mc^2, which has hitherto attracted our attention, is nothing else than the energy possessed by the body[1] before it absorbed the energy E_0.

A direct comparison of this relation with experiment is not possible at the present time (1920; see Note, p. 53), owing to the fact that the changes in energy E_0 to which we can subject a system are not large enough to make themselves perceptible as a change in the inertial mass of the system. $\dfrac{E_0}{c^2}$ is too small in comparison with the mass m, which was present before the alteration of the energy. It is owing to this circumstance that classical mechanics was able to establish successfully the conservation of mass as a law of independent validity.

Let me add a final remark of a fundamental nature. The success of the Faraday-Maxwell interpretation of electromagnetic action at a distance resulted in physicists becoming convinced that there are no such things as instantaneous actions at a distance (not involving an intermediary medium) of the type of Newton's law of gravitation. According to the theory of relativity, action at a distance with the velocity of light always takes the place of instantaneous action at a distance or of action at a distance with an infinite velocity of transmission. This is connected with the fact that the velocity c plays a fundamental rôle in this theory. In Part II we shall see in what

---

[1] As judged from a co-ordinate system moving with the body.

way this result becomes modified in the general theory of
relativity.

NOTE.—With the advent of nuclear transformation processes, which result from the
bombardment of elements by α-particles, protons, deuterons, neutrons or γ-rays, the
equivalence of mass and energy expressed by the relation $E = mc^2$ has been amply
confirmed. The sum of the reacting masses, together with the mass equivalent of the
kinetic energy of the bombarding particle (or photon), is always greater than the sum
of the resulting masses. The difference is the equivalent mass of the kinetic energy
of the particles generated, or of the released electromagnetic energy (γ-photons). In
the same way, the mass of a spontaneously disintegrating radioactive atom is always
greater than the sum of the masses of the resulting atoms by the mass equivalent of
the kinetic energy of the particles generated (or of the photonic energy). Measurements of the energy of the rays emitted in nuclear reactions, in combination with the
equations of such reactions, render it possible to evaluate atomic weights to a high
degree of accuracy.

R. W. L.

SIXTEEN

Experience and the Special Theory of Relativity

To what extent is the special theory of relativity supported by experience? This question is not easily answered for the reason already mentioned in connection with the fundamental experiment of Fizeau. The special theory of relativity has crystallised out from the Maxwell-Lorentz theory of electromagnetic phenomena. Thus all facts of experience which support the electromagnetic theory also support the theory of relativity. As being of particular importance, I mention here the fact that the theory of relativity enables us to predict the effects produced on the light reaching us from the fixed stars. These results are obtained in an exceedingly simple manner, and the effects indicated, which are due to the relative motion of the earth with reference to those fixed stars, are found to be in accord with experience. We refer to the yearly movement of the apparent position of the fixed stars resulting from the motion of the earth round the sun (aberration), and to the influence of the radial components of the relative motions of the fixed stars with respect to the earth on the colour of the light reaching us from them. The latter effect manifests itself

in a slight displacement of the spectral lines of the light transmitted to us from a fixed star, as compared with the position of
the same spectral lines when they are produced by a terrestrial
source of light (Doppler principle). The experimental arguments in favour of the Maxwell-Lorentz theory, which are at
the same time arguments in favour of the theory of relativity,
are too numerous to be set forth here. In reality they limit the
theoretical possibilities to such an extent, that no other theory
than that of Maxwell and Lorentz has been able to hold its own
when tested by experience.

But there are two classes of experimental facts hitherto
obtained which can be represented in the Maxwell-Lorentz
theory only by the introduction of an auxiliary hypothesis,
which in itself—*i.e.* without making use of the theory of relativity—appears extraneous.

It is known that cathode rays and the so-called β-rays emitted by radioactive substances consist of negatively electrified
particles (electrons) of very small inertia and large velocity. By
examining the deflection of these rays under the influence of
electric and magnetic fields, we can study the law of motion of
these particles very exactly.

In the theoretical treatment of these electrons, we are faced
with the difficulty that electrodynamic theory of itself is unable to give an account of their nature. For since electrical
masses of one sign repel each other, the negative electrical
masses constituting the electron would necessarily be scattered under the influence of their mutual repulsions, unless
there are forces of another kind operating between them, the

nature of which has hitherto remained obscure to us.[1] If we now assume that the relative distances between the electrical masses constituting the electron remain unchanged during the motion of the electron (rigid connection in the sense of classical mechanics), we arrive at a law of motion of the electron which does not agree with experience. Guided by purely formal points of view, H. A. Lorentz was the first to introduce the hypothesis that the form of the electron experiences a contraction in the direction of motion in consequence of that motion, the contracted length being proportional to the expession $\sqrt{1 - \dfrac{v^2}{c^2}}$. This hypothesis, which is not justifiable by any electrodynamical facts, supplies us then with that particular law of motion which has been confirmed with great precision in recent years.

The theory of relativity leads to the same law of motion, without requiring any special hypothesis whatsoever as to the structure and the behaviour of the electron. We arrived at a similar conclusion of Section 13 in connection with the experiment of Fizeau, the result of which is foretold by the theory of relativity without the necessity of drawing on hypotheses as to the physical nature of the liquid.

The second class of facts to which we have alluded has reference to the question whether or not the motion of the earth in space can be made perceptible in terrestrial experiments. We have already remarked in Section 5 that all attempts of this

---

[1] The general theory of relativity renders it likely that the electrical masses of an electron are held together by gravitational forces.

nature led to a negative result. Before the theory of relativity was put forward, it was difficult to become reconciled to this negative result, for reasons now to be discussed. The inherited prejudices about time and space did not allow any doubt to arise as to the prime importance of the Galileian transformation for changing over from one body of reference to another. Now assuming that the Maxwell-Lorentz equations hold for a reference-body K, we then find that they do not hold for a reference-body K' moving uniformly with respect to K, if we assume that the relations of the Galileian transformation exist between the co-ordinates of K and K'. It thus appears that, of all Galileian co-ordinate systems, one (K) corresponding to a particular state of motion is physically unique. This result was interpreted physically by regarding K as at rest with respect to a hypothetical æther of space. On the other hand, all co-ordinate systems K' moving relatively to K were to be regarded as in motion with respect to the æther. To this motion of K' against the æther ("æther-drift" relative to K') were attributed the more complicated laws which were supposed to hold relative to K'. Strictly speaking, such an æther-drift ought also to be assumed relative to the earth, and for a long time the efforts of physicists were devoted to attempts to detect the existence of an æther-drift at the earth's surface.

In one of the most notable of these attempts Michelson devised a method which appears as though it must be decisive. Imagine two mirrors so arranged on a rigid body that the reflecting surfaces face each other. A ray of light requires a perfectly definite time T to pass from one mirror to the other and back again, if the whole system be at rest with respect to the æther. It is found by calculation, however, that a slightly different time T' is required for this process, if the body, together with the mirrors, be moving relatively to the æther. And yet another point: it is shown by calculation that for a given velocity v with reference to the æther, this time T' is different when the body is moving perpendicularly to the planes of the mirrors from that resulting when the motion is parallel to these planes. Although the estimated difference between these two times is exceedingly small, Michelson and Morley performed an experiment involving interference in which this difference should have been clearly detectable. But the experiment gave a negative result—a fact very perplexing to physicists. Lorentz and FitzGerald rescued the theory from this difficulty by assuming that the motion of the body relative to the æther produces a contraction of the body in the direction of motion, the amount of contraction being just sufficient to compensate for the difference in time mentioned above. Comparison with the discussion in Section 12 shows that also from the standpoint of the theory of relativity this solution of the difficulty was the right one. But on the basis of the theory of relativity the method of interpretation is incomparably more satisfactory. According to this theory there is no such thing as a "specially favoured" (unique) co-ordinate system to occasion the introduction of the æther-idea, and hence there can be no æther-drift, nor any experiment with which to demonstrate it. Here the contraction of moving bodies follows from the two fundamental principles of the theory, without the introduction of particular hypotheses; and as the prime factor involved in this contraction we find, not the motion in itself, to which we cannot attach any meaning, but the motion with respect to the body of reference chosen in the particular case in point. Thus for a co-ordinate system moving with the earth the mirror system of Michelson and Morley is not shortened, but it *is* shortened for a co-ordinate system which is at rest relatively to the sun.

SEVENTEEN

Minkowski's Four-Dimensional Space

The non-mathematician is seized by a mysterious shuddering when he hears of "four-dimensional" things, by a feeling not unlike that awakened by thoughts of the occult. And yet there is no more common-place statement than that the world in which we live is a four-dimensional space-time continuum.

Space is a three-dimensional continuum. By this we mean that it is possible to describe the position of a point (at rest) by means of three numbers (co-ordinates) x, y, z, and that there is an indefinite number of points in the neighbourhood of this one, the position of which can be described by co-ordinates such as x_1, y_1, z_1, which may be as near as we choose to the respective values of the co-ordinates x, y, z of the first point. In virtue of the latter property we speak of a "continuum," and owing to the fact that there are three co-ordinates we speak of it as being "three-dimensional."

Similarly, the world of physical phenomena which was briefly called "world" by Minkowski is naturally four-dimensional in the space-time sense. For it is composed of individual events, each of which is described by four numbers, namely, three space co-ordinates x, y, z and a time co-ordinate, the time-value t. The "world" is in this sense also a continuum; for to every event there are as many "neighbouring" events (realised or at least thinkable) as we care to choose, the co-ordinates x_1, y_1, z_1, t_1 of which differ by an indefinitely small amount from those of the event x, y, z, t originally considered. That we have not been accustomed to regard the world in this sense as a four-dimensional continuum is due to the fact that in physics, before the advent of the theory of relativity, time played a different and more independent rôle, as compared with the space co-ordinates. It is for this reason that we have been in the habit of treating time as an independent continuum. As a matter of fact, according to classical mechanics, time is absolute, *i.e.* it is independent of the position and the condition of motion of the system of co-ordinates. We see this expressed in the last equation of the Galileian transformation $(t' = t)$.

The four-dimensional mode of consideration of the "world" is natural on the theory of relativity, since according to this theory time is robbed of its independence. This is shown by the fourth equation of the Lorentz transformation:

$$t' = \frac{t - \frac{v}{c^2} x}{\sqrt{1 - \frac{v^2}{c^2}}}.$$

Moreover, according to this equation the time difference $\Delta t'$ of two events with respect to K' does not in general vanish, even when the time difference Δt of the same events with reference to K vanishes. Pure "space-distance" of two events with respect to K results in "time-distance" of the same events with respect to K'. But the discovery of Minkowski, which was of importance for the formal development of the theory of relativity, does not lie here. It is to be found rather in the fact of his recognition that the four-dimensional space-time continuum of the theory of relativity, in its most essential formal properties, shows a pronounced relationship to the three-dimensional continuum of Euclidean geometrical space.[1] In order to give due prominence to this relationship, however, we must replace the usual time co-ordinate t by an imaginary magnitude $\sqrt{-1} \cdot ct$ proportional to it. Under these conditions, the natural laws satisfying the demands of the (special) theory of relativity assume mathematical forms, in which the time co-ordinate plays exactly the same rôle as the three space co-ordinates. Formally, these four co-ordinates correspond exactly to the three space co-ordinates in Euclidean geometry. It must be clear even to the non-mathematician that, as a consequence of this purely formal addition to our knowledge, the theory perforce gained clearness in no mean measure.

These inadequate remarks can give the reader only a vague notion of the important idea contributed by Minkowski. Without it the general theory of relativity, of which the fundamental ideas are developed in the following pages, would perhaps have got no farther than its long clothes. Minkowski's work is doubtless difficult of access to anyone inexperienced in math-

---

[1] Cf. the somewhat more detailed discussion in Appendix 2.

ematics, but since it is not necessary to have a very exact grasp of this work in order to understand the fundamental ideas of either the special or the general theory of relativity, I shall leave it here at present, and revert to it only towards the end of Part II.

Part II

The General Theory of Relativity

EIGHTEEN

Special and General Principle of Relativity

The basal principle, which was the pivot of all our previous considerations, was the *special* principle of relativity, *i.e.* the principle of the physical relativity of all *uniform* motion. Let us once more analyse its meaning carefully.

It was at all times clear that, from the point of view of the idea it conveys to us, every motion must be considered only as a relative motion. Returning to the illustration we have frequently used of the embankment and the railway carriage, we can express the fact of the motion here taking place in the following two forms, both of whch are equally justifiable:

(*a*) The carriage is in motion relative to the embankment.

(*b*) The embankment is in motion relative to the carriage.

In (*a*) the embankment, in (*b*) the carriage, serves as the body of reference in our statement of the motion taking place. If it is simply a question of detecting or of describing the motion involved, it is in principle immaterial to what reference-body we refer the motion. As already mentioned, this is self-evident, but it must not be confused with the much more comprehensive statement called "the principle of relativity," which we have taken as the basis of our investigations.

The principle we have made use of not only maintains that we may equally well choose the carriage or the embankment as our reference-body for the description of any event (for this, too, is self-evident). Our principle rather asserts what follows: If we formulate the general laws of nature as they are obtained from experience, by making use of

(*a*) the embankment as reference-body,

(*b*) the railway carriage as reference-body,

then these general laws of nature (*e.g.* the laws of mechanics or the law of the propagation of light *in vacuo*) have exactly the same form in both cases. This can also be expressed as follows: For the *physical* description of natural processes, neither of the reference-bodies K, K' is unique (lit. "specially marked out") as compared with the other. Unlike the first, this latter statement need not of necessity hold *a priori*; it is not contained in the conceptions of "motion" and "reference-body" and derivable from them; only *experience* can decide as to its correctness or incorrectness.

Up to the present, however, we have by no means maintained the equivalence of *all* bodies of reference K in connection with the formulation of natural laws. Our course was more on the following lines. In the first place, we started out from the assumption that there exists a reference-body K, whose condition of motion is such that the Galileian law holds with respect to it: A particle left to itself and sufficiently far removed from all other particles moves uniformly in a straight line. With reference to K (Galileian reference-body) the laws of nature were to be as simple as possible. But in addition to *K*, all bodies of reference *K'* should be given preference in this sense, and they should be exactly equivalent to *K* for the formulation of natural laws, provided that they are in a state of *uniform rectilinear and non-rotary motion* with respect to *K*; all these bodies of reference are to be regarded as Galileian reference-bodies. The validity of the principle of relativity was assumed only for these reference-bodies, but not for others (*e.g.* those possessing motion of a different kind). In this sense we speak of the *special* principle of relativity, or special theory of relativity.

In contrast to this we wish to understand by the "general principle of relativity" the following statement: All bodies of reference *K*, *K'*, etc., are equivalent for the description of natural phenomena (formulation of the general laws of nature), whatever may be their state of motion. But before proceeding farther, it ought to be pointed out that this formulation must be replaced later by a more abstract one, for reasons which will become evident at a later stage.

Since the introduction of the special principle of relativity has been justified, every intellect which strives after generalisation must feel the temptation to venture the step towards the general principle of relativity. But a simple and apparently quite reliable consideration seems to suggest that, for the present at any rate, there is little hope of success in such an attempt. Let us imagine ourselves transferred to our old friend the railway carriage, which is travelling at a uniform rate. As long as it is moving uniformly, the occupant of the carriage is not sensible of its motion, and it is for this reason that he can without reluctance interpret the facts of the case as indicating that the carriage is at rest, but the embankment in motion. Moreover, according to the special principle of relativity, this interpretation is quite justified also from a physical point of view.

If the motion of the carriage is now changed into a non-uniform motion, as for instance by a powerful application of the brakes, then the occupant of the carriage experiences a correspondingly powerful jerk forwards. The retarded motion is manifested in the mechanical behaviour of bodies relative to the person in the railway carriage. The mechanical behaviour is different from that of the case previously considered, and for this reason it would appear to be impossible that the same mechanical laws hold relatively to the non-uniformly moving carriage, as hold with reference to the carriage when at rest or in uniform motion. At all events it is clear that the Galileian law does not hold with respect to the non-uniformly moving carriage. Because of this, we feel compelled at the present juncture to grant a kind of absolute physical reality to non-uniform motion, in opposition to the general principle of relativity. But in what follows we shall soon see that this conclusion cannot be maintained.

NINETEEN

The Gravitational Field

If we pick up a stone and then let it go, why does it fall to the ground?" The usual answer to this question is: "Because it is attracted by the earth." Modern physics formulates the answer rather differently for the following reason. As a result of the more careful study of electromagnetic phenomena, we have come to regard action at a distance as a process impossible without the intervention of some intermediary medium. If, for instance, a magnet attracts a piece of iron, we cannot be content to regard this as meaning that the magnet acts directly on the iron through the intermediate empty space, but we are constrained to imagine—after the manner of Faraday—that the magnet always calls into being something physically real in the space around it, that something being what we call a "magnetic field." In its turn this magnetic field operates on the piece of iron, so that the latter strives to move towards the magnet. We shall not discuss here the justification for this incidental conception, which is indeed a somewhat arbitrary one. We shall only mention that with its aid electromagnetic phenomena can be theoretically represented much more satisfactorily than without it, and this applies particularly to the transmission of electromagnetic waves. The effects of gravitation also are regarded in an analogous manner.

The action of the earth on the stone takes place indirectly. The earth produces in its surroundings a gravitational field, which acts on the stone and produces its motion of fall. As we know from experience, the intensity of the action on a body diminishes according to a quite definite law, as we proceed farther and farther away from the earth. From our point of view this means: The law governing the properties of the gravitational field in space must be a perfectly definite one, in order correctly to represent the diminution of gravitational action with the distance from operative bodies. It is something like this: The body (*e.g.* the earth) produces a field in its immediate neighbourhood directly; the intensity and direction of the field at points farther removed from the body are thence determined by the law which governs the properties in space of the gravitational fields themselves.

In contrast to electric and magnetic fields, the gravitational field exhibits a most remarkable property, which is of fundamental importance for what follows. Bodies which are moving under the sole influence of a gravitational field receive an acceleration, *which does not in the least depend either on the material or on the physical state of the body.* For instance, a piece of lead and a piece of wood fall in exactly the same manner in a gravitational field (*in vacuo*), when they start off from rest or with the same initial velocity. This law, which holds most accurately, can be expressed in a different form in the light of the following consideration.

According to Newton's law of motion, we have

$$(\text{Force}) = (\text{inertial mass}) \times (\text{acceleration}),$$

where the "inertial mass" is a characteristic constant of the accelerated body. If now gravitation is the cause of the acceleration, we then have

$$(\text{Force}) = (\text{gravitational mass}) \times (\text{intensity of the gravitational field}),$$

where the "gravitational mass" is likewise a characteristic constant for the body. From these two relations follows:

$$(\text{acceleration}) = \frac{(\text{gravitational mass})}{(\text{inertial mass})} \ (\text{intensity of the gravitational field}).$$

If now, as we find from experience, the acceleration is to be independent of the nature and the condition of the body and always the same for a given gravitational field, then the ratio of the gravitational to the inertial mass must likewise be the same for all bodies. By a suitable choice of units we can thus make this ratio equal to unity. We then have the following law: The *gravitational* mass of a body is equal to its *inertial* mass.

It is true that this important law had hitherto been recorded in mechanics, but it had not been *interpreted*. A satisfactory interpretation can be obtained only if we recognise the following fact: *The same* quality of a body manifests itself according to circumstances as "inertia" or as "weight" (lit. "heaviness"). In the following section we shall show to what extent this is actually the case, and how this question is connected with the general postulate of relativity.

TWENTY

The Equality of Inertial and Gravitational Mass as an Argument for the General Postulate of Relativity

We imagine a large portion of empty space, so far removed from stars and other appreciable masses, that we have before us approximately the conditions required by the fundamental law of Galilei. It is then possible to choose a Galileian reference-body for this part of space (world), relative to which points at rest remain at rest and points in motion continue permanently in uniform rectilinear motion. As reference-body let us imagine a spacious chest resembling a room with an observer inside who is equipped with apparatus. Gravitation naturally does not exist for this observer. He must fasten himself with strings to the floor, otherwise the slightest impact against the floor will cause him to rise slowly towards the ceiling of the room.

To the middle of the lid of the chest is fixed externally a hook with rope attached, and now a "being" (what kind of a being is immaterial to us) begins pulling at this with a constant force. The chest together with the observer then begins to move "upwards" with a uniformly accelerated motion. In course of time their velocity will reach unheard-of values—

provided that we are viewing all this from another reference-body which is not being pulled with a rope.

But how does the man in the chest regard the process? The acceleration of the chest will be transmitted to him by the reaction of the floor of the chest. He must therefore take up this pressure by means of his legs if he does not wish to be laid out full length on the floor. He is then standing in the chest in exactly the same way as anyone stands in a room of a house on our earth. If he releases a body which he previously had in his hand, the acceleration of the chest will no longer be transmitted to this body, and for this reason the body will approach the floor of the chest with an accelerated relative motion. The observer will further convince himself *that the acceleration of the body towards the floor of the chest is always of the same magnitude, whatever kind of body he may happen to use for the experiment.*

Relying on his knowledge of the gravitational field (as it was discussed in the preceding section), the man in the chest will thus come to the conclusion that he and the chest are in a gravitational field which is constant with regard to time. Of course he will be puzzled for a moment as to why the chest does not fall in this gravitational field. Just then, however, he discovers the hook in the middle of the lid of the chest and the rope which is attached to it, and he consequently comes to the conclusion that the chest is suspended at rest in the gravitational field.

Ought we to smile at the man and say that he errs in his conclusion? I do not believe we ought to if we wish to remain consistent; we must rather admit that his mode of grasping the situation violates neither reason nor known mechanical laws.

Even though it is being accelerated with respect to the "Galileian space" first considered, we can nevertheless regard the chest as being at rest. We have thus good grounds for extending the principle of relativity to include bodies of reference which are accelerated with respect to each other, and as a result we have gained a powerful argument for a generalised postulate of relativity.

We must note carefully that the possibility of this mode of interpretation rests on the fundamental property of the gravitational field of giving all bodies the same acceleration, or, what comes to the same thing, on the law of the equality of inertial and gravitational mass. If this natural law did not exist, the man in the accelerated chest would not be able to interpret the behaviour of the bodies around him on the supposition of a gravitational field, and he would not be justified on the grounds of experience in supposing his reference-body to be "at rest."

Suppose that the man in the chest fixes a rope to the inner side of the lid, and that he attaches a body to the free end of the rope. The result of this will be to stretch the rope so that it will hang "vertically" downwards. If we ask for an opinion of the cause of tension in the rope, the man in the chest will say: "The suspended body experiences a downward force in the gravitational field, and this is neutralised by the tension of the rope; what determines the magnitude of the tension of the rope is the *gravitational mass* of the suspended body." On the other hand, an observer who is poised freely in space will interpret the condition of things thus: "The rope must perforce take part in the accelerated motion of the chest, and it transmits this motion to the body attached to it. The tension of the rope is just large enough to effect the acceleration of the body. That which determines the magnitude of the tension of the rope is the *inertial mass* of the body." Guided by this example, we see that our extension of the principle of relativity implies the *necessity* of the law of the equality of inertial and gravitational mass. Thus we have obtained a physical interpretation of this law.

From our consideration of the accelerated chest we see that a general theory of relativity must yield important results on the laws of gravitation. In point of fact, the systematic pursuit of the general idea of relativity has supplied the laws satisfied by the gravitational field. Before proceeding farther, however, I must warn the reader against a misconception suggested by these considerations. A gravitational field exists for the man in the chest, despite the fact that there was no such field for the co-ordinate system first chosen. Now we might easily suppose that the existence of a gravitational field is always only an *apparent* one. We might also think that, regardless of the kind of gravitational field which may be present, we could always choose another reference-body such that *no* gravitational field exists with reference to it. This is by no means true for all gravitational fields, but only for those of quite special form. It is, for instance, impossible to choose a body of reference such that, as judged from it, the gravitational field of the earth (in its entirety) vanishes.

We can now appreciate why that argument is not convincing, which we brought forward against the general principle of relativity at the end of Section 18. It is certainly true that the observer in the railway carriage experiences a jerk forwards as a result of the application of the brake, and that he recognises in this the non-uniformity of motion (retardation) of the carriage. But he is compelled by nobody to refer this jerk to a "real" acceleration (retardation) of the carriage. He might also interpret his experience thus: "My body of reference (the carriage) remains permanently at rest. With reference to it, however, there exists (during the period of application of the brakes) a gravitational field which is directed forwards and which is variable with respect to time. Under the influence of this field, the embankment together with the earth moves nonuniformly in such a manner that their original velocity in the backwards direction is continuously reduced."

TWENTY-ONE

In What Respects Are the Foundations of Classical Mechanics and of the Special Theory of Relativity Unsatisfactory?

We have already stated several times that classical mechanics starts out from the following law: Material particles sufficiently far removed from other material particles continue to move uniformly in a straight line or continue in a state of rest. We have also repeatedly emphasised that this fundamental law can only be valid for bodies of reference K which possess certain unique states of motion, and which are in uniform translational motion relative to each other. Relative to other reference-bodies K the law is not valid. Both in classical mechanics and in the special theory of relativity we therefore differentiate between reference-bodies K relative to which the recognised "laws of nature" can be said to hold, and reference-bodies K relative to which these laws do not hold.

But no person whose mode of thought is logical can rest satisfied with this condition of things. He asks: "How does it come that certain reference-bodies (or their states of motion) are given priority over other reference-bodies (or their states of motion)? *What is the reason for this preference?* In order to show clearly what I mean by this question, I shall make use of a comparison.

I am standing in front of a gas range. Standing alongside of each other on the range are two pans so much alike that one may be mistaken for the other. Both are half full of water. I notice that steam is being emitted continuously from the one pan, but not from the other. I am surprised at this, even if I have never seen either a gas range or a pan before. But if I now notice a luminous something of bluish colour under the first pan but not under the other, I cease to be astonished, even if I have never before seen a gas flame. For I can only say that this bluish something will cause the emission of the steam, or at least *possibly* it may do so. If, however, I notice the bluish something in neither case, and if I observe that the one continuously emits steam whilst the other does not, then I shall remain astonished and dissatisfied until I have discovered some circumstance to which I can attribute the different behaviour of the two pans.

Analogously, I seek in vain for a real something in classical mechanics (or in the special theory of relativity) to which I can attribute the different behaviour of bodies considered with respect to the reference-systems K and K''.[1] Newton saw this objection and attempted to invalidate it, but without success. But E. Mach recognised it most clearly of all, and because of

---

[1] The objection is of importance more especially when the state of motion of the reference-body is of such a nature that it does not require any external agency for its maintenance, *e.g.* in the case when the reference-body is rotating uniformly.

this objection he claimed that mechanics must be placed on a new basis. It can only be got rid of by means of a physics which is comformable to the general principle of relativity, since the equations of such a theory hold for every body of reference, whatever may be its state of motion.

TWENTY-TWO

A *Few Inferences from the General Principle of Relativity*

The considerations of Section 20 show that the general principle of relativity puts us in a position to derive properties of the gravitational field in a purely theoretical manner. Let us suppose, for instance, that we know the space-time "course" for any natural process whatsoever, as regards the manner in which it takes place in the Galileian domain relative to a Galileian body of reference K. By means of purely theoretical operations (*i.e.* simply by calculation) we are then able to find how this known natural process appears, as seen from a reference-body K' which is accelerated relatively to K. But since a gravitational field exists with respect to this new body of reference K', our consideration also teaches us how the gravitational field influences the process studied.

For example, we learn that a body which is in a state of uniform rectilinear motion with respect to K (in accordance with the law of Galilei) is executing an accelerated and in general curvilinear motion with respect to the accelerated reference-body K' (chest). This acceleration or curvature corresponds to the influence on the moving body of the gravitational field prevailing relatively to K'. It is known that a gravitational field influences the movement of bodies in this way, so that our consideration supplies us with nothing essentially new.

However, we obtain a new result of fundamental importance when we carry out the analogous consideration for a ray of light. With respect to the Galileian reference-body K, such a ray of light is transmitted rectilinearly with the velocity c. It can easily be shown that the path of the same ray of light is no longer a straight line when we consider it with reference to the accelerated chest (reference-body K'). From this we conclude, *that, in general, rays of light are propagated curvilinearly in gravitational fields*. In two respects this result is of great importance.

In the first place, it can be compared with the reality. Although a detailed examination of the question shows that the curvature of light rays required by the general theory of relativity is only exceedingly small for the gravitational fields at our disposal in practice, its estimated magnitude for light rays passing the sun at grazing incidence is nevertheless 1.7 seconds of arc. This ought to manifest itself in the following way. As seen from the earth, certain fixed stars appear to be in the neighbourhood of the sun, and are thus capable of observation during a total eclipse of the sun. At such times, these stars ought to appear to be displaced outwards from the sun by an amount indicated above, as compared with their apparent position in the sky when the sun is situated at another part of the heavens. The examination of the correctness or otherwise of this deduction is a problem of the greatest importance, the early solution of which is to be expected of astronomers.[1]

In the second place our result shows that, according to the general theory of relativity, the law of the constancy of the velocity of light *in vacuo*, which constitutes one of the two fundamental assumptions in the special theory of relativity and to which we have already frequently referred, cannot claim any unlimited validity. A curvature of rays of light can only take place when the velocity of propagation of light varies with position. Now we might think that as a consequence of this, the special theory of relativity and with it the whole theory of relativity would be laid in the dust. But in reality this is not the case. We can only conclude that the special theory of relativity cannot claim an unlimited domain of validity; its results hold only so long as we are able to disregard the influences of gravitational fields on the phenomena (*e.g.* of light).

Since it has often been contended by opponents of the theory of relativity that the special theory of relativity is overthrown by the general theory of relativity, it is perhaps advisable to make the facts of the case clearer by means of an appropriate comparison. Before the development of electrodynamics the laws of electrostatics were looked upon as the laws of electricity. At the present time we know that electric fields can be derived correctly from electrostatic considerations only for the case, which is never strictly realised, in which the electrical masses are quite at rest relatively to each

---

[1] By means of the star photographs of two expeditions equipped by a Joint Committee of the Royal and Royal Astronomical Societies, the existence of the deflection of light demanded by theory was first confirmed during the solar eclipse of 29th May, 1919. (Cf. Appendix 3.)

other, and to the co-ordinate system. Should we be justified in saying that for this reason electrostatics is overthrown by the field-equations of Maxwell in electrodynamics? Not in the least. Electrostatics is contained in electrodynamics as a limiting case; the laws of the latter lead directly to those of the former for the case in which the fields are invariable with regard to time. No fairer destiny could be allotted to any physical theory, than that it should of itself point out the way to the introduction of a more comprehensive theory, in which it lives on as a limiting case.

In the example of the transmission of light just dealt with, we have seen that the general theory of relativity enables us to derive theoretically the influence of a gravitational field on the course of natural processes, the laws of which are already known when a gravitational field is absent. But the most attractive problem, to the solution of which the general theory of relativity supplies the key, concerns the investigation of the laws satisfied by the gravitational field itself. Let us consider this for a moment.

We are acquainted with space-time domains which behave (approximately) in a "Galileian" fashion under suitable choice of reference-body, *i.e.* domains in which gravitational fields are absent. If we now refer such a domain to a reference-body K' possessing any kind of motion, then relative to K' there exists a gravitational field which is variable with respect to space and time.[1] The character of this field will of course depend on the motion chosen for K'. According to the general theory of rel-

---

[1] This follows from a generalisation of the discussion in Section 20.

ativity, the general law of the gravitational field must be satisfied for all gravitational fields obtainable in this way. Even
though by no means all gravitational fields can be produced in
this way, yet we may entertain the hope that the general law
of gravitation will be derivable from such gravitational fields of
a special kind. This hope has been realised in the most beautiful manner. But between the clear vision of this goal and its
actual realisation it was necessary to surmount a serious difficulty, and as this lies deep at the root of things, I dare not
withhold it from the reader. We require to extend our ideas of
the space-time continuum still farther.

TWENTY-THREE

Behaviour of Clocks and Measuring-Rods on a Rotating Body of Reference

Hitherto I have purposely refrained from speaking about the physical interpretation of space- and time-data in the case of the general theory of relativity. As a consequence, I am guilty of a certain slovenliness of treatment, which, as we know from the special theory of relativity, is far from being unimportant and pardonable. It is now high time that we remedy this defect; but I would mention at the outset, that this matter lays no small claims on the patience and on the power of abstraction of the reader.

We start off again from quite special cases, which we have frequently used before. Let us consider a space-time domain in which no gravitational field exists relative to a reference-body K whose state of motion has been suitably chosen. K is then a Galilean reference-body as regards the domain considered, and the results of the special theory of relativity hold relative to K. Let us suppose the same domain referred to a second body of reference K', which is rotating uniformly with respect to K. In order to fix our ideas, we shall imagine K' to be in the form of a plane circular disc, which rotates uniformly in its own plane about its centre. An observer who is sitting eccentrically on the disc K' is sensible of a force which acts outwards in a radial direction, and which would be interpreted as an effect of inertia (centrifugal force) by an observer who was at rest with respect to the original reference-body K. But the observer on the disc may regard his disc as a reference-body which is "at rest"; on the basis of the general principle of relativity he is justified in doing this. The force acting on himself, and in fact on all other bodies which are at rest relative to the disc, he regards as the effect of a gravitational field. Nevertheless, the space-distribution of this gravitational field is of a kind that would not be possible on Newton's theory of gravitation.[1] But since the observer believes in the general theory of relativity, this does not disturb him; he is quite in the right when he believes that a general law of gravitation can be formulated—a law which not only explains the motion of the stars correctly, but also the field of force experienced by himself.

The observer performs experiments on his circular disc with clocks and measuring-rods. In doing so, it is his intention to arrive at exact definitions for the signification of time- and space-data with reference to the circular disc K', these definitions being based on his observations. What will be his experience in this enterprise?

To start with, he places one of two identically constructed clocks at the centre of the circular disc, and the other on the

---

[1] The field disappears at the centre of the disc and increases proportionally to the distance from the centre as we proceed outwards.

edge of the disc, so that they are at rest relative to it. We now ask ourselves whether both clocks go at the same rate from the standpoint of the non-rotating Galileian reference-body *K*. As judged from this body, the clock at the centre of the disc has no velocity, whereas the clock at the edge of the disc is in motion relative to *K* in consequence of the rotation. According to a result obtained in Section 12, it follows that the latter clock goes at a rate permanently slower than that of the clock at the centre of the circular disc, *i.e.* as observed from *K*. It is obvious that the same effect would be noted by an observer whom we will imagine sitting alongside his clock at the centre of the circular disc. Thus on our circular disc, or, to make the case more general, in every gravitational field, a clock will go more quickly or less quickly, according to the position in which the clock is situated (at rest). For this reason it is not possible to obtain a reasonable definition of time with the aid of clocks which are arranged at rest with respect to the body of reference. A similar difficulty presents itself when we attempt to apply our earlier definition of simultaneity in such a case, but I do not wish to go any farther into this question.

Moreover, at this stage the definition of the space co-ordinates also presents insurmountable difficulties. If the observer applies his standard measuring-rod (a rod which is short as compared with the radius of the disc) tangentially to the edge of the disc, then, as judged from the Galileian system, the length of this rod will be less than 1, since, according to Section 12, moving bodies suffer a shortening in the direction of the motion. On the other hand, the measuring-rod will not experience a shortening in length, as judged from *K*, if it is applied to the disc in the direction of the radius. If, then, the observer first measures the circumference of the disc with his measuring-rod and then the diameter of the disc, on dividing the one by the other, he will not obtain as quotient the familiar number $\pi = 3 \cdot 14 \ldots$, but a larger number,[1] whereas of course, for a disc which is at rest with respect to K, this operation would yield π exactly. This proves that the propositions of Euclidean geometry cannot hold exactly on the rotating disc, nor in general in a gravitational field, at least if we attribute the length 1 to the rod in all positions and in every orientation. Hence the idea of a straight line also loses its meaning. We are therefore not in a position to define exactly the co-ordinates x, y, z relative to the disc by means of the method used in discussing the special theory, and as long as the co-ordinates and times of events have not been defined, we cannot assign an exact meaning to the natural laws in which these occur.

Thus all our previous conclusions based on general relativity would appear to be called in question. In reality we must make a subtle detour in order to be able to apply the postulate of general relativity exactly. I shall prepare the reader for this in the following paragraphs.

---

[1] Throughout this consideration we have to use the Galileian (non-rotating) system K as reference-body, since we may only assume the validity of the results of the special theory of relativity relative to K (relative to K' a gravitational field prevails).

TWENTY-FOUR

Euclidean and Non-Euclidean Continuum

The surface of a marble table is spread out in front of me. I can get from any one point on this table to any other point by passing continuously from one point to a "neighbouring" one, and repeating this process a (large) number of times, or, in other words, by going from point to point without executing "jumps." I am sure the reader will appreciate with sufficient clearness what I mean here by "neighbouring" and by "jumps" (if he is not too pedantic). We express this property of the surface by describing the latter as a continuum.

Let us now imagine that a large number of little rods of equal length have been made, their lengths being small compared with the dimensions of the marble slab. When I say they are of equal length, I mean that one can be laid on any other without the ends overlapping. We next lay four of these little rods on the marble slab so that they constitute a quadrilateral figure (a square), the diagonals of which are equally long. To ensure the equality of the diagonals, we make use of a little testing-rod. To this square we add similar ones, each of which has one rod in common with the first. We proceed in like manner with each of these squares until finally the whole marble slab is laid out with squares. The arrangement is such, that each side of a square belongs to two squares and each corner to four squares.

It is a veritable wonder that we can carry out this business without getting into the greatest difficulties. We only need to think of the following. If at any moment three squares meet at a corner, then two sides of the fourth square are already laid, and, as a consequence, the arrangement of the remaining two sides of the square is already completely determined. But I am now no longer able to adjust the quadrilateral so that its diagonals may be equal. If they are equal of their own accord, then this is an especial favour of the marble slab and of the little rods, about which I can only be thankfully surprised. We must needs experience many such surprises if the construction is to be successful.

If everything has really gone smoothly, then I say that the points of the marble slab constitute a Euclidean continuum with respect to the little rod, which has been used as a "distance" (line-interval). By choosing one corner of a square as "origin," I can characterize every other corner of a square with reference to this origin by means of two numbers. I only need state how many rods I must pass over when, starting from the origin, I proceed towards the "right" and then "upwards," in order to arrive at the corner of the square under consideration. These two numbers are then the "Cartesian co-ordinates" of this corner with reference to the "Cartesian co-ordinate system" which is determined by the arrangement of little rods.

By making use of the following modification of this abstract experiment, we recognise that there must also be cases in which the experiment would be unsuccessful. We shall suppose that the rods "expand" by an amount proportional to the increase of temperature. We heat the central part of the marble slab, but not the periphery, in which case two of our little rods can still be brought into coincidence at every position on the table. But our construction of squares must necessarily come into disorder during the heating, because the little rods on the central region of the table expand, whereas those on the outer part do not.

With reference to our little rods—defined as unit lengths— the marble slab is no longer a Euclidean continuum, and we are also no longer in the position of defining Cartesian co-ordinates directly with their aid, since the above construction can no longer be carried out. But since there are other things which are not influenced in a similar manner to the little rods (or perhaps not at all) by the temperature of the table, it is possible quite naturally to maintain the point of view that the marble slab is a "Euclidean continuum." This can be done in a satisfactory manner by making a more subtle stipulation about the measurement or the comparison of lengths.

But if rods of every kind (*i.e.* of every material) were to behave *in the same way* as regards the influence of temperature when they are on the variably heated marble slab, and if we had no other means of detecting the effect of temperature than the geometrical behaviour of our rods in experiments analogous to the one described above, then our best plan would be to assign the distance *one* to two points on the slab, provided that the ends of one of our rods could be made to coincide with these two points; for how else should we define the distance without our proceeding being in the highest measure grossly arbitrary? The method of Cartesian co-ordinates must then be discarded, and replaced by another which does not assume the validity of Euclidean geometry for rigid bodies.[1] The reader will notice that the situation depicted here corresponds to the one brought about by the general postulate of relativity (Section 23).

---

[1] Mathematicians have been confronted with our problem in the following form. If we are given a surface (*e.g.* an ellipsoid) in Euclidean three-dimensional space, then there exists for this surface a two-dimensional geometry, just as much as for a plane surface. Gauss undertook the task of treating this two-dimensional geometry from first principles, without making use of the fact that the surface belongs to a Euclidean continuum of three dimensions. If we imagine constructions to be made with rigid rods *in the surface* (similar to that above with the marble slab), we should find that different laws hold for these from those resulting on the basis of Euclidean plane geometry. The surface is not a Euclidean continuum with respect to the rods, and we cannot define Cartesian co-ordinates *in the surface*. Gauss indicated the principles according to which we can treat the geometrical relationships in the surface, and thus pointed out the way to the method of Riemann of treating multi-dimensional, non-Euclidean *continua*. Thus it is that mathematicians long ago solved the formal problems to which we are led by the general postulate of relativity.

TWENTY-FIVE

Gaussian Co-ordinates

According to Gauss, this combined analytical and geometrical mode of handling the problem can be arrived at in the following way. We imagine a system of arbitrary curves (see Fig. 4) drawn on the surface of the table.

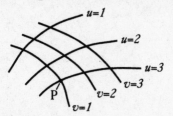

FIG. 4

These we designate as *u*-curves, and we indicate each of them by means of a number. The curves $u = 1$, $u = 2$ and $u = 3$ are drawn in the diagram. Between the curves $u = 1$ and $u = 2$ we must imagine an infinitely large number to be drawn, all of which correspond to real numbers lying between 1 and 2. We have then a system of *u*-curves, and this "infinitely dense" system covers the whole surface of the table. These *u*-curves must not intersect each other, and through each point of the surface one and only one curve must pass. Thus a perfectly definite value of u belongs to every point on the surface of the marble slab. In like manner we imagine a system of v-curves drawn on the surface. These satisfy the same conditions as the u-curves, they are provided with numbers in a corresponding manner, and they may likewise be of arbitrary shape. It follows that a value of u and a value of v belong to every point on the surface of the table. We call these two numbers the co-ordinates of the surface of the table (Gaussian co-ordinates). For example, the point P in the diagram has the Gaussian co-ordinates $u = 3, v = 1$. Two neighbouring points P and P' on the surface then correspond to the co-ordinates

$$P: \qquad u, v$$
$$P': \qquad u + du, v + dv,$$

where du and dv signify very small numbers. In a similar manner we may indicate the distance (line-interval) between P and P', as measured with a little rod, by means of the very small number ds. Then according to Gauss we have

$$ds^2 = g_{11}du^2 + 2g_{12}dudv + g_{22}\,dv^2,$$

where g_{11}, g_{12}, g_{22}, are magnitudes which depend in a perfectly definite way to u and v. The magnitudes g_{11}, g_{12} and g_{22} determine the behaviour of the rods relative to the u-curves and v-curves, and thus also relative to the surface of the table. For the case in which the points of the surface considered form a Euclidean continuum with reference to the measuring-rods, but only in this case, it is possible to draw the *u*-curves and *v*-curves and to attach numbers to them, in such a manner, that we simply have:

$$ds^2 = du^2 + dv^2.$$

Under these conditions, the *u*-curves and *v*-curves are straight lines in the sense of Euclidean geometry, and they are perpendicular to each other. Here the Gaussian co-ordinates are simply Cartesian ones. It is clear that Gauss co-ordinates are nothing more than an association of two sets of numbers with the points of the surface considered, of such a nature that numerical values differing very slightly from each other are associated with neighbouring points "in space."

So far, these considerations hold for a continuum of two dimensions. But the Gaussian method can be applied also to a continuum of three, four or more dimensions. If, for instance, a continuum of four dimensions be supposed available, we may represent it in the following way. With every point of the continuum we associate arbitrarily four numbers, x_1, x_2, x_3, x_4, which are known as "co-ordinates." Adjacent points correspond to adjacent values of the co-ordinates. If a distance ds is associated with the adjacent points P and P', this distance being measurable and well-defined from a physical point of view, then the following formula holds:

$$ds^2 = g_{11}dx_1{}^2 + 2g_{12}dx_1dx_2 \ldots . + g_{44}dx_4{}^2,$$

where the magnitudes g_{11}, etc., have values which vary with the position in the continuum. Only when the continuum is a Euclidean one is it possible to associate the co-ordinates x_1 . . x_4 with the points of the continuum so that we have simply

$$ds^2 = dx_1{}^2 + dx_2{}^2 + dx_3{}^2 + dx_4{}^2.$$

In this case relations hold in the four-dimensional continuum which are analogous to those holding in our three-dimensional measurements.

However, the Gauss treatment for ds^2 which we have given above is not always possible. It is only possible when sufficiently small regions of the continuum under consideration may be regarded as Euclidean continua. For example, this obviously holds in the case of the marble slab of the table and local variation of temperature. The temperature is practically constant for a small part of the slab, and thus the geometrical behaviour of the rods is *almost* as it ought to be according to the rules of Euclidean geometry. Hence the imperfections of the construction of squares in the previous section do not show themselves clearly until this construction is extended over a considerable portion of the surface of the table.

We can sum this up as follows: Gauss invented a method for the mathematical treatment of continua in general, in which "size-relations" ("distances" between neighbouring points) are defined. To every point of a continuum are assigned as many numbers (Gaussian co-ordinates) as the continuum has dimensions. This is done in such a way, that only one meaning can be attached to the assignment, and that numbers (Gaus-

sian co-ordinates) which differ by an indefinitely small amount
are assigned to adjacent points. The Gaussian co-ordinate system is a logical generalisation of the Cartesian co-ordinate
system. It is also applicable to non-Euclidean continua, but
only when, with respect to the defined "size" or "distance,"
small parts of the continuum under consideration behave more
nearly like a Euclidean system, the smaller the part of the
continuum under our notice.

TWENTY-SIX

The Space-Time Continuum of the Special Theory of Relativity Considered as a Euclidean Continuum

We are now in a position to formulate more exactly the idea of Minkowski, which was only vaguely indicated in Section 17. In accordance with the special theory of relativity, certain co-ordinate systems are given preference for the description of the four-dimensional, space-time continuum. We called these "Galileian co-ordinate systems." For these systems, the four co-ordinates x, y, z, t, which determine an event or—in other words—a point of the four-dimensional continuum, are defined physically in a simple manner, as set forth in detail in the first part of this book. For the transition from one Galileian system to another, which is moving uniformly with reference to the first, the equations of the Lorentz transformation are valid. These last form the basis for the derivation of deductions from the special theory of relativity, and in themselves they are nothing more than the expression of the universal validity of the law of transmission of light for all Galileian systems of reference.

Minkowski found that the Lorentz transformations satisfy the following simple conditions. Let us consider two neighbouring events, the relative position of which in the four-dimensional continuum is given with respect to a Galileian reference-body K by the space co-ordinate differences dx, dy, dz and the time-difference dt. With reference to a second Galileian system we shall suppose that the corresponding differences for these two events are dx', dy', dz', dt'. Then these magnitudes always fulfil the condition[1]

$$dx^2 + dy^2 + dz^2 - c^2 dt^2 = dx'^2 + dy'^2 + dz'^2 - c^2 dt'^2.$$

The validity of the Lorentz transformation follows from this condition. We can express this as follows: The magnitude

$$ds^2 = dx^2 + dy^2 + dz^2 - c^2 dt^2,$$

which belongs to two adjacent points of the four-dimensional space-time continuum, has the same value for all selected (Galileian) reference-bodies. If we replace $x, y, z \sqrt{-1}\, ct$, by x_1, x_2, x_3, x_4, we also obtain the result that

$$ds^2 = dx_1^2 + dx_2^2 + dx_3^2 + dx_4^2$$

is independent of the choice of the body of reference. We call the magnitude ds the "distance" apart of the two events or four-dimensional points.

---

[1] Cf. Appendices 1 and 2. The relations which are derived there for the co-ordinates themselves are valid also for co-ordinate *differences*, and thus also for co-ordinate differentials (indefinitely small differences).

Thus, if we choose as time-variable the imaginary variable $\sqrt{-1}\, ct$ instead of the real quantity t, we can regard the space-time continuum—in accordance with the special theory of relativity—as a "Euclidean" four-dimensional continuum, a result which follows from the considerations of the preceding section.

TWENTY-SEVEN

The Space-Time Continuum
of the General Theory of Relativity
Is Not a Euclidean Continuum

In the first part of this book we were able to make use of space-time co-ordinates which allowed of a simple and direct physical interpretation, and which, according to Section 26, can be regarded as four-dimensional Cartesian co-ordinates. This was possible on the basis of the law of the constancy of the velocity of light. But according to Section 21, the general theory of relativity cannot retain this law. On the contrary, we arrived at the result that according to this latter theory the velocity of light must always depend on the co-ordinates when a gravitational field is present. In connection with a specific illustration in Section 23, we found that the presence of a gravitational field invalidates the definition of the co-ordinates and the time, which led us to our objective in the special theory of relativity.

In view of the results of these considerations we are led to the conviction that, according to the general principle of relativity, the space-time continuum cannot be regarded as a Euclidean one, but that here we have the general case, corresponding to the marble slab with local variations of temperature, and with which we made acquaintance as an example of a two-dimensional continuum. Just as it was there impossible to construct a Cartesian co-ordinate system from equal rods, so here it is impossible to build up a system (reference-body) from rigid bodies and clocks, which shall be of such a nature that measuring-rods and clocks, arranged rigidly with respect to one another, shall indicate position and time directly. Such was the essence of the difficulty with which we were confronted in Section 23.

But the considerations of Sections 25 and 26 show us the way to surmount this difficulty. We refer the four-dimensional space-time continuum in an arbitrary manner to Gauss co-ordinates. We assign to every point of the continuum (event) four numbers, x_1, x_2, x_3, x_4 (co-ordinates), which have not the least direct physical significance, but only serve the purpose of numbering the points of the continuum in a definite but arbitrary manner. This arrangement does not even need to be of such a kind that we must regard x_1, x_2, x_3 as "space" co-ordinates and x_4 as a "time" co-ordinate.

The reader may think that such a description of the world would be quite inadequate. What does it mean to assign to an event the particular co-ordinates x_1, x_2, x_3, x_4, if in themselves these co-ordinates have no significance? More careful consideration shows, however, that this anxiety is unfounded. Let us consider, for instance, a material point with any kind of motion. If this point had only a momentary existence without duration, then it would be described in space-time by a single system of values x_1, x_2, x_3, x_4. Thus its permanent existence must be characterised by an infinitely large number of such systems of values, the co-ordinate values of which are so close together as to give continuity; corresponding to the material point, we thus have a (uni-dimensional) line in the four-dimensional continuum. In the same way, any such lines in our continuum correspond to many points in motion. The only statements having regard to these points which can claim a physical existence are in reality the statements about their encounters. In our mathematical treatment, such an encounter is expressed in the fact that the two lines which represent the motions of the points in question have a particular system of co-ordinate values, x_1, x_2, x_3, x_4, in common. After mature consideration the reader will doubtless admit that in reality such encounters constitute the only actual evidence of a time-space nature with which we meet in physical statements.

When we were describing the motion of a material point relative to a body of reference, we stated nothing more than the encounters of this point with particular points of the reference-body. We can also determine the corresponding values of the time by the observation of encounters of the body with clocks, in conjunction with the observation of the encounter of the hands of clocks with particular points on the dials. It is just the same in the case of space-measurements by means of measuring-rods, as a little consideration will show.

The following statements hold generally: Every physical description resolves itself into a number of statements, each of which refers to the space-time coincidence of two events A and B. In terms of Gaussian co-ordinates, every such statement is expressed by the agreement of their four co-ordinates

x_1, x_2, x_3, x_4. Thus in reality, the description of the time-space continuum by means of Gauss co-ordinates completely replaces the description with the aid of a body of reference, without suffering from the defects of the latter mode of description; it is not tied down to the Euclidean character of the continuum which has to be represented.

TWENTY-EIGHT

Exact Formulation of the General Principle of Relativity

We are now in a position to replace the provisional formulation of the general principle of relativity given in Section 18 by an exact formulation. The form there used, "All bodies of reference K, K', etc., are equivalent for the description of natural phenomena (formulation of the general laws of nature), whatever may be their state of motion," cannot be maintained, because the use of rigid reference-bodies, in the sense of the method followed in the special theory of relativity, is in general not possible in space-time description. The Gauss co-ordinate system has to take the place of the body of reference. The following statement corresponds to the fundamental idea of the general principle of relativity: *"All Gaussian co-ordinate systems are essentially equivalent for the formulation of the general laws of nature."*

We can state this general principle of relativity in still another form, which renders it yet more clearly intelligible than it is when in the form of the natural extension of the special principle of relativity. According to the special theory of relativity, the equations which express the general laws of nature pass over into equations of the same form when, by making use of the Lorentz transformation, we replace the space-time variables x, y, z, t, of a (Galileian) reference-body K by the space-time variables x', y', z', t', of a new reference-body K'. According to the general theory of relativity, on the other hand, by application of *arbitrary substitutions* of the Gauss variables x_1, x_2, x_3, x_4, the equations must pass over into equations of the same form; for every transformation (not only the Lorentz transformation) corresponds to the transition of one Gauss co-ordinate system into another.

If we desire to adhere to our "old-time" three-dimensional view of things, then we can characterise the development which is being undergone by the fundamental idea of the general theory of relativity as follows: The special theory of relativity has reference to Galileian domains, *i.e.* to those in which no gravitational field exists. In this connection a Galileian reference-body serves as body of reference, *i.e.* a rigid body the state of motion of which is so chosen that the Galileian law of the uniform rectilinear motion of "isolated" material points holds relatively to it.

Certain considerations suggest that we should refer the same Galileian domains to *non-Galileian* reference-bodies also. A gravitational field of a special kind is then present with respect to these bodies (cf. Sections 20 and 23).

In gravitational fields there are no such things as rigid bodies with Euclidean properties; thus the fictitious rigid body of reference is of no avail in the general theory of relativity. The motion of clocks is also influenced by gravitational fields, and in such a way that a physical definition of time which is made directly with the aid of clocks has by no means the same degree of plausibility as in the special theory of relativity.

For this reason non-rigid reference-bodies are used, which are as a whole not only moving in any way whatsoever, but which also suffer alterations in form *ad lib.* during their motion. Clocks, for which the law of motion is of any kind, however irregular, serve for the definition of time. We have to imagine each of these clocks fixed at a point on the non-rigid reference-body. These clocks satisfy only the one condition, that the "readings" which are observed simultaneously on adjacent clocks (in space) differ from each other by an indefinitely small amount. This non-rigid reference-body, which might appropriately be termed a "reference-mollusc," is in the main equivalent to a Gaussian four-dimensional co-ordinate system chosen arbitrarily. That which gives the "mollusc" a certain comprehensibility as compared with the Gauss co-ordinate system is the (really unjustified) formal retention of the separate existence of the space co-ordinates as opposed to the time co-ordinate. Every point on the mollusc is treated as a space-point, and every material point which is at rest relatively to it as at rest, so long as the mollusc is considered as reference-body. The general principle of relativity requires that all these molluscs can be used as reference-bodies with equal right and equal success in the formulation of the general laws of nature; the laws themselves must be quite independent of the choice of mollusc.

The great power possessed by the general principle of relativity lies in the comprehensive limitation which is imposed on the laws of nature in consequence of what we have seen above.

TWENTY-NINE

The Solution of the Problem of Gravitation on the Basis of the General Principle of Relativity

If the reader has followed all our previous considerations, he will have no further difficulty in understanding the methods leading to the solution of the problem of gravitation.

We start off from a consideration of a Galileian domain, *i.e.* a domain in which there is no gravitational field relative to the Galileian reference-body K. The behaviour of measuring-rods and clocks with reference to K is known from the special theory of relativity, likewise the behaviour of "isolated" material points; the latter move uniformly and in straight lines.

Now let us refer this domain to a random Gauss co-ordinate system or to a "mollusc" as reference-body K'. Then with respect to K' there is a gravitational field G (of a particular kind). We learn the behaviour of measuring-rods and clocks and also of freely-moving material points with reference to K' simply by mathematical transformation. We interpret this behaviour as the behaviour of measuring-rods, clocks and material points under the influence of the gravitational field G. Hereupon we introduce a hypothesis: that the influence of the gravitational field on measuring-rods, clocks and freely-moving material points continues to take place according to the same laws, even in the case where the prevailing gravitational field is *not* derivable from the Galileian special case, simply by means of a transformation of co-ordinates.

The next step is to investigate the space-time behaviour of the gravitational field *G*, which was derived from the Galileian special case simply by transformation of the co-ordinates. This behaviour is formulated in a law, which is always valid, no matter how the reference-body (mollusc) used in the description may be chosen.

This law is not yet the *general* law of the gravitational field, since the gravitational field under consideration is of a special kind. In order to find out the general law-of-field of gravitation we still require to obtain a generalisation of the law as found above. This can be obtained without caprice, however, by taking into consideration the following demands:

(*a*) The required generalisation must likewise satisfy the general postulate of relativity.

(*b*) If there is any matter in the domain under consideration, only its inertial mass, and thus according to Section 15 only its energy is of importance for its effect in exciting a field.

(*c*) Gravitational field and matter together must satisfy the law of the conservation of energy (and of impulse).

Finally, the general principle of relativity permits us to determine the influence of the gravitational field on the course of all those processes which take place according to known laws when a gravitational field is absent, *i.e.* which have al-

ready been fitted into the frame of the special theory of relativity. In this connection we proceed in principle according to
the method which has already been explained for measuring-
rods, clocks and freely-moving material points.

The theory of gravitation derived in this way from the general postulate of relativity excels not only in its beauty; nor in
removing the defect attaching to classical mechanics which
was brought to light in Section 21; nor in interpreting the
empirical law of the equality of inertial and gravitational mass;
but it has also already explained a result of observation in
astronomy, against which classical mechanics is powerless.

If we confine the application of the theory to the case where
the gravitational fields can be regarded as being weak, and in
which all masses move with respect to the co-ordinate system
with velocities which are small compared with the velocity of
light, we then obtain as a first approximation the Newtonian
theory. Thus the latter theory is obtained here without any
particular assumption, whereas Newton had to introduce the
hypothesis that the force of attraction between mutually at-
tracting material points is inversely proportional to the square
of the distance between them. If we increase the accuracy of
the calculation, deviations from the theory of Newton make
their appearance, practically all of which must nevertheless
escape the test of observation owing to their smallness.

We must draw attention here to one of these deviations.
According to Newton's theory, a planet moves round the sun
in an ellipse, which would permanently maintain its position
with respect to the fixed stars, if we could disregard the motion of the fixed stars themselves and the action of the other

planets under consideration. Thus, if we correct the observed motion of the planets for these two influences, and if Newton's theory be strictly correct, we ought to obtain for the orbit of the planet an ellipse, which is fixed with reference to the fixed stars. This deduction, which can be tested with great accuracy, has been confirmed for all the planets save one, with the precision that is capable of being obtained by the delicacy of observation attainable at the present time. The sole exception is Mercury, the planet which lies nearest the sun. Since the time of Leverrier, it has been known that the ellipse corresponding to the orbit of Mercury, after it has been corrected for the influences mentioned above, is not stationary with respect to the fixed stars, but that it rotates exceedingly slowly in the plane of the orbit and in the sense of the orbital motion. The value obtained for this rotary movement of the orbital ellipse was 43 seconds of arc per century, an amount ensured to be correct to within a few seconds of arc. This effect can be explained by means of classical mechanics only on the assumption of hypotheses which have little probability, and which were devised solely for this purpose.

On the basis of the general theory of relativity, it is found that the ellipse of every planet round the sun must necessarily rotate in the manner indicated above; that for all the planets, with the exception of Mercury, this rotation is too small to be detected with the delicacy of observation possible at the present time; but that in the case of Mercury it must amount to 43 seconds of arc per century, a result which is strictly in agreement with observation.

Apart from this one, it has hitherto been possible to make

only two deductions from the theory which admit of being tested by observation, to wit, the curvature of light rays by the gravitational field of the sun,[1] and a displacement of the spectral lines of light reaching us from large stars, as compared with the corresponding lines for light produced in an analogous manner terrestrially (*i.e.* by the same kind of atom).[2] These two deductions from the theory have both been confirmed.

---

[1] First observed by Eddington and others in 1919. (Cf. Appendix 3, pp. 145–151).

[2] Established by Adams in 1924. (Cf. p. 151).

Part III

Considerations on the Universe as a Whole

THIRTY

Cosmological Difficulties of Newton's Theory

Apart from the difficulty discussed in Section 21, there is a second fundamental difficulty attending classical celestial mechanics, which, to the best of my knowledge, was first discussed in detail by the astronomer Seeliger. If we ponder over the questions as to how the universe, considered as a whole, is to be regarded, the first answer that suggests itself to us is surely this: As regards space (and time) the universe is infinite. There are stars everywhere, so that the density of matter, although very variable in detail, is nevertheless on the average everywhere the same. In other words: However far we might travel through space, we should find everywhere an attenuated swarm of fixed stars of approximately the same kind and density.

This view is not in harmony with the theory of Newton. The latter theory rather requires that the universe should have a kind of centre in which the density of the stars is a maximum, and that as we proceed outwards from this centre the group-density of the stars should diminish, until finally, at great distances, it is succeeded by an infinite region of emptiness. The stellar universe ought to be a finite island in the infinite ocean of space.[1]

This conception is in itself not very satisfactory. It is still less satisfactory because it leads to the result that the light emitted by the stars and also individual stars of the stellar system are perpetually passing out into infinite space, never to return, and without ever again coming into interaction with other objects of nature. Such a finite material universe would be destined to become gradually but systematically impoverished.

In order to escape this dilemma, Seeliger suggested a modification of Newton's law, in which he assumes that for great distances the force of attraction between two masses diminishes more rapidly than would result from the inverse square law. In this way it is possible for the mean density of matter to be constant everywhere, even to infinity, without infinitely large gravitational fields being produced. We thus free ourselves from the distasteful conception that the material universe ought to possess something of the nature of a centre. Of course we purchase our emancipation from the fundamental difficulties mentioned, at the cost of a modification and complication of Newton's law which has neither empirical nor

---

[1] *Proof*—According to the theory of Newton, the number of "lines of force" which come from infinity and terminate in a mass m is proportional to the mass m. If, on the average, the mass density p_0 is constant throughout the universe, then a sphere of volume V will enclose the average mass p_0V. Thus the number of lines of force passing through the surface F of the sphere into its interior is proportional to p_0V. For unit area of the surface of the sphere the number of lines of force which enters the sphere is thus proportional to $p_0 \frac{V}{F}$ or to p_0R. Hence the intensity of the field at the surface would ultimately become infinite with increasing radius R of the sphere, which is impossible.

theoretical foundation. We can imagine innumerable laws which would serve the same purpose, without our being able to state a reason why one of them is to be preferred to the others; for any one of these laws would be founded just as little on more general theoretical principles as is the law of Newton.

THIRTY-ONE

The Possibility of a "Finite" and Yet "Unbounded" Universe

B
ut speculations on the structure of the universe also move in quite another direction. The development of non-Euclidean geometry led to the recognition of the fact, that we can cast doubt on the *infiniteness* of our space without coming into conflict with the laws of thought or with experience (Riemann, Helmholtz). These questions have already been treated in detail and with unsurpassable lucidity by Helmholtz and Poincaré, whereas I can only touch on them briefly here.

In the first place, we imagine an existence in two-dimensional space. Flat beings with flat implements, and in particular flat rigid measuring-rods, are free to move in a *plane*. For them nothing exists outside of this plane: that which they observe to happen to themselves and to their flat "things" is the all-inclusive reality of their plane. In particular, the constructions of plane Euclidean geometry can be carried out by means of the rods, *e.g.* the lattice construction, considered in Section 24. In contrast to ours, the universe of these beings is two-dimensional; but, like ours, it extends to infinity. In their universe there is room for an infinite number of identical squares made up of rods, *i.e.* its volume (surface) is infinite. If these beings say their universe is "plane," there is sense in the statement, because they mean that they can perform the constructions of plane Euclidean geometry with their rods. In this connection the individual rods always represent the same distance, independently of their position.

Let us consider now a second two-dimensional existence, but this time on a spherical surface instead of on a plane. The flat beings with their measuring-rods and other objects fit exactly on this surface and they are unable to leave it. Their whole universe of observation extends exclusively over the surface of the sphere. Are these beings able to regard the geometry of their universe as being plane geometry and their rods withal as the realisation of "distance"? They cannot do this. For if they attempt to realise a straight line, they will obtain a curve, which we "three-dimensional beings" designate as a great circle, *i.e.* a self-contained line of definite finite length, which can be measured up by means of a measuring-rod. Similarly, this universe has a finite area that can be compared with the area of a square constructed with rods. The great charm resulting from this consideration lies in the recognition of the fact that *the universe of these beings is finite and yet has no limits.*

But the spherical-surface beings do not need to go on a world-tour in order to perceive that they are not living in a Euclidean universe. They can convince themselves of this on every part of their "world," provided they do not use too small a piece of it. Starting from a point, they draw "straight lines"

(arcs of circles as judged in three-dimensional space) of equal
length in all directions. They will call the line joining the free
ends of these lines a "circle." For a plane surface, the ratio of
the circumference of a circle to its diameter, both lengths
being measured with the same rod, is, according to Euclidean
geometry of the plane, equal to a constant value π, which is
independent of the diameter of the circle. On their spherical
surface our flat beings would find for this ratio the value

$$\pi = \frac{\sin\left(\dfrac{r}{R}\right)}{\left(\dfrac{v}{R}\right)},$$

i.e. a smaller value than π, the difference being the more
considerable, the greater is the radius of the circle in comparison with the radius R of the "world-sphere." By means of this
relation the spherical beings can determine the radius of their
universe ("world"), even when only a relatively small part of
their world-sphere is available for their measurements. But if
this part is very small indeed, they will no longer be able to
demonstrate that they are on a spherical "world" and not on
a Euclidean plane, for a small part of a spherical surface differs
only slightly from a piece of a plane of the same size.

Thus if the spherical-surface beings are living on a planet of
which the solar system occupies only a negligibly small part of
the spherical universe, they have no means of determining
whether they are living in a finite or in an infinite universe,

because the "piece of universe" to which they have access is in both cases practically plane, or Euclidean. It follows directly from this discussion, that for our sphere-beings the circumference of a circle first increases with the radius until the "circumference of the universe" is reached, and that it thenceforward gradually decreases to zero for still further increasing values of the radius. During this process the area of the circle continues to increase more and more, until finally it becomes equal to the total area of the whole "world-sphere."

Perhaps the reader will wonder why we have placed our "beings" on a sphere rather than on another closed surface. But this choice has its justification in the fact that, of all closed surfaces, the sphere is unique in possessing the property that all points on it are equivalent. I admit that the ratio of the circumference c of circle to its radius r depends on r, but for a given value of r it is the same for all points of the "world-sphere"; in other words, the "world-sphere" is a "surface of constant curvature."

To this two-dimensional sphere-universe there is a three-dimensional analogy, namely, the three-dimensional spherical space which was discovered by Riemann. Its points are likewise all equivalent. It possesses a finite volume, which is determined by its "radius" $(2\pi^2 R^3)$. Is it possible to imagine a spherical space? To imagine a space means nothing else than that we imagine an epitome of our "space" experience, *i.e.* of experience that we can have in the movement of "rigid" bodies. In this sense we *can* imagine a spherical space.

Suppose we draw lines or stretch strings in all directions

from a point, and mark off from each of these the distance γ
with a measuring-rod. All the free end-points of these lengths
lie on a spherical surface. We can specially measure up the
area (F) of this surface by means of a square made up of
measuring-rods. If the universe is Euclidean, then $F = 4\pi\gamma^2$; if
it is spherical, then F is always less than $4\pi\gamma^2$. With increasing
values of γ, F increases from zero up to a maximum value
which is determined by the "world-radius," but for still further increasing values of γ, the area gradually diminishes to
zero. At first, the straight lines which radiate from the starting
point diverge farther and farther from one another, but later
they approach each other, and finally they run together again
at a "counter-point" to the starting point. Under such conditions they have traversed the whole spherical space. It is easily
seen that the three-dimensional spherical space is quite analogous to the two-dimensional spherical surface. It is finite (*i.e.*
of finite volume), and has no bounds.

It may be mentioned that there is yet another kind of curved
space: "elliptical space." It can be regarded as a curved space
in which the two "counter-points" are identical (indistinguish-
able from each other). An elliptical universe can thus be considered to some extent as a curved universe possessing central
symmetry.

It follows from what has been said, that closed spaces without limits are conceivable. From amongst these, the spherical
space (and the elliptical) excels in its simplicity, since all
points on it are equivalent. As a result of this discussion, a
most interesting question arises for astronomers and physicists, and that is whether the universe in which we live is

infinite, or whether it is finite in the manner of the spherical universe. Our experience is far from being sufficient to enable us to answer this question. But the general theory of relativity permits of our answering it with a moderate degree of certainty, and in this connection the difficulty mentioned in Section 30 finds its solution.

THIRTY-TWO

The Structure of Space
According to the General Theory
of Relativity

According to the general theory of relativity, the geometrical properties of space are not independent, but they are determined by matter. Thus we can draw conclusions about the geometrical structure of the universe only if we base our considerations on the state of the matter as being something that is known. We know from experience that, for a suitably chosen co-ordinate system, the velocities of the stars are small as compared with the velocity of transmission of light. We can thus as a rough approximation arrive at a conclusion as to the nature of the universe as a whole, if we treat the matter as being at rest.

We already know from our previous discussion that the behaviour of measuring-rods and clocks is influenced by gravitational fields, *i.e.* by the distribution of matter. This in itself is sufficient to exclude the possibility of the exact validity of Euclidean geometry in our universe. But it is conceivable that our universe differs only slightly from a Euclidean one, and this notion seems all the more probable, since calculations show that the metrics of surrounding space is influenced only to an exceedingly small extent by masses even of the magnitude of our sun. We might imagine that, as regards geometry, our universe behaves analogously to a surface which is irregularly curved in its individual parts, but which nowhere departs appreciably from a plane: something like the rippled surface of a lake. Such a universe might fittingly be called a quasi-Euclidean universe. As regards its space it would be infinite. But calculation shows that in a quasi-Euclidean universe the average density of matter would necessarily be *nil*. Thus such a universe could not be inhabited by matter everywhere; it would present to us that unsatisfactory picture which we portrayed in Section 30.

If we are to have in the universe an average density of matter which differs from zero, however small may be that difference, then the universe cannot be quasi-Euclidean. On the contrary, the results of calculation indicate that if matter be distributed uniformly, the universe would necessarily be spherical (or elliptical). Since in reality the detailed distribution of matter is not uniform, the real universe will deviate in individual parts from the spherical, *i.e.* the universe will be quasi-spherical. But it will be necessarily finite. In fact, the theory supplies us with a simple connection[1] between the space-expanse of the universe and the average density of matter in it.

---

[1] For the "radius" R of the universe we obtain the equation

$$R^2 = \frac{2}{\kappa \rho}.$$

The use of the C.G.S. system in this equation gives $\frac{2}{\kappa} = 108.10^{37}$; ρ is the average density of the matter and x is a constant connected with the Newtonian constant of gravitational.

Simple Derivation of the
Lorentz Transformation

For the relative orientation of the co-ordinate systems indicated in Fig. 2, the x-axes of both systems permanently coincide. In the present case we can divide the problem into parts by considering first only events which are localised on the x-axis. Any such event is represented with respect to the co-ordinate system K by the abscissa x and the time t, and with respect to the system K' by the abscissa x' and the time t'. We require to find x' and t' when x and t are given.

A light-signal, which is proceeding along the positive axis of x, is transmitted according to the equation

$$x = ct$$

or

$$x - ct = 0 \qquad . \quad . \quad . \quad (1).$$

Since the same light-signal has to be transmitted relative to K' with the velocity c, the propagation relative to the system K' will be represented by the analogous formula

$$x' - ct' = 0 \qquad . \quad . \quad . \quad (2).$$

Those space-time points (events) which satisfy (1) must also satisfy (2). Obviously this will be the case when the relation

$$(x' - ct' = \lambda(x - ct) \qquad . \quad . \quad . \quad (3),$$

is fulfilled in general, where λ indicates a constant; for, according to (3), the disappearance of $(x - ct)$ involves the disappearance of $(x' - ct')$.

If we apply quite similar considerations to light rays which are being transmitted along the negative x-axis, we obtain the condition

$$(x' + ct') = \mu(x + ct) \qquad . \quad . \quad . \quad (4).$$

By adding (or subtracting) equations (3) and (4), and introducing for convenience the constants a and b in place of the constants λ and μ, where

$$a = \frac{\gamma + \mu}{2}$$

and

$$b = \frac{\gamma - \mu}{2},$$

we obtain the equations

$$\left.\begin{array}{l} x' = ax - bct \\ ct' = act - bx \end{array}\right\} \qquad . \quad . \quad . \quad (5).$$

We should thus have the solution of our problem, if the constants a and b were known. These result from the following discussion.

For the origin of K' we have permanently $x' = 0$, and hence according to the first of the equations (5)

$$x = \frac{bc}{a}t.$$

If we call v the velocity with which the origin of K' is moving relative to K, we then have

$$v = \frac{bc}{a} \qquad . \quad . \quad . \quad (6).$$

The same value v can be obtained from equations (5), if we calculate the velocity of another point of K' relative to K, or the velocity (directed towards the negative x-axis) of a point of K with respect to K'. In short, we can designate v as the relative velocity of the two systems.

Furthermore, the principle of relativity teaches us that, as judged from K, the length of a unit measuring-rod which is at rest with reference to K' must be exactly the same as the length, as judged from K', of a unit measuring-rod which is at rest relative to K. In order to see how the points of the x'-axis appear as viewed from K, we only require to take a "snapshot" of K' from K; this means that we have to insert a particular value of t (time of K), *e.g.* $t = 0$. For this value of t we then obtain from the first of the equations (5)

$$x' = ax.$$

Two points of the x'-axis which are separated by the distance $\Delta x' = 1$ when measured in the K' system are thus separated in our instantaneous photograph by the distance

$$\Delta x = \frac{1}{a} \qquad \qquad . \quad . \quad . \quad (7).$$

But if the snapshot be taken from $K'(t' = 0)$, and if we eliminate t from the equations (5), taking into account the expression (6), we obtain

$$x' = a\left(1 - \frac{v^2}{c^2}\right)x.$$

From this we conclude that two points of the x-axis separated by the distance 1 (relative to K) will be represented on our snapshot by the distance

$$\Delta x' = a\left(1 - \frac{v^2}{c^2}\right) \qquad . \quad . \quad . \quad (7a).$$

But from what has been said, the two snapshots must be identical; hence Δx in (7) must be equal to $\Delta x'$ in (7a), so that we obtain

$$a^2 = \frac{1}{1 - \dfrac{v^2}{c^2}} \qquad . \quad . \quad . \quad (7b).$$

The equations (6) and (7b) determine the constants a and b. By inserting the values of these constants in (5), we obtain the first and the fourth of the equations given in Section XI.

$$\left. \begin{aligned} x' &= \frac{x - vt}{\sqrt{1 - \dfrac{v^2}{c^2}}} \\[2em] t' &= \frac{t - \dfrac{v}{c^2}x}{\sqrt{1 - \dfrac{v^2}{c^2}}} \end{aligned} \right\} \qquad . \quad . \quad . \quad (8).$$

Thus we have obtained the Lorentz transformation for events on the x-axis. It satisfies the condition

$$x'^2 - c^2 t'^2 = x^2 - c^2 t^2 \qquad . \quad . \quad . \quad (8a).$$

The extension of this result, to include events which take place outside the x-axis, is obtained by retaining equations (8) and supplementing them by the relations

$$\left. \begin{array}{l} y' = y \\ z' = z \end{array} \right\} \qquad . \quad . \quad . \quad (9).$$

In this way we satisfy the postulate of the constancy of the velocity of light *in vacuo* for rays of light of arbitrary directions, both for the system K and for the system K'. This may be shown in the following manner.

We suppose a light-signal sent out from the origin of K at the time $t = 0$. It will be propagated according to the equation

$$r = \sqrt{x^2 + y^2 + z^2} = ct,$$

or, if we square this equation, according to the equation

$$x^2 + y^2 + z^2 - c^2 t^2 = 0 \quad . \qquad . \qquad . \quad (10).$$

It is required by the law of propagation of light, in conjunction with the postulate of relativity, that the transmission of the signal in question should take place—as judged from K'—in accordance with the corresponding formula

$$r' = ct',$$

or,

$$x'^2 + y'^2 + z'^2 - c^2 t'^2 = 0 \quad . \qquad . \quad (10a).$$

In order that equation (10*a*) may be a consequence of equation (10), we must have

$$x' + y'^2 + z'^2 - c^2t'^2 = \sigma(x^2 + y^2 + z^2 - c^2t^2) \qquad (11).$$

Since equation (8*a*) must hold for points on the *x*-axis, we thus have $\sigma = 1$. It is easily seen that the Lorentz transformation really satisfies equation (11) for $\sigma = 1$; for (11) is a consequence of (8*a*) and (9), and hence also of (8) and (9). We have thus derived the Lorentz transformation.

The Lorentz transformation represented by (8) and (9) still requires to be generalised. Obviously it is immaterial whether the axes of *K'* be chosen so that they are spatially parallel to those of *K*. It is also not essential that the velocity of translation of *K'* with respect to *K* should be in the direction of the *x*-axis. A simple consideration shows that we are able to construct the Lorentz transformation in this general sense from two kinds of transformations, viz. from Lorentz transformations in the special sense and from purely spatial transformations, which corresponds to the replacement of the rectangular co-ordinate system by a new system with its axes pointing in other directions.

Mathematically, we can characterise the generalised Lorentz transformation thus:

It expresses x', y', z', t', in terms of linear homogeneous functions of x, y, z, t, of such a kind that the relation

$$x'^2 + y'^2 + z'^2 - c^2t'^2 = x^2 + y^2 + z^2 - c^2t^2 \qquad (11a)$$

is satisfied identically. That is to say: If we substitute their expressions in x, y, z, t in place of x', y', z', t', on the left-hand side, then the left-hand side of (11*a*) agrees with the right-hand side.

Minkowski's Four-Dimensional Space ("World")

[SUPPLEMENTARY TO SECTION 17]

We can characterise the Lorentz transformation still more simply if we introduce the imaginary $\sqrt{-1}$. ct in place of t, as time-variable. If, in accordance with this, we insert

$$x_1 = x$$
$$x_2 = y$$
$$x_3 = z$$
$$x_4 = \sqrt{-1}.\,ct,$$

and similarly for the accented system K', then the condition which is identically satisfied by the transformation can be expressed thus:

$$x_1'^2 + x_2'^2 + x_3'^2 + x_4'^2 = x_1^2 + x_2^2 + x_3^2 + x_4^2 \qquad (12).$$

That is, by the afore-mentioned choice of "co-ordinates," (11a) is transformed into this equation.

We see from (12) that the imaginary time co-ordinate x_4 enters into the condition of transformation in exactly the same way as the space co-ordinates x_1, x_2, x_3. It is due to this fact that, according to the theory of relativity, the "time" x_4 enters into natural laws in the same form as the space co-ordinates x_1, x_2, x_3.

A four-dimensional continuum described by the "co-ordinates" x_1, x_2, x_3, x_4, was called "world" by Minkowski, who also termed a point-event a "world-point." From a "happening" in three-dimensional space, physics becomes, as it were, an "existence" in the four-dimensional "world."

This four-dimensional "world" bears a close similarity to the three-dimensional "space" of (Euclidean) analytical geometry. If we introduce into the latter a new Cartesian co-ordinate system (x'_1, x'_2, x'_3) with the same origin, then x'_1, x'_2, x'_3, are linear homogeneous functions of x_1, x_2, x_3, which identically satisfy the equation

$$x_1'^2 + x_2'^2 + x_3'^2 = x_1^2 + x_2^2 + x_3^2.$$

The analogy with (12) is a complete one. We can regard Minkowski's "world" in a formal manner as a four-dimensional Euclidean space (with imaginary time co-ordinate); the Lorentz transformation corresponds to a "rotation" of the co-ordinate system in the four-dimensional "world."

The Experimental Confirmation of the General Theory of Relativity

From a systematic theoretical point of view, we may imagine the process of evolution of an empirical science to be a continuous process of induction. Theories are evolved and are expressed in short compass as statements of a large number of individual observations in the form of empirical laws, from which the general laws can be ascertained by comparison. Regarded in this way, the development of a science bears some resemblance to the compilation of a classified catalogue. It is, as it were, a purely empirical enterprise.

But this point of view by no means embraces the whole of the actual process; for it slurs over the important part played by intuition and deductive thought in the development of an exact science. As soon as a science has emerged from its initial stages, theoretical advances are no longer achieved merely by a process of arrangement. Guided by empirical data, the investigator rather develops a system of thought which, in general, is built up logically from a small number of fundamental assumptions, the so-called axioms. We call such a system of thought a *theory*. The theory finds the justification for its existence in the fact that it correlates a large number of single observations, and it is just here that the "truth" of the theory lies.

Corresponding to the same complex of empirical data, there may be several theories, which differ from one another to a considerable extent. But as regards the deductions from the theories which are capable of being tested, the agreement between the theories may be so complete, that it becomes difficult to find any deductions in which the two theories differ from each other. As an example, a case of general interest is available in the province of biology, in the Darwinian theory of the development of species by selection in the struggle for existence, and in the theory of development which is based on the hypothesis of the hereditary transmission of acquired characters.

We have another instance of far-reaching agreement between the deductions from two theories in Newtonian mechanics on the one hand, and the general theory of relativity on the other. This agreement goes so far, that up to the present we have been able to find only a few deductions from the general theory of relativity which are capable of investigation, and to which the physics of pre-relativity days does not also lead, and this despite the profound difference in the fundamental assumptions of the two theories. In what follows, we shall again consider these important deductions, and we shall also discuss the empirical evidence appertaining to them which has hitherto been obtained.

(A) MOTION OF THE PERIHELION OF MERCURY

According to Newtonian mechanics and Newton's law of gravitation, a planet which is revolving round the sun would describe an ellipse round the latter, or, more correctly, round the common centre of gravity of the sun and the planet. In such a system, the sun, or the common centre of gravity, lies in one of the foci of the orbital ellipse in such a manner that, in the course of a planet-year, the distance sun-planet grows from a minimum to a maximum, and then decreases again to a minimum. If instead of Newton's law we insert a somewhat different law of attraction into the calculation, we find that, according to this new law, the motion would still take place in such a manner that the distance sun-planet exhibits periodic variations; but in this case the angle described by the line joining sun and planet during such a period (from perihelion—closest proximity to the sun—to perihelion) would differ from 360°. The line of the orbit would not then be a closed one but in the course of time it would fill up an annular part of the orbital plane, viz. between the circle of least and the circle of greatest distance of the planet from the sun.

According also to the general theory of relativity, which differs of course from the theory of Newton, a small variation from the Newton-Kepler motion of a planet in its orbit should take place, and in such a way, that the angle described by the radius sun-planet between one perihelion and the next should exceed that corresponding to one complete revolution by an amount given by

$$+ \frac{24\pi^3 a^2}{T^2 c^2 (1 - e^2)}.$$

(*N.B.*—One complete revolution corresponds to the angle 2π in the absolute angular measure customary in physics, and the above expression gives the amount by which the radius sun-planet exceeds this angle during the interval between one perihelion and the next.) In this expression a represents the major semi-axis of the ellipse, e its eccentricity, c the velocity of light, and T the period of revolution of the planet. Our result may also be stated as follows: According to the general theory of relativity, the major axis of the ellipse rotates round the sun in the same sense as the orbital motion of the planet. Theory requires that this rotation should amount to 43 seconds of arc per century for the planet Mercury, but for the other planets of our solar system its magnitude should be so small that it would necessarily escape detection.[1]

In point of fact, astronomers have found that the theory of Newton does not suffice to calculate the observed motion of Mercury with an exactness corresponding to that of the delicacy of observation attainable at the present time. After taking account of all the disturbing influences exerted on Mercury by the remaining planets, it was found (Leverrier—1859—and Newcomb—1895) that an unexplained perihelial movement of the orbit of Mercury remained over, the amount of which does not differ sensibly from the above-mentioned +43 sec-

---

[1] Especially since the next planet Venus has an orbit that is almost an exact circle, which makes it more difficult to locate the perihelion with precision.

onds of arc per century. The uncertainty of the empirical result amounts to a few seconds only.

(B) DEFLECTION OF LIGHT BY A GRAVITATIONAL FIELD

In Section 12 it has been already mentioned that according to the general theory of relativity, a ray of light will experience a curvature of its path when passing through a gravitational field, this curvature being similar to that experienced by the path of a body which is projected through a gravitational field. As a result of this theory, we should expect that a ray of light which is passing close to a heavenly body would be deviated towards the latter. For a ray of light which passes the sun at a distance of Δ sun-radii from its centre, the angle of deflection (a) should amount to

$$a = \frac{1.7 \text{ seconds of arc}}{\Delta}.$$

It may be added that, according to the theory, half of this deflection is produced by the Newtonian field of attraction of the sun, and the other half by the geometrical modification ("curvature") of space caused by the sun.

This result admits of an experimental test by means of the photographic registration of stars during a total eclipse of the sun. The only reason why we must wait for a total eclipse is because at every

FIG. 5

other time the atmosphere is so strongly illuminated by the light from the sun that the stars situated near the sun's disc are invisible. The predicted effect can be seen clearly from the accompanying diagram. If the sun (S) were not present, a star which is practically infinitely distant would be seen in the direction D_1, as observed from the earth. But as a consequence of the deflection of light from the star by the sun, the star will be seen in the direction D_2, *i.e.* at a somewhat greater distance from the centre of the sun that corresponds to its real position.

In practice, the question is tested in the following way. The stars in the neighbourhood of the sun are photographed during a solar eclipse. In addition, a second photograph of the same stars is taken when the sun is situated at another position in the sky, *i.e.* a few months earlier or later. As compared with the standard photograph, the positions of the stars on the eclipse-photograph ought to appear displaced radially outwards (away from the centre of the sun) by an amount corresponding to the angle *a*.

We are indebted to the Royal Society and to the Royal Astronomical Society for the investigation of this important deduction. Undaunted by the war and by difficulties of both a material and a psychological nature aroused by the war, these societies equipped two expeditions—to Sobral (Brazil), and to the island of Principe (West Africa)—and sent several of Britain's most celebrated astronomers (Eddington, Cottingham, Crommelin, Davidson), in order to obtain photographs of the solar eclipse of 29th May, 1919. The relative discrepancies to be expected between the stellar photographs obtained during the eclipse and the comparison photographs amounted to a few hundredths of a millimetre only. Thus great accuracy was necessary in making the adjustments required for the taking of the photographs, and in their subsequent measurement.

The results of the measurements confirmed the theory in a thoroughly satisfactory manner. The rectangular components of the observed and of the calculated deviations of the stars (in seconds of arc) are set forth in the following table of results:

Number of the Star.	First Co-ordinate.		Second Co-ordinate.	
	Observed.	Calculated.	Observed.	Calculated.
11	−0.19	−0.22	+0.16	+0.02
5	+0.29	+0.31	−0.46	−0.43
4	+0.11	+0.10	+0.83	+0.74
3	+0.20	+0.12	+1.00	+0.87
6	+0.10	+0.04	+0.57	+0.40
10	−0.08	+0.09	+0.35	+0.32
2	+0.95	+0.85	−0.27	−0.09

(c) DISPLACEMENT OF SPECTRAL LINES TOWARDS THE RED

In Section 23 it has been shown that in a system K' which is in rotation with regard to a Galileian system K, clocks of identical construction, and which are considered at rest with respect to the rotating reference-body, go at rates which are dependent on the positions of the clocks. We shall now examine this dependence quantitatively. A clock, which is situated at a distance γ from the centre of the disc, has a velocity relative to K which is given by

$$v = \omega\gamma$$

where ω represents the angular velocity of rotation of the disc K' with respect to K. If ν_0 represents the number of ticks of the clock per unit time ("rate" of the clock) relative to K when the clock is at rest, then the "rate" of the clock (ν) when it is moving relative to K with a velocity v, but at rest with respect to the disc, will, in accordance with Section 12, be given by

$$\nu = \nu_0\sqrt{1 - \frac{v^2}{c^2}},$$

or with sufficient accuracy by

$$\nu = \nu_0\left(1 - \frac{1}{2}\frac{v^2}{c^2}\right).$$

This expression may also be stated in the following form:

$$\nu = \nu_0\left(1 - \frac{1}{c^2}\frac{\omega^2\gamma^2}{2}\right).$$

If we represent the difference of potential of the centrifugal force between the position of the clock and the centre of the disc by ϕ, *i.e.* the work, considered negatively, which must be performed on the unit of mass against the centrifugal force in order to transport it from the position of the clock on the rotating disc to the centre of the disc, then we have

$$\phi = -\frac{\omega^2 \gamma^2}{2}.$$

From this it follows that

$$\nu = \nu_0 \left(1 + \frac{\phi}{c^2}\right).$$

In the first place, we see from this expression that two clocks of identical construction will go at different rates when situated at different distances from the centre of the disc. This result is also valid from the standpoint of an observer who is rotating with the disc.

Now, as judged from the disc, the latter is in a gravitational field of potential ϕ, hence the result we have obtained will hold quite generally for gravitational fields. Furthermore, we can regard an atom which is emitting spectral lines as a clock, so that the following statement will hold:

An atom absorbs or emits light of a frequency which is dependent on the potential of the gravitational field in which it is situated.

The frequency of an atom situated on the surface of a heavenly body will be somewhat less than the frequency of an atom of the same element which is situated in free space (or on the surface of a smaller celestial body). Now $\phi = - K\dfrac{M}{\gamma}$, where K is Newton's constant of gravitation, and M is the mass of the heavenly body. Thus a displacement towards the red ought to take place for spectral lines produced at the surface of stars as compared with the spectral lines of the same element produced at the surface of the earth, the amount of this displacement being

$$\frac{\nu_0 - \nu}{\nu_0} = \frac{K}{c^2}\frac{M}{\gamma}.$$

For the sun, the displacement towards the red predicted by theory amounts to about two millionths of the wave-length. A trustworthy calculation is not possible in the case of the stars, because in general neither the mass M nor the radius γ are known.

It is an open question whether or not this effect exists, and at the present time (1920) astronomers are working with great zeal towards the solution. Owing to the smallness of the effect in the case of the sun, it is difficult to form an opinion as to its existence. Whereas Grebe and Bachem (Bonn), as a result of their own measurements and those of Evershed and Schwarzschild on the cyanogen bands, have placed the existence of the effect almost beyond doubt, other investigators, particularly St. John, have been led to the opposite opinion in consequence of their measurements.

Mean displacements of lines towards the less refrangible end of the spectrum are certainly revealed by statistical investigations of the fixed stars; but up to the present the examination of the available data does not allow of any definite decision being arrived at, as to whether or not these displacements are to be referred in reality to the effect of gravitation. The results of observation have been collected together, and discussed in detail from the standpoint of the question which has been engaging our attention here, in a paper by E. Freundlich entitled "Zur Prüfung der aligemeinen Relativitäts-Theorie" (*Die Naturwissenschaften*, 1919, No. 35, p. 520: Julius Springer, Berlin).

At all events, a definite decision will be reached during the next few years. If the displacement of spectral lines towards the red by the gravitational potential does not exist, then the general theory of relativity will be untenable. On the other hand, if the cause of the displacement of spectral lines be definitely traced to the gravitational potential, then the study of this displacement will furnish us with important information as to the mass of the heavenly bodies.

NOTE.—The displacement of spectral lines towards the red end of the spectrum was definitely established by Adams in 1924, by observations on the dense companion of Sirius, for which the effect is about thirty times greater than for the sun.

R . W . L .

The Structure of Space According to the General Theory of Relativity

[SUPPLEMENTARY TO SECTION 32]

Since the publication of the first edition of this little book, our knowledge about the structure of space in the large ("cosmological problem") has had an important development, which ought to be mentioned even in a popular presentation of the subject.

My original considerations on the subject were based on two hypotheses:

1. There exists an average density of matter in the whole of space which is everywhere the same and different from zero.
2. The magnitude ("radius") of space is independent of time.

Both these hypotheses proved to be consistent, according to the general theory of relativity, but only after a hypothetical term was added to the field equations, a term which was not required by the theory as such nor did it seem natural from a theoretical point of view ("cosmological term of the field equations").

Hypothesis (2) appeared unavoidable to me at the time, since I thought that one would get into bottomless speculations if one departed from it.

However, already in the 'twenties, the Russian mathematician Friedman showed that a different hypothesis was natural from a purely theoretical point of view. He realized that it was possible to preserve hypothesis (1) without introducing the less natural cosmological term into the field equations of gravitation, if one was ready to drop hypothesis (2). Namely, the original field equations admit a solution in which the "world-radius" depends on time (expanding space). In that sense one can say, according to Friedman, that the theory demands an expansion of space.

A few years later Hubble showed, by a special investigation of the extra-galactic nebulae ("milky ways"), that the spectral lines emitted showed a red shift which increased regularly with the distance of the nebulae. This can be interpreted in regard to our present knowledge only in the sense of Doppler's principle, as an expansive motion of the system of stars in the large—as required, according to Friedman, by the field equations of gravitation. Hubble's discovery can, therefore, be considered to some extent as a confirmation of the theory.

There does arise, however, a strange difficulty. The interpretation of the galactic line-shift discovered by Hubble as an expansion (which can hardly be doubted from a theoretical point of view), leads to an origin of this expansion which lies "only" about 10^9 years ago, while physical astronomy makes it appear likely that the development of individual stars and systems of stars takes considerably longer. It is in no way known how this incongruity is to be overcome.

I further want to remark that the theory of expanding space, together with the empirical data of astronomy, permit no decision to be reached about the finite or infinite character of (three-dimensional) space, while the original "static" hypothesis of space yielded the closure (finiteness) of space.

Relativity and the Problem of Space[1]

It is characteristic of Newtonian physics that it has to ascribe independent and real existence to space and time as well as to matter, for in Newton's law of motion the idea of acceleration appears. But in this theory, acceleration can only denote "acceleration with respect to space." Newton's space must thus be thought of as "at rest," or at least as "unaccelerated," in order that one can consider the acceleration, which appears in the law of motion, as being a magnitude with any meaning. Much the same holds with time, which of course likewise enters into the concept of acceleration. Newton himself and his most critical contemporaries felt it to be disturbing that one had to ascribe physical reality both to space itself as well as to its state of motion; but there was at that time no other alternative, if one wished to ascribe to mechanics a clear meaning.

[1] As with the original translation of this book in 1920, my old friend Emeritus Professor S. R. Milner, F.R.S. has again given me the benefit of his unique experience in this field, by reading the translation of this new appendix and making numerous suggestions for improvement. I am deeply grateful to him and to Professor A. G. Walker of the Mathematics Department of Liverpool University, who also read this appendix and offered various helpful suggestions.

R . W . L .

It is indeed an exacting requirement to have to ascribe physical reality to space in general, and especially to empty space. Time and again since remotest times philosophers have resisted such a presumption. Descartes argued somewhat on these lines: space is identical with extension, but extension is connected with bodies; thus there is no space without bodies and hence no empty space. The weakness of this argument lies primarily in what follows. It is certainly true that the concept extension owes its origin to our experiences of laying out or bringing into contact solid bodies. But from this it cannot be concluded that the concept of extension may not be justified in cases which have not themselves given rise to the formation of this concept. Such an enlargement of concepts can be justified indirectly by its value for the comprehension of empirical results. The assertion that extension is confined to bodies is therefore of itself certainly unfounded. We shall see later, however, that the general theory of relativity confirms Descartes' conception in a roundabout way. What brought Descartes to his remarkably attractive view was certainly the feeling that, without compelling necessity, one ought not to ascribe reality to a thing like space, which is not capable of being "directly experienced."[1]

The psychological origin of the idea of space, or of the necessity for it, is far from being so obvious as it may appear to be on the basis of our customary habit of thought. The old geometers deal with conceptual objects (straight line, point, surface), but not really with space as such, as was done later in

---

[1] This expression is to be taken *cum grano salis*.

analytical geometry. The idea of space, however, is suggested by certain primitive experiences. Suppose that a box has been constructed. Objects can be arranged in a certain way inside the box, so that it becomes full. The possibility of such arrangements is a property of the material object "box," something that is given with the box, the "space enclosed" by the box. This is something which is different for different boxes, something that is thought quite naturally at being independent of whether or not, at any moment, there are any objects at all in the box. When there are no objects in the box, its space appears to be "empty."

So far, our concept of space has been associated with the box. It turns out, however, that the storage possibilities that make up this box-space are independent of the thickness of the walls of the box. Cannot this thickness be reduced to zero, without the "space" being lost as a result? The naturalness of such a limiting process is obvious, and now there remains for our thought the space without the box, a self-evident thing, yet it appears to be so unreal if we forget the origin of this concept. One can understand that it was repugnant to Descartes to consider space as independent of material objects, a thing that might exist without matter.[1] (At the same time, this does not prevent him from treating space as a fundamental concept in his analytical geometry.) The drawing of attention to the vacuum in a mercury barometer has certainly disarmed

---

[1] Kant's attempt to remove the embarrassment by denial of the objectivity of space can, however, hardly be taken seriously. The possibilities of packing inherent in the inside space of a box are objective in the same sense as the box itself, and as the objects which can be packed inside it.

the last of the Cartesians. But it is not to be denied that, even at this primitive stage, something unsatisfactory clings to the concept of space, or to space thought of as an independent real thing.

The ways in which bodies can be packed into space (*e.g.* the box) are the subject of three-dimensional Euclidean geometry, whose axiomatic structure readily deceives us into forgetting that it refers to realisable situations.

If now the concept of space is formed in the manner outlined above, and following on from experience about the "filling" of the box, then this space is primarily a *bounded* space. This limitation does not appear to be essential, however, for apparently a larger box can always be introduced to enclose the smaller one. In this way space appears as something unbounded.

I shall not consider here how the concepts of the three-dimensional and the Euclidean nature of space can be traced back to relatively primitive experiences. Rather, I shall consider first of all from other points of view the rôle of the concept of space in the development of physical thought.

When a smaller box s is situated, relatively at rest, inside the hollow space of a larger box S, then the hollow space of s is a part of the hollow space of S, and the same "space," which contains both of them, belongs to each of the boxes. When s is in motion with respect to S, however, the concept is less simple. One is then inclined to think that s encloses always the same space, but a variable part of the space S. It then becomes necessary to apportion to each box its particular space, not thought of as bounded, and to assume that these two spaces are in motion with respect to each other.

Before one has become aware of this complication, space appears as an unbounded medium or container in which material objects swim around. But it must now be remembered that there is an infinite number of spaces, which are in motion with respect to each other. The concept of space as something existing objectively and independent of things belongs to pre-scientific thought, but not so the idea of the existence of an infinite number of spaces in motion relatively to each other. This latter idea is indeed logically unavoidable, but is far from having played a considerable rôle even in scientific thought.

But what about the psychological origin of the concept of time? This concept is undoubtedly associated with the fact of "calling to mind," as well as with the differentiation between sense experiences and the recollection of these. Of itself it is doubtful whether the differentiation between sense experience and recollection (or simple re-presentation) is something psychologically directly given to us. Everyone has experienced that he has been in doubt whether he has actually experienced something with his senses or has simply dreamt about it. Probably the ability to discriminate between these alternatives first comes about as the result of an activity of the mind creating order.

An experience is associated with a "recollection," and it is considered as being "earlier" in comparison with "present experiences." This is a conceptual ordering principle for recollected experiences, and the possibility of its accomplishment gives rise to the subjective concept of time, *i.e.* that concept of time which refers to the arrangement of the experiences of the individual.

What do we mean by rendering objective the concept of time? Let us consider an example. A person A ("I") has the experience "it is lightning." At the same time the person A also experiences such a behaviour of the person B as brings the behaviour of B into relation with his own experience "it is lightning." Thus it comes about that A associates with B the experience "it is lightning." For the person A the idea arises that other persons also participate in the experience "it is lightning." "It is lightning" is now no longer interpreted as an exclusively personal experience, but as an experience of other persons (or eventually only as a "potential experience"). In this way arises the interpretation that "it is lightning," which originally entered into the consciousness of an "experience," is now also interpreted as an (objective) "event." It is just the sum total of all events that we mean when we speak of the "real external world."

We have seen that we feel ourselves impelled to ascribe a temporal arrangement to our experiences, somewhat as follows. If β is later than α and γ later than β, then γ is also later than α ("sequence of experiences"). Now what is the position in this respect with the "events" which we have associated with the experiences? At first sight it seems obvious to assume that a temporal arrangement of events exists which agrees with the temporal arrangement of the experiences. In general, and unconsciously this was done, until sceptical doubts made themselves felt.[1] In order to arrive at the idea of an objective world, an additional constructive concept still is necessary: the event is localised not only in time, but also in space.

In the previous paragraphs we have attempted to describe how the concepts space, time and event can be put psychologically into relation with experiences. Considered logically, they are free creations of the human intelligence, tools of thought, which are to serve the purpose of bringing experiences into relation with each other, so that in this way they can be better surveyed. The attempt to become conscious of the empirical sources of these fundamental concepts should show to what extent we are actually bound to these concepts. In this way we become aware of our freedom, of which, in case of necessity, it is always a difficult matter to make sensible use.

We still have something essential to add to this stretch concerning the psychological origin of the concepts space-time-event (we will call them more briefly "space-like," in contrast to concepts from the psychological sphere). We have linked up the concept of space with experiences using boxes and the arrangement of material objects in them. Thus this formation of concepts already presupposes the concept of material objects (*e.g.* "boxes"). In the same way persons, who had to be introduced for the formation of an objective concept of time, also play the rôle of material objects in this connection. It appears to me, therefore, that the formation of the concept

---

[1] For example, the order of experiences in time obtained by acoustical means can differ from the temporal order gained visually, so that one cannot simply identify the time sequence of events with the time sequence of experiences.

of the material object must precede our concepts of time and space.

All these space-like concepts already belong to pre-scientific thought, along with concepts like pain, goal, purpose, etc. from the field of psychology. Now it is characteristic of thought in physics, as of thought in natural science generally, that it endeavours in principle to make do with "space-like" concepts *alone*, and strives to express with their aid all relations having the form of laws. The physicist seeks to reduce colours and tones to vibrations, the physiologist thought and pain to nerve processes, in such a way that the psychical element as such is eliminated from the causal nexus of existence, and thus nowhere occurs as an independent link in the causal associations. It is no doubt this attitude, which considers the comprehension of all relations by the exclusive use of only "space-like" concepts as being possible in principle, that is at the present time understood by the term "materialism" (since "matter" has lost its rôle as a fundamental concept).

Why is it necessary to drag down from the Olympian fields of Plato the fundamental ideas of thought in natural science, and to attempt to reveal their earthly lineage? Answer: In order to free these ideas from the taboo attached to them, and thus to achieve greater freedom in the formation of ideas or concepts. It is to the immortal credit of D. Hume and E. Mach that they, above all others, introduced this critical conception.

Science has taken over from pre-scientific thought the concepts space, time, and material object (with the important special case "solid body"), and has modified them and rendered them more precise. Its first significant accomplishment was the development of Euclidean geometry, whose axiomatic formulation must not be allowed to blind us to its empirical origin (the possibilities of laying out or juxtaposing solid bodies). In particular, the three-dimensional nature of space as well as its Euclidean character are of empirical origin (it can be wholly filled by like constituted "cubes").

The subtlety of the concept of space was enhanced by the discovery that there exist no completely rigid bodies. All bodies are elastically deformable and alter in volume with change in temperature. The structures, whose possible congruences are to be described by Euclidean geometry, cannot therefore be represented apart from physical concepts. But since physics after all must make use of geometry in the establishment of its concepts, the empirical content of geometry can be stated and tested only in the framework of the whole of physics.

In this connection atomistics must also be borne in mind, and its conception of finite divisibility; for spaces of subatomic extension cannot be measured up. Atomistics also compels us to give up, in principle, the idea of sharply and statically defined bounding surfaces of solid bodies. Strictly speaking, there are no *precise* laws, even in the macro-region, for the possible configurations of solid bodies touching each other.

In spite of this, no one thought of giving up the concept of space, for it appeared indispensable in the eminently satisfactory whole system of natural science. Mach, in the nineteenth century, was the only one who thought seriously of an elimination of the concept of space, in that he sought to replace it by the notion of the totality of the instantaneous distances between all material points. (He made this attempt in order to arrive at a satisfactory understanding of inertia).

The Field

In Newtonian mechanics, space and time play a dual rôle. First, they play the part of carrier or frame for things that happen in physics, in reference to which events are described by the space co-ordinates and the time. In principle, matter is thought of as consisting of "material points," the motions of which constitute physical happening. When matter is thought of as being continuous, this is done as it were provisionally in those cases where one does not wish to or cannot describe the discrete structure. In this case small parts (elements of volume) of the matter are treated similarly to material points, at least in so far as we are concerned merely with motions and not with occurrences which, at the moment, it is not possible or serves no useful purpose to attribute to motion (*e.g.* temperature changes, chemical processes). The second rôle of space and time was that of being an "inertial system." From all conceivable systems of reference, inertial systems were considered to be advantageous in that, with respect to them, the law of inertia claimed validity.

In this, the essential thing is that "physical reality," thought of as being independent of the subjects experiencing it, was conceived as consisting, at least in principle, of space and time on one hand, and of permanently existing material points, moving with respect to space and time, on the other. The idea of the independent existence of space and time can be expressed drastically in this way: If matter were to disappear, space and time alone would remain behind (as a kind of stage for physical happening).

The surmounting of this standpoint resulted from a development which, in the first place, appeared to have nothing to do with the problem of space-time, namely, the appearance of the *concept of field* and its final claim to replace, in principle, the idea of a particle (material point). In the framework of classical physics, the concept of field appeared as an auxiliary concept, in cases in which matter was treated as a continuum. For example, in the consideration of the heat conduction in a solid body, the state of the body is described by giving the temperature at every point of the body for every definite time. Mathematically, this means that the temperature T is represented as a mathematical expression (function) of the space co-ordinates and the time t (Temperature field). The law of heat conduction is represented as a local relation (differential equation), which embraces all special cases of the conduction of heat. The temperature is here a simple example of the concept of field. This is a quantity (or a complex of quantities), which is a function of the co-ordinates and the time. Another example is the description of the motion of a liquid. At every point there exists at any time a velocity, which is quantitatively described by its three "components" with respect to the axes of a co-ordinate system (vector). The components of the velocity at a point (field components), here also, are functions of the co-ordinates (x, y, z) and the time (t).

It is characteristic of the fields mentioned that they occur only within a ponderable mass; they serve only to describe a state of this matter. In accordance with the historical development of the field concept, where no matter was available there could also exist no field. But in the first quarter of the nineteenth century it was shown that the phenomena of the interference and motion of light could be explained with astonishing clearness when light was regarded as a wave-field, completely analogous to the mechanical vibration field in an elastic solid body. It was thus felt necessary to introduce a field, that could also exist in "empty space" in the absence of ponderable matter.

This state of affairs created a paradoxical situation, because, in accordance with its origin, the field concept appeared to be restricted to the description of states in the inside of a ponderable body. This seemed to be all the more certain, inasmuch as the conviction was held that every field is to be regarded as a state capable of mechanical interpretation, and this presupposed the presence of matter. One thus felt compelled, even in the space which had hitherto been regarded as empty, to assume everywhere the existence of a form of matter, which was called "æther."

The emancipation of the field concept from the assumption of its association with a mechanical carrier finds a place among the psychologically most interesting events in the development of physical thought. During the second half of the nineteenth century, in connection with the researches of Faraday and Maxwell, it became more and more clear that the description of electromagnetic processes in terms of field was vastly superior to a treatment on the basis of the mechanical concepts of material points. By the introduction of the field concept in electrodynamics, Maxwell succeeded in predicting the existence of electromagnetic waves, the essential identity of which with light waves could not be doubted, because of the equality of their velocity of propagation. As a result of this, optics was, in principle, absorbed by electrodynamics. *One* psychological effect of this immense success was that the field concept, as opposed to the mechanistic framework of classical physics, gradually won greater independence.

Nevertheless, it was at first taken for granted that electromagnetic fields had to be interpreted as states of the æther, and it was zealously sought to explain these states as mechanical ones. But as these efforts always met with frustration, science gradually became accustomed to the idea of renouncing such a mechanical interpretation. Nevertheless, the conviction still remained that electromagnetic fields must be states of the æther, and this was the position at the turn of the century.

The æther-theory brought with it the question: How does the æther behave from the mechanical point of view with respect to ponderable bodies? Does it take part in the motions of the bodies, or do its parts remain at rest relatively to each other? Many ingenious experiments were undertaken to decide this question. The following important facts should be mentioned in this connection: the "aberration" of the fixed stars in consequence of the annual motion of the earth, and the "Doppler effect," *i.e.* the influence of the relative motion of the fixed stars on the frequency of the light reaching us from them, for known frequencies of emission. The results of all these facts and experiments, except for one, the Michelson-

Morley experiment, were explained by H. A. Lorentz on the assumption that the æther does not take part in the motions of ponderable bodies, and that the parts of the æther have no relative motions at all with respect to each other. Thus the æther appeared, as it were, as the embodiment of a space absolutely at rest. But the investigation of Lorentz accomplished still more. It explained all the electromagnetic and optical processes within ponderable bodies known at that time, on the assumption that the influence of ponderable matter on the electric field—and conversely—is due solely to the fact that the constituent particles of matter carry electrical charges, which share the motion of the particles. Concerning the experiment of Michelson and Morley, H. A. Lorentz showed that the result obtained at least does not contradict the theory of an æther at rest.

In spite of all these beautiful successes the state of the theory was not yet wholly satisfactory, and for the following reasons. Classical mechanics, of which it could not be doubted that it holds with a close degree of approximation, teaches the equivalence of all inertial systems or inertial "spaces" for the formulation of natural laws, *i.e.* the invariance of natural laws with respect to the transition from one inertial system to another. Electromagnetic and optical *experiments* taught the same thing with considerable accuracy. But the foundation of electromagnetic *theory* taught that a particular inertial system must be given preference, namely that of the luminiferous æther at rest. This view of the theoretical foundation was much too unsatisfactory. Was there no modification that, like classical mechanics, would uphold the equivalence of inertial systems (special principle of relativity)?

The answer to this question is the special theory of relativity. This takes over from the theory of Maxwell–Lorentz the assumption of the constancy of the velocity of light in empty space. In order to bring this into harmony with the equivalence of inertial systems (special principle of relativity), the idea of the absolute character of simultaneity must be given up; in addition, the Lorentz transformations for the time and the space co-ordinates follow for the transition from one inertial system to another. The whole content of the special theory of relativity is included in the postulate: The laws of Nature are invariant with respect to the Lorentz transformations. The important thing of this requirement lies in the fact that it limits the possible natural laws in a definite manner.

What is the position of the special theory of relativity in regard to the problem of space? In the first place we must guard against the opinion that the four-dimensionality of reality has been newly introduced for the first time by this theory. Even in classical physics the event is localised by four numbers, three spatial co-ordinates and a time co-ordinate; the totality of physical "events" is thus thought of as being embedded in a four-dimensional continuous manifold. But the basis of classical mechanics this four-dimensional continuum breaks up objectively into the one-dimensional time and into three-dimensional spatial sections, only the latter of which contain simultaneous events. This resolution is the same for all inertial systems. The simultaneity of two definite events with reference to one inertial system involves the simultaneity of these events in reference to all inertial systems. This is what is meant when we say that the time of classical mechanics is absolute. According to the special theory of relativity it is otherwise. The sum total of events which are simultaneous with a selected event exist, it is true, in relation to a particular inertial system, but no longer independently of the choice of the inertial system. The four-dimensional continuum is now no longer resolvable objectively into sections, all of which contain simultaneous events; "now" loses for the spatially extended world its objective meaning. It is because of this that space and time must be regarded as a four-dimensional continuum that is objectively unresolvable, if it is desired to express the purport of objective relations without unnecessary conventional arbitrariness.

Since the special theory of relativity revealed the physical equivalence of all inertial systems, it proved the untenability of the hypothesis of an æther at rest. It was therefore necessary to renounce the idea that the electromagnetic field is to be regarded as a state of a material carrier. The field thus becomes an irreducible element of physical description, irreducible in the same sense as the concept of matter in the theory of Newton.

Up to now we have directed our attention to finding in what respect the concepts of space and time were *modified* by the special theory of relativity. Let us now focus our attention on those elements which this theory has taken over from classical mechanics. Here also, natural laws claim validity only when an inertial system is taken as the basis of space-time description. The principle of inertia and the principle of the constancy of the velocity of light are valid only with respect to an *inertial system*. The field-laws also can claim to have a meaning and validity only in regard to inertial systems. Thus, as in classical mechanics, space is here also an independent component in the representation of physical reality. If we imagine matter and field to be removed, inertial-space or, more accurately, this space together with the associated time remains behind. The four-dimensional structure (Minkowski-space) is thought of as being the carrier of matter and of the field. Inertial spaces, with their associated times, are only privileged four-dimensional co-ordinate systems, that are linked together by the linear Lorentz transformations. Since there exist in this four-dimensional structure no longer any sections which represent "now" objectively, the concepts of happening and becoming are indeed not completely suspended, but yet complicated. It appears therefore more natural to think of physical reality as a four-dimensional existence, instead of, as hitherto, the *evolution* of a three-dimensional existence.

This rigid four-dimensional space of the special theory of relativity is to some extent a four-dimensional analogue of H. A. Lorentz's rigid three-dimensional æther. For this theory also the following statement is valid: The description of physical states postulates space as being initially given and as existing independently. Thus even this theory does not dispel Descartes' uneasiness concerning the independent, or indeed, the *a priori* existence of "empty space." The real aim of the elementary discussion given here is to show to what extent these doubts are overcome by the general theory of relativity.

The Concept of Space in the General Theory of Relativity

This theory arose primarily from the endeavour to understand the equality of inertial and gravitational mass. We start out from an inertial system S_1, whose space is, from the physical point of view, empty. In other words, there exists in the part of space contemplated neither matter (in the usual sense) nor a field (in the sense of the special theory of relativity). With reference to S_1 let there be a second system of reference S_2 in uniform acceleration. Then S_2 is thus not an inertial system. With respect to S_2 every test mass would move with an acceleration, which is independent of its physical and chemical nature. Relative to S_2, therefore, there exists a state which, at least to a first approximation, cannot be distinguished from a gravitational field. The following concept is thus compatible with the observable facts: S_2 is also equivalent to an "inertial system"; but with respect to S_2 a (homogeneous) gravitational field is present (about the origin of which one does not worry in this connection). Thus when the gravitational field is included in the framework of the consideration, the inertial system loses its objective significance, assuming that this "principle of equivalence" can be extended to any relative motion whatsoever of the systems of reference. If it is possible to base a consistent theory on these fundamental ideas, it will satisfy of itself the fact of the equality of inertial and gravitational mass, which is strongly confirmed empirically.

Considered four-dimensionally, a non-linear transformation of the four co-ordinates corresponds to the transition from S_1 to S_2. The question now arises: What kind of non-linear transformations are to be permitted, or, how is the Lorentz transformation to be generalised? In order to answer this question, the following consideration is decisive.

We ascribe to the inertial system of the earlier theory this property: Differences in co-ordinates are measured by stationary "rigid" measuring rods, and differences in time by clocks at rest. The first assumption is supplemented by another, namely, that for the relative laying out and fitting together of measuring rods at rest, the theorems on "lengths" in Euclidean geometry hold. From the results of the special theory of relativity it is then concluded, by elementary considerations, that this direct physical interpretation of the co-ordinates is lost for systems of reference (S_2) accelerated relatively to inertial systems (S_1). But if this is the case, the co-ordinates now express only the order or rank of the "contiguity" and hence also the dimensional grade of the space, but do not express any of its metrical properties. We are thus led to extend the transformations to arbitrary continuous transformations.[1] This implies the general principle of relativity: Natural laws must be covariant with respect to arbitrary continuous transformations of the co-ordinates. This requirement (combined with that of the greatest possible logical simplicity of the laws) limits the natural laws concerned incomparably more strongly than the special principle of relativity.

---

[1] This inexact mode of expression will perhaps suffice here.

This train of ideas is based essentially on the field as an independent concept. For the conditions prevailing with respect to S_2 are interpreted as a gravitational field, without the question of the existence of masses which produce this field being raised. By virtue of this train of ideas it can also be grasped why the laws of the pure gravitational field are more directly linked with the idea of general relativity than the laws for fields of a general kind (when, for instance, an electromagnetic field is present). We have, namely, good ground for the assumption that the "field-free" Minkowski-space represents a special case possible in natural law, in fact, the simplest conceivable special case. With respect to its metrical character, such a space is characterised by the fact that $dx_1^2 + dx_2^2 + dx_3^2$ is the square of the spatial separation, measured with a unit gauge, of two infinitesimally neighbouring points of a three-dimensional "space-like" cross section (Pythagorean theorem), whereas dx_4 is the temporal separation, measured with a suitable time gauge, of two events with common (x_1, x_2, x_3). All this simply means that an objective metrical significance is attached to the quantity

$$ds^2 = dx_1^2 + dx_2^2 + dx_3^2 - dx_4^2 \tag{1}$$

as is readily shown with the aid of the Lorentz transformations. Mathematically, this fact corresponds to the condition that ds^2 is invariant with respect to Lorentz transformations.

If now, in the sense of the general principle of relativity, this space (cf. eq. (1)) is subjected to an arbitrary continuous transformation of the co-ordinates, then the objectively significant quantity ds is expressed in the new system of co-ordinates by the relation

$$ds^2 = g_{ik} dx_i dx_k \qquad . \qquad . \qquad . \qquad (1a)$$

which has to be summed up over the indices i and k for all combinations 11, 12, . . . up to 44. The term g_{ik} now are not constants, but functions of the co-ordinates, which are determined by the arbitrarily chosen transformation. Nevertheless, the terms g_{ik} are not arbitrary functions of the new co-ordinates, but just functions of such a kind that the form $(1a)$ can be transformed back into the form (1) by a continuous transformation of the four co-ordinates. In order that this may be possible, the function g_{ik} must satisfy certain general covariant equations of condition, which were derived by B. Riemann more than half a century before the formulation of the general theory of relativity ("Riemann condition"). According to the principle of equivalence, $(1a)$ describes in general covariant form a gravitational field of a special kind, when the functions g_{ik} satisfy the Riemann condition.

It follows that the law for the pure gravitational field of a general kind must be satisfied when the Riemann condition is satisfied; but it must be weaker or less restricting than the Riemann condition. In this way the field law of pure gravitation is practically completely determined, a result which will not be justified in greater detail here.

We are now in a position to see how far the transition to the general theory of relativity modifies the concept of space. In accordance with classical mechanics and according to the special theory of relativity, space (space-time) has an existence independent of matter or field. In order to be able to describe at all that which fills up space and is dependent on the co-ordinates, space-time or the inertial system with its metrical properties must be thought of at once as existing, for otherwise the description of "that which fills up space" would have no meaning.[1] On the basis of the general theory of relativity, on the other hand, space as opposed to "what fills space," which is dependent on the co-ordinates, has no separate existence. Thus a pure gravitational field might have been described in terms of the g_{ik} (as functions of the co-ordinates), by solution of the gravitational equations. If we imagine the gravitational field, *i.e.* the functions g_{ik}, to be removed, there does not remain a space of the type (1), but absolutely *nothing*, and also no "topological space." For the functions g_{ik} describe not only the field, but at the same time also the topological and metrical structural properties of the manifold. A space of the type (1), judged from the standpoint of the general theory of relativity, is not a space without field, but a special case of the g_{ik} field, for which—for the co-ordinate system used, which in itself has no objective significance—the functions g_{ik} have values that do not depend on the co-ordinates. There is no such thing as an empty space, *i.e.* a space without field. Space-time does not claim existence on its own, but only as a structural quality of the field.

[1] If we consider that which fills space (e.g. the field) to be removed, there still remains the metric space in accordance with (1), which would also determine the inertial behaviour of a test body introduced into it.

Thus Descartes was not so far from the truth when he believed he must exclude the existence of an empty space. The notion indeed appears absurd, as long as physical reality is seen exclusively in ponderable bodies. It requires the idea of the field as the representative of reality, in combination with the general principle of relativity, to show the true kernel of Descartes' idea; there exists no space "empty of field."

Generalised Theory of Gravitation

The theory of the pure gravitational field on the basis of the general theory of relativity is therefore readily obtainable, because we may be confident that the "field-free" Minkowski space with its metric in conformity with (1) must satisfy the general laws of field. From this special case the law of gravitation follows by a generalisation which is practically free from arbitrariness. The further development of the theory is not so unequivocally determined by the general principle of relativity; it has been attempted in various directions during the last few decades. It is common to all these attempts, to conceive physical reality as a field, and moreover, one which is a generalisation of the gravitational field, and in which the field law is a generalisation of the law for the pure gravitational field. After long probing I believe that I have now found[1] the most

---

[1] The generalisation can be characterised in the following way. In accordance with its derivation from empty "Minkowski space," the pure gravitational field of the functions g_{ik} has the property of symmetry given by $g_{ik} = g_{ki}$ ($g_{12} = g_{21}$, etc.). The generalised field is of the same kind, but without this property of symmetry. The derivation of the field law is completely analogous to that of the special case of pure gravitation.

natural form for this generalisation, but I have not yet been able to find out whether this generalised law can stand up against the facts of experience.

The question of the particular field law is secondary in the preceding general considerations. At the present time, the main question is whether a field theory of the kind here contemplated can lead to the goal at all. By this is meant a theory which describes exhaustively physical reality, including four-dimensional space, by a field. The present-day generation of physicists is inclined to answer this question in the negative. In conformity with the present form of the quantum theory, it believes that the state of a system cannot be specified directly, but only in an indirect way by a statement of the statistics of the results of measurement attainable on the system. The conviction prevails that the experimentally assured duality of nature (corpuscular and wave structure) can be realised only by such a weakening of the concept of reality. I think that such a far-reaching theoretical renunciation is not for the present justified by our actual knowledge, and that one should not desist from pursuing to the end the path of the relativistic field theory.

Bibliography

BIOGRAPHICAL

Out of My Later Years: Albert Einstein. (Constable, 1950).
Einstein—His Life and Times: Philipp Frank. (Cape, 1948).

INTRODUCTORY OR GENERAL

The Special Theory of Relativity: H. Dingle. (Methuen, 1940).
The Expanding Universe: A. Eddington. (Cambridge, 1933).
Space, Time and Gravitation: A. Eddington. (Cambridge, 1923).
The Meaning of Relativity: A. Einstein. (Fifth revised edition; Methuen, 1951).
Evolution of Physics: A. Einstein and L. Infeld. (Cambridge, 1947).
Relativity Physics: W. H. McCrea. (Methuen, 1947).
Albert Einstein: Philosopher—Scientist. (*The Library of Living Philosophers, Vol. VII.*) Edited by P. A. Schilpp. (Cambridge, 1950).
Space-Time Structure: E. Schrödinger. (Cambridge, 1950).
The Structure of the Universe: G. J. Whitrow. (Hutchinson's University Library, No. 29, 1949).

MATHEMATICAL

Introduction to the Theory of Relativity: P. G. Bergmann. (Prentice-Hall, 1942).
The Mathematical Theory of Relativity: A. Eddington. (Cambridge, 1924).
Relativity, Gravitation and World Structure: E. A. Milne. (Oxford, 1935).

179

Kinematic Relativity: E. A. Milne. (Oxford, 1948).

The Theory of Relativity: C. Møller. (Oxford, 1952).

Relativitätstheorie: W. Pauli, Jr. (Sonderabdruck aus der Enzyklopädie der mathematischen Wissenschaften, V (2), 543–773). (Teubner, Leipzig, 1921).

Relativity, Thermodynamics and Cosmology: R. C. Tolman. (Oxford, 1934).

Space, Time and Matter: H. Weyl. (Methuen, 1922).

I am indebted to my former colleagues Dr. B. Donovan (Northern Polytechnic, London) and Professor A. G. Walker (Liverpool University) for suggestions in the choice of books.

R. W. L.

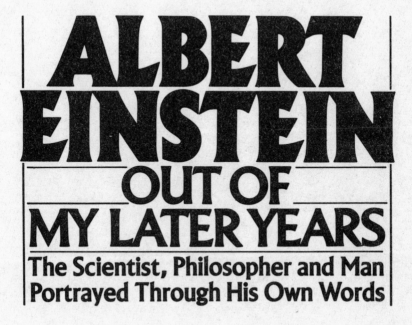

ALBERT EINSTEIN

OUT OF
MY LATER YEARS

The Scientist, Philosopher and Man
Portrayed Through His Own Words

PORTLAND HOUSE

Contents

Convictions and Beliefs

Science

Physics and Reality (1936)

Public Affairs

Science and Life

Military Intrusion in Science (1947)

Personalities

My People

1

PUBLISHER'S PREFACE

THIS SECOND VOLUME of collected essays by Albert Einstein covers a period of about fifteen years—1934 to 1950; the first anthology, published under the title *The World As I See It*, comprising material from 1922 to 1934.

Albert Einstein does not belong to that group of scholars who live in the "ivory tower" of their research work, oblivious to the world around them. On the contrary, he has always been an astute and critical observer of the trends and needs of his time. Indeed, frequently did he intervene by written as well as spoken appeal, and always, we should like to emphasize, for a humanitarian cause.

In this sense *Out of My Later Years* mirrors the philosophical, as well as political and social attitudes of its author. The chapters themselves represent addresses, articles, letters, appeals and miscellaneous papers hitherto unpublished.

We feel privileged to offer them to the public with hardly any editorial change—a moving document of the workings of a conscientious, profound and deeply humane mind.

Convictions and Beliefs

2

SELF-PORTRAIT

OF WHAT IS SIGNIFICANT in one's own existence one is hardly aware, and it certainly should not bother the other fellow. What does a fish know about the water in which he swims all his life?

The bitter and the sweet come from the outside, the hard from within, from one's own efforts. For the most part I do the thing which my own nature drives me to do. It is embarrassing to earn so much respect and love for it. Arrows of hate have been shot at me too; but they never hit me, because somehow they belonged to another world, with which I have no connection whatsoever.

I live in that solitude which is painful in youth, but delicious in the years of maturity.

3

TEN FATEFUL YEARS

Reading once again the lines I wrote almost ten years ago,* I receive two strangely contrasting impressions. What I wrote then still seems essentially as true as ever; yet, it all seems curiously remote and strange. How can that be? Has the world changed so profoundly in ten years, or is it merely that I have grown ten years older, and my eyes see everything in a changed, dimmer light? What are ten years in the history of humanity? Must not all those forces that determine the life of man be regarded as constant compared with such a trifling interval? Is my critical reason so susceptible that the physiological change in my body during those ten years has been able to influence my concept of life so deeply? It seems clear to me that such considerations cannot throw light upon a change in the emotional approach to the general problems of life. Nor may the reasons for this curious change be sought in my own external circumstances; for I know that these have always played a subordinate part in my thoughts and emotions.

No, something quite different is involved. In these ten years confidence in the stability, yes, even the very basis for existence, of human society has largely vanished. One senses not only a threat to man's cultural heritage, but also that a lower value is placed upon all that one would like to see defended at all costs.

Conscious man, to be sure, has at all times been keenly

* To the volume *Living Philosophy*.

aware that life is an adventure, that life must, forever, be wrested from death. In part the dangers were external: one might fall downstairs and break one's neck, lose one's livelihood without fault, be condemned though innocent, or ruined by calumny. Life in human society meant dangers of all sorts; but these dangers were chaotic in nature, subject to chance. Human society, as a whole, seemed stable. Measured by the ideals of taste and morals it was decidedly imperfect. But, all in all, one felt at home with it and, apart from the many kinds of accidents, comparatively safe in it. One accepted its intrinsic qualities as a matter of course, as the air one breathed. Even standards of virtue, aspiration, and practical truth were taken for granted as an inviolable heritage, common to all civilized humanity.

To be sure, the first World War had already shaken this feeling of security. The sanctity of life vanished and the individual was no longer able to do as he pleased and to go where he liked. The lie was raised to the dignity of a political instrument. The war was, however, widely regarded as an external event, hardly or not at all as the result of man's conscious planful action. It was thought of as an interruption of man's normal life from the outside, universally considered unfortunate and evil. The feeling of security in regard to human aims and values remained, for the main part, unshaken.

The subsequent development is sharply marked by political events that are not as far-reaching as the less easily grasped socio-psychological background. First a brief, promising step forward characterized by the creation of the League of Nations through the grandiose initiative of Wilson, and the establishment of a system of collective security among the nations. Then the formation of Fascist states, attended by a series of broken pacts and undisguised acts of violence against humanity and against weaker nations. The system of collective security collapsed like a house of cards—a collapse the consequences of which cannot be measured even today. It was a manifestation of weakness of character and lack of responsibility on the part of the leaders in the affected countries, and of shortsighted selfishness in the democracies—those that still remain outwardly intact—which prevented any vigorous counterattack.

Things grew even worse than a pessimist of the deepest dye would have dared prophesy. In Europe to the east of the Rhine free exercise of the intellect exists no longer, the population is terrorized by gangsters who have seized power, and youth is poisoned by systematic lies. The pseudo-success of political adventurers has dazzled the rest of the world; it becomes apparent everywhere that this generation lacks the strength and force which enabled previous generations to win, in painful struggle and at great sacrifice, the political and individual freedom of man.

Awareness of this state of affairs overshadows every hour of my present existence, while ten years ago it did not yet occupy my thoughts. It is this that I feel so strongly in re-reading the words written in the past.

And yet I know that, all in all, man changes but little, even though prevailing notions make him appear in a very different light at different times, and even though current trends like the present bring him unimaginable sorrow. Nothing of all that will remain but a few pitiful pages in the history books, briefly picturing to the youth of future generations the follies of its ancestors.

4

MORAL DECAY

ALL RELIGIONS, arts and sciences are branches of the same tree. All these aspirations are directed toward ennobling man's life, lifting it from the sphere of mere physical existence and leading the individual toward freedom. It is no mere chance that our older universities have developed from clerical schools. Both churches and universities—insofar as they live up to their true function—serve the ennoblement of the individual. They seek to fulfill this great task by spreading moral and cultural understanding, renouncing the use of brute force.

The essential unity of ecclesiastical and secular cultural institutions was lost during the 19th century, to the point of senseless hostility. Yet there never was any doubt as to the striving for culture. No one doubted the sacredness of the goal. It was the approach that was disputed.

The political and economic conflicts and complexities of the last few decades have brought before our eyes dangers which even the darkest pessimists of the last century did not dream of. The injunctions of the Bible concerning human conduct were then accepted by believer and infidel alike as self-evident demands for individuals and society. No one would have been taken seriously who failed to acknowledge the quest for objective truth and knowledge as man's highest and eternal aim.

Yet today we must recognize with horror that these pillars of civilized human existence have lost their firmness. Nations that once ranked high bow down before tyrants who dare openly to assert: Right is that which serves us! The quest for truth for its own sake has no justification and is not to be tolerated. Arbitrary rule, oppression, persecution of individuals, faiths and communities are openly practiced in those countries and accepted as justifiable or inevitable.

And the rest of the world has slowly grown accustomed to these symptoms of moral decay. One misses the elementary reaction against injustice and for justice—that reaction which in the long run represents man's only protection against a relapse into barbarism. I am firmly convinced that the passionate will for justice and truth has done more to improve man's condition than calculating political shrewdness which in the long run only breeds general distrust. Who can doubt that Moses was a better leader of humanity than Machiavelli?

During the War someone tried to convince a great Dutch scientist that might went before right in the history of man. "I cannot disprove the accuracy of your assertion," he replied, "but I do know that I should not care to live in such a world!"

Let us think, feel and act like this man, refusing to accept fateful compromise. Let us not even shun the fight when it is unavoidable to preserve right and the dignity of man. If we do this we shall soon return to conditions that will allow us to rejoice in humanity.

5

MESSAGE FOR POSTERITY

Our time is rich in inventive minds, the inventions of which could facilitate our lives considerably. We are crossing the seas by power and utilize power also in order to relieve humanity from all tiring muscular work. We have learned to fly and we are able to send messages and news without any difficulty over the entire world through electric waves.

However, the production and distribution of commodities is entirely unorganized so that everybody must live in fear of being eliminated from the economic cycle, in this way suffering for the want of everything. Furthermore, people living in different countries kill each other at irregular time intervals, so that also for this reason any one who thinks about the future must live in fear and terror. This is due to the fact that the intelligence and the character of the masses are incomparably lower than the intelligence and character of the few who produce something valuable for the community.

I trust that posterity will read these statements with a feeling of proud and justified superiority.

6

ON FREEDOM

I KNOW THAT IT IS a hopeless undertaking to debate about fundamental value judgments. For instance if someone approves, as a goal, the extirpation of the human race from the earth, one cannot refute such a viewpoint on rational grounds. But if there is agreement on certain goals and values, one can argue rationally about the means by which these objectives may be attained. Let us, then, indicate two goals which may well be agreed upon by nearly all who read these lines.

1. Those instrumental goods which should serve to maintain the life and health of all human beings should be produced by the least possible labor of all.

2. The satisfaction of physical needs is indeed the indispensable precondition of a satisfactory existence, but in itself it is not enough. In order to be content men must also have the possibility of developing their intellectual and artistic powers to whatever extent accord with their personal characteristics and abilities.

The first of these two goals requires the promotion of all knowledge relating to the laws of nature and the laws of social processes, that is, the promotion of all scientific endeavor. For scientific endeavor is a natural whole the parts of which mutually support one another in a way which, to be sure, no one can anticipate. However, the progress of science presupposes the possibility of unrestricted communication of all results and judgments—freedom of expression and instruction in all realms of intellectual endeavor. By freedom I understand social conditions of such a kind that the expression of opinions and assertions about general and particular matters of knowledge will not involve dangers or serious disadvantages for him who expresses them. This freedom of communication is indispensable for the development and extension of scientific knowledge, a consideration of much practical import. In the first instance it must be guaranteed by law. But laws alone cannot secure freedom of expression; in order that every man may present his views without penalty there must be a spirit of tolerance in the entire population. Such an ideal of external liberty can never be fully attained but must be sought unremittingly if scientific thought, and philosophical and creative thinking in general, are to be advanced as far as possible.

If the second goal, that is, the possibility of the spiritual development of all individuals, is to be secured, a second kind of outward freedom is necessary. Man should not have to work for the achievement of the necessities of life to such an extent that he has neither time nor strength for personal activities. Without this second kind of outward liberty, freedom of expression is useless for him. Advances in technology would provide the possibility of this kind of freedom if the problem of a reasonable division of labor were solved.

The development of science and of the creative activities of the spirit in general requires still another kind of freedom, which may be characterized as inward freedom. It is this freedom of the spirit which consists in the independence of thought from the restrictions of authoritarian and social prejudices as well as from unphilosophical routinizing and habit in general. This inward freedom is an infrequent gift of nature and a worthy objective for the individual. Yet the community can do much to further this achievement, too, at least by not interfering with its development. Thus schools may interfere with the development of inward freedom through authoritarian influences and through imposing on young people excessive spiritual burdens; on the other hand schools may favor such freedom by encouraging independent thought. Only if outward and inner freedom are constantly and consciously pursued is there a possibility of spiritual development and perfection and thus of improving man's outward and inner life.

7

MORALS AND EMOTIONS

We all know, from what we experience with and within ourselves, that our conscious acts spring from our desires and our fears. Intuition tells us that that is true also of our fellows and of the higher animals. We all try to escape pain and death, while we seek what is pleasant. We all are ruled in what we do by impulses; and these impulses are so organized that our actions in general serve for our self-preservation and that of the race. Hunger, love, pain, fear are some of those inner forces which rule the individual's instinct for self-preservation. At the same time, as social beings, we are moved in the relations with our fellow beings by such feelings as sympathy, pride, hate, need for power, pity, and so on. All these primary impulses, not easily described in words, are the springs of man's actions. All such action would cease if those powerful elemental forces were to cease stirring within us.

Though our conduct seems so very different from that of the higher animals, the primary instincts are much alike in them and in us. The most evident difference springs from the important part which is played in man by a relatively strong power of imagination and by the capacity to think, aided as it is by language and other symbolical devices. Thought is the organizing factor in man, intersected between the causal primary instincts and the resulting actions. In that way imagination and intelligence enter into our existence in the part of servants of the primary instincts. But their intervention makes our acts to serve ever less merely the immediate claims of our instincts. Through them the primary instinct attaches itself to ends which become ever more distant. The instincts bring thought into action, and thought provokes intermediary actions inspired by emotions which are likewise related to the ultimate end. Through repeated performance, this process brings it about that ideas and beliefs acquire and retain a strong effective power even after the ends which gave them that power are long forgotten. In abnormal cases of such intensive borrowed emotions, which cling to objects emptied of their erstwhile effective meaning, we speak of fetishism.

Yet the process which I have indicated plays a very important part also in ordinary life. Indeed there is no doubt that to this process—which one may describe as a spiritualizing of the emotions and of thought—that to it man owes the most subtle and refined pleasures of which he is capable: the pleasure in the beauty of artistic creation and of logical trains of thought.

As far as I can see, there is one consideration which stands at the threshold of all moral teaching. If men as individuals surrender to the call of their elementary instincts, avoiding pain and seeking satisfaction only for their own selves, the result for them all taken together must be a state of insecurity, of fear, and of promiscuous misery. If, besides that, they use their intelligence from an individualist, i.e., a selfish standpoint, building up their life on the illusion of a happy unattached existence, things will be hardly better. In comparison with the other elementary instincts and impulses, the emotions of love, of pity and of friendship are too weak and too cramped to lead to a tolerable state of human society.

The solution of this problem, when freely considered, is simple enough, and it seems also to echo from the teachings of the wise men of the past always in the same strain: All men should let their conduct be guided by the same principles; and those principles should be such, that by following them there should accrue to all as great a measure as possible of security and satisfaction, and as small a measure as possible of suffering.

Of course, this general requirement is much too vague that we should be able to draw from it with confidence specific rules to guide the individuals in their actions. And indeed, these specific rules will have to change in keeping with changing circumstances. If this were the main difficulty that stands in the way of that keen conception, the millenary fate of man would have been incomparably happier than it actually was, or still is. Man would not have killed man, tortured each other, exploited each other by force and by guile.

The real difficulty, the difficulty which has baffled the sages of all times, is rather this: how can we make our teaching so potent in the emotional life of man, that its influence should withstand the pressure of the elemental psychic forces in the individual? We do not know, of course, if the sages of the past have really asked themselves this question, consciously and in this form; but we do know how they have tried to solve the problem.

Long before men were ripe, namely, to be faced with such a universal moral attitude, fear of the dangers of life had led them to attribute to various imaginary personal beings, not physically tangible, power to release those natural forces which men feared or perhaps welcomed. And they believed that those beings, which everywhere dominated their imagination, were psychically made in their own image, but were endowed with superhuman powers. These were the primitive precursors of the idea of God. Sprung in the first place from the fears which filled man's daily life, the belief in the existence of such beings, and in their extraordinary powers, has had so strong an influence on men and their conduct, that it is difficult for us to imagine. Hence it is not surprising that those who set out to establish the moral idea, as embracing all men equally, did so by linking it closely with religion. And the fact that those moral claims were the same for all men, may have had much to do with the development of mankind's religious culture from polytheism to monotheism.

The universal moral idea thus owed its original psychological potency to that link with religion. Yet in another sense that close association was fatal for the moral idea. Monotheistic religion acquired different forms with various peoples and groups. Although those differences were by no means fundamental, yet they soon were felt more strongly than the essentials that were common. And in that way religion often caused enmity and conflict, instead of binding mankind together with the universal moral idea.

Then came the growth of the natural sciences, with their great influence on thought and practical life, weakening still more in modern times the religious sentiment of the peoples. The causal and objective mode of thinking—though not necessarily in contradiction with the religious sphere—leaves in most people little room for a deepening religious sense. And because of the traditional close link between religion and morals, that has brought with it, in the last hundred years or so, a serious weakening of moral thought and sentiment. That, to my mind, is a main cause for the barbarization of political ways in our time. Taken together with the terrifying efficiency of the new technical means, the barbarization already forms a fearful threat for the civilized world.

Needless to say, one is glad that religion strives to work for the realization of the moral principle. Yet the moral imperative is not a matter for church and religion alone, but the most precious traditional possession of all mankind. Consider from this standpoint the position of the Press, or of the schools with their competitive method! Everything is dominated by the cult of efficiency and of success and not by the value of things and men in relation to the moral ends of human society. To that must be added the moral deterioration resulting from a ruthless economic struggle. The deliberate nurturing of the moral sense also outside the religious sphere, however, should help also in this, to lead men to look upon social problems as so many opportunities for joyous service towards a better life. For looked at from a simple human point of view, moral conduct does not mean merely a stern demand to renounce some of the desired joys of life, but rather a sociable interest in a happier lot for all men.

This conception implies one requirement above all—that every individual should have the opportunity to develop the gifts which may be latent in him. Alone in that way can the individual obtain the satisfaction to which he is justly entitled; and alone in that way can the community achieve its richest flowering. For everything that is really great and inspiring is created by the individual who can labour in freedom. Restriction is justified only in so far as it may be needed for the security of existence.

There is one other thing which follows from that conception—that we must not only tolerate differences between individuals and between groups, but we should indeed welcome them and look upon them as an enriching of our existence. That is the essence of all true tolerance; without tolerance in this widest sense there can be no question of true morality.

Morality in the sense here briefly indicated is not a fixed and stark system. It is rather a standpoint from which all questions which arise in life could and should be judged. It is a task never finished, something always present to guide our judgment and to inspire our conduct. Can you imagine that any man truly filled with this ideal could be content:—

Were he to receive from his fellow men a much greater return in goods and services than most other men ever receive?

Were his country, because it feels itself for the time being militarily secure, to stand aloof from the aspiration to create a supra-national system of security and justice?

Could he look on passively, or perhaps even with indifference, when elsewhere in the world innocent people are being brutally persecuted, deprived of their rights or even massacred?

To ask these questions is to answer them!

8

SCIENCE AND RELIGION

I

During the last century, and part of the one before, it was widely held that there was an unreconcilable conflict between knowledge and belief. The opinion prevailed among advanced minds that it was time that belief should be replaced increasingly by knowledge; belief that did not itself rest on knowledge was superstition, and as such had to be opposed. According to this conception, the sole function of education was to open the way to thinking and knowing, and the school, as the outstanding organ for the people's education, must serve that end exclusively.

One will probably find but rarely, if at all, the rationalistic standpoint expressed in such crass form; for any sensible man would see at once how one-sided is such a statement of the position. But it is just as well to state a thesis starkly and nakedly, if one wants to clear up one's mind as to its nature.

It is true that convictions can best be supported with experience and clear thinking. On this point one must agree unreservedly with the extreme rationalist. The weak point of his conception is, however, this, that those convictions which are necessary and determinant for our conduct and judgments, cannot be found solely along this solid scientific way.

For the scientific method can teach us nothing else beyond how facts are related to, and conditioned by, each other. The aspiration toward such objective knowledge belongs to the highest of which man is capable, and you will certainly not suspect me of wishing to belittle the achievements and the heroic efforts of man in this sphere. Yet it is equally clear that knowledge of what *is* does not open the door directly to what *should be*. One can have the clearest and most complete knowledge of what *is*, and yet not be able to deduct from that what should be the *goal* of our human aspirations. Objective knowledge provides us with powerful instruments for the achievements of certain ends, but the ultimate goal itself and the longing to reach it must come from another source. And it is hardly necessary to argue for the view that our existence and our activity acquire meaning only by the setting up of such a goal and of corresponding values. The knowledge of truth as such is wonderful, but it is so little capable of acting as a guide that it cannot prove even the justification and the value of the aspiration towards that very knowledge of truth. Here we face, therefore, the limits of the purely rational conception of our existence.

But it must not be assumed that intelligent thinking can play no part in the formation of the goal and of ethical judgments. When someone realizes that for the achievement of an end certain means would be useful, the means itself becomes thereby an end. Intelligence makes clear to us the interrelation of means and ends. But mere thinking cannot give us a sense of the ultimate and fundamental ends. To make clear these fundamental ends and valuations, and to set them fast in the emotional life of the individual, seems to me precisely the most important function which religion has to perform in the social life of man. And if one asks whence derives the authority of such fundamental ends, since they cannot be stated and justified merely by reason, one can only answer: they exist in a healthy society as powerful traditions, which act upon the conduct and aspirations and judgments of the individuals; they are there, that is, as something living, without its being necessary to find justification for their existence. They come into being not through demonstration but

through revelation, through the medium of powerful personalities. One must not attempt to justify them, but rather to
sense their nature simply and clearly.

The highest principles for our aspirations and judgments
are given to us in the Jewish-Christian religious tradition.
It is a very high goal which, with our weak powers, we can
reach only very inadequately, but which gives a sure foundation to our aspirations and valuations. If one were to take
that goal out of its religious form and look merely at its purely
human side, one might state it perhaps thus: free and responsible development of the individual, so that he may place
his powers freely and gladly in the service of all mankind.

There is no room in this for the divinization of a nation, of
a class, let alone of an individual. Are we not all children of
one father, as it is said in religious language? Indeed, even
the divinization of humanity, as an abstract totality, would
not be in the spirit of that ideal. It is only to the individual
that a soul is given. And the high destiny of the individual
is to serve rather than to rule, or to impose himself in any
other way.

If one looks at the substance rather than at the form, then
one can take these words as expressing also the fundamental
democratic position. The true democrat can worship his nation as little as can the man who is religious, in our sense of
the term.

What, then, in all this, is the function of education and
of the school? They should help the young person to grow up
in such a spirit that these fundamental principles should be
to him as the air which he breathes. Teaching alone cannot
do that.

If one holds these high principles clearly before one's eyes,
and compares them with the life and spirit of our times, then
it appears glaringly that civilized mankind finds itself at present in grave danger. In the totalitarian states it is the rulers
themselves who strive actually to destroy that spirit of hu-

manity. In less threatened parts it is nationalism and intolerance, as well as the oppression of the individuals by economic
means, which threaten to choke these most precious traditions.

A realization of how great is the danger is spreading, however, among thinking people, and there is much search for
means with which to meet the danger—means in the field of
national and international politics, of legislation, of organization in general. Such efforts are, no doubt, greatly needed.
Yet the ancients knew something which we seem to have
forgotten. All means prove but a blunt instrument, if they
have not behind them a living spirit. But if the longing for
the achievement of the goal is powerfully alive within us,
then shall we not lack the strength to find the means for
reaching the goal and for translating it into deeds.

II

It would not be difficult to come to an agreement as to
what we understand by science. Science is the century-old
endeavor to bring together by means of systematic thought
the perceptible phenomena of this world into as thorough-
going an association as possible. To put it boldly, it is the
attempt at the posterior reconstruction of existence by the
process of conceptualization. But when asking myself what
religion is I cannot think of the answer so easily. And even
after finding an answer which may satisfy me at this particular moment I still remain convinced that I can never under
any circumstances bring together, even to a slight extent, all
those who have given this question serious consideration.

At first, then, instead of asking what religion is I should
prefer to ask what characterizes the aspirations of a person
who gives me the impression of being religious: A person
who is religiously enlightened appears to me to be one who
has, to the best of his ability, liberated himself from the

fetters of his selfish desires and is preoccupied with thoughts, feelings, and aspirations to which he clings because of their super-personal value. It seems to me that what is important is the force of this super-personal content and the depth of the conviction concerning its overpowering meaningfulness, regardless of whether any attempt is made to unite this content with a divine Being, for otherwise it would not be possible to count Buddha and Spinoza as religious personalities. Accordingly, a religious person is devout in the sense that he has no doubt of the significance and loftiness of those super-personal objects and goals which neither require nor are capable of rational foundation. They exist with the same necessity and matter-of-factness as he himself. In this sense religion is the age-old endeavor of mankind to become clearly and completely conscious of these values and goals and constantly to strengthen and extend their effect. If one conceives of religion and science according to these definitions then a conflict between them appears impossible. For science can only ascertain what *is*, but not what *should be*, and outside of its domain value judgments of all kinds remain necessary. Religion, on the other hand, deals only with evaluations of human thought and action: it cannot justifiably speak of facts and relationships between facts. According to this interpretation the well-known conflicts between religion and science in the past must all be ascribed to a misapprehension of the situation which has been described.

For example, a conflict arises when a religious community insists on the absolute truthfulness of all statements recorded in the Bible. This means an intervention on the part of religion into the sphere of science; this is where the struggle of the Church against the doctrines of Galileo and Darwin belongs. On the other hand, representatives of science have often made an attempt to arrive at fundamental judgments with respect to values and ends on the basis of scientific method, and in this way have set themselves in opposition to religion. These conflicts have all sprung from fatal errors.

Now, even though the realms of religion and science in themselves are clearly marked off from each other, nevertheless there exist between the two strong reciprocal relationships and dependencies. Though religion may be that which determines the goal, it has, nevertheless, learned from science, in the broadest sense, what means will contribute to the attainment of the goals it has set up. But science can only be created by those who are thoroughly imbued with the aspiration towards truth and understanding. This source of feeling, however, springs from the sphere of religion. To this there also belongs the faith in the possibility that the regulations valid for the world of existence are rational, that is, comprehensible to reason. I cannot conceive of a genuine scientist without that profound faith. The situation may be expressed by an image: Science without religion is lame, religion without science is blind.

Though I have asserted above that in truth a legitimate conflict between religion and science cannot exist I must nevertheless qualify this assertion once again on an essential point, with reference to the actual content of historical religions. This qualification has to do with the concept of God. During the youthful period of mankind's spiritual evolution human fantasy created gods in man's own image, who, by the operations of their will were supposed to determine, or at any rate to influence the phenomenal world. Man sought to alter the disposition of these gods in his own favor by means of magic and prayer. The idea of God in the religions taught at present is a sublimation of that old conception of the gods. Its anthropomorphic character is shown, for instance, by the fact that men appeal to the Divine Being in prayers and plead for the fulfilment of their wishes.

Nobody, certainly, will deny that the idea of the existence of an omnipotent, just and omnibeneficent personal God is able to accord man solace, help, and guidance; also, by virtue of its simplicity it is accessible to the most undeveloped mind. But, on the other hand, there are decisive weaknesses attached to this idea in itself, which have been painfully felt since the beginning of history. That is, if this being is omnipotent then every occurrence, including every human action, every human thought, and every human feeling and aspiration is also His work; how is it possible to think of holding men responsible for their deeds and thoughts before such an almighty Being? In giving out punishment and rewards He would to a certain extent be passing judgment on Himself. How can this be combined with the goodness and righteousness ascribed to Him?

The main source of the present-day conflicts between the spheres of religion and of science lies in this concept of a personal God. It is the aim of science to establish general rules which determine the reciprocal connection of objects and events in time and space. For these rules, or laws of nature, absolutely general validity is required—not proven. It is mainly a program, and faith in the possibility of its accomplishment in principle is only founded on partial successes. But hardly anyone could be found who would deny these partial successes and ascribe them to human self-deception. The fact that on the basis of such laws we are able to predict the temporal behavior of phenomena in certain domains with great precision and certainty is deeply embedded in the consciousness of the modern man, even though he may have grasped very little of the contents of those laws. He need only consider that planetary courses within the solar system may be calculated in advance with great exactitude on the basis of a limited number of simple laws. In a similar way, though not with the same precision, it is possible to calculate in advance the mode of operation of an electric motor, a transmission system, or of a wireless apparatus, even when dealing with a novel development.

To be sure, when the number of factors coming into play in a phenomenological complex is too large scientific method in most cases fails us. One need only think of the weather, in which case prediction even for a few days ahead is impossible. Nevertheless no one doubts that we are confronted with a causal connection whose causal components are in the main known to us. Occurrences in this domain are beyond the reach of exact prediction because of the variety of factors in operation, not because of any lack of order in nature.

We have penetrated far less deeply into the regularities obtaining within the realm of living things, but deeply enough nevertheless to sense at least the rule of fixed necessity. One need only think of the systematic order in heredity, and in the effect of poisons, as for instance alcohol, on the behavior of organic beings. What is still lacking here is a grasp of connections of profound generality, but not a knowledge of order in itself.

The more a man is imbued with the ordered regularity of all events the firmer becomes his conviction that there is no room left by the side of this ordered regularity for causes of a different nature. For him neither the rule of human nor the rule of divine will exists as an independent cause of natural events. To be sure, the doctrine of a personal God interfering with natural events could never be *refuted*, in the real sense, by science, for this doctrine can always take refuge in those domains in which scientific knowledge has not yet been able to set foot.

But I am persuaded that such behavior on the part of the representatives of religion would not only be unworthy but also fatal. For a doctrine which is able to maintain itself not in clear light but only in the dark, will of necessity lose its effect on mankind, with incalculable harm to human progress. In their struggle for the ethical good, teachers of religion must have the stature to give up the doctrine of a personal God, that is, give up that source of fear and hope which in the past placed such vast power in the hands of priests. In their labors they will have to avail themselves of those forces which are capable of cultivating the Good, the True, and the Beautiful in humanity itself. This is, to be sure, a more difficult but an incomparably more worthy task.[1] After religious teachers accomplish the refining process indicated they will surely recognize with joy that true religion has been ennobled and made more profound by scientific knowledge.

If it is one of the goals of religion to liberate mankind as far as possible from the bondage of egocentric cravings, desires, and fears, scientific reasoning can aid religion in yet another sense. Although it is true that it is the goal of science to discover rules which permit the association and foretelling of facts, this is not its only aim. It also seeks to reduce the connections discovered to the smallest possible number of mutually independent conceptual elements. It is in this striving after the rational unification of the manifold that it encounters its greatest successes, even though it is precisely this attempt which causes it to run the greatest risk of falling a prey to illusions. But whoever has undergone the intense experience of successful advances made in this domain, is moved by profound reverence for the rationality made manifest in existence. By way of the understanding he achieves a far-reaching emancipation from the shackles of personal hopes and desires, and thereby attains that humble attitude of mind towards the grandeur of reason incarnate in existence, and which, in its profoundest depths, is inaccessible to man. This attitude, however, appears to me to be religious, in the highest sense of the word. And so it seems to me that science not only purifies the religious impulse of the dross of its anthropomorphism but also contributes to a religious spiritualization of our understanding of life.

The further the spiritual evolution of mankind advances,

[1] This thought is convincingly presented in Herbert Samuel's book, *Belief and Action*.

the more certain it seems to me that the path to genuine religiosity does not lie through the fear of life, and the fear of death, and blind faith, but through striving after rational knowledge. In this sense I believe that the priest must become a teacher if he wishes to do justice to his lofty educational mission.

9

ON EDUCATION

A DAY OF CELEBRATION generally is in the first place dedicated to retrospect, especially to the memory of personages
who have gained special distinction for the development of
the cultural life. This friendly service for our predecessors
must indeed not be neglected, particularly as such a memory
of the best of the past is proper to stimulate the well-disposed
of today to a courageous effort. But this should be done by
someone who, from his youth, has been connected with this
State and is familiar with its past, not by one who like a gypsy
has wandered about and gathered his experiences in all kinds
of countries.

Thus, there is nothing else left for me but to speak about
such questions as, independently of space and time, always
have been and will be connected with educational matters.
In this attempt I cannot lay any claim to being an authority,
especially as intelligent and well-meaning men of all times
have dealt with educational problems and have certainly repeatedly expressed their views clearly about these matters.
From what source shall I, as a partial layman in the realm
of pedagogy, derive courage to expound opinions with no
foundations except personal experience and personal conviction? If it were really a scientific matter, one would probably
be tempted to silence by such considerations.

However, with the affairs of active human beings it is different. Here knowledge of truth alone does not suffice; on the
contrary this knowledge must continually be renewed by
ceaseless effort, if it is not to be lost. It resembles a statue of

marble which stands in the desert and is continuously threatened with burial by the shifting sand. The hands of service must ever be at work, in order that the marble continue lastingly to shine in the sun. To these serving hands mine also shall belong.

The school has always been the most important means of transferring the wealth of tradition from one generation to the next. This applies today in an even higher degree than in former times for, through modern development of the economic life, the family as bearer of tradition and education has been weakened. The continuance and health of human society is therefore in a still higher degree dependent on the school than formerly.

Sometimes one sees in the school simply the instrument for transferring a certain maximum quantity of knowledge to the growing generation. But that is not right. Knowledge is dead; the school, however, serves the living. It should develop in the young individuals those qualities and capabilities which are of value for the welfare of the commonwealth. But that does not mean that individuality should be destroyed and the individual become a mere tool of the community, like a bee or an ant. For a community of standardized individuals without personal originality and personal aims would be a poor community without possibilities for development. On the contrary, the aim must be the training of independently acting and thinking individuals, who, however, see in the service of the community their highest life problem. As far as I can judge, the English school system comes nearest to the realization of this ideal.

But how shall one try to attain this ideal? Should one perhaps try to realize this aim by moralizing? Not at all. Words are and remain an empty sound, and the road to perdition has ever been accompanied by lip service to an ideal. But personalities are not formed by what is heard and said, but by labor and activity.

The most important method of education accordingly always has consisted of that in which the pupil was urged to actual performance. This applies as well to the first attempts at writing of the primary boy as to the doctor's thesis on graduation from the university, or as to the mere memorizing of a poem, the writing of a composition, the interpretation and translation of a text, the solving of a mathematical problem or the practice of physical sport.

But behind every achievement exists the motivation which is at the foundation of it and which in turn is strengthened and nourished by the accomplishment of the undertaking. Here there are the greatest differences and they are of greatest importance to the educational value of the school. The same work may owe its origin to fear and compulsion, ambitious desire for authority and distinction, or loving interest in the object and a desire for truth and understanding, and thus to that divine curiosity which every healthy child possesses, but which so often early is weakened. The educational influence which is exercised upon the pupil by the accomplishment of one and the same work may be widely different, depending upon whether fear of hurt, egoistic passion or desire for pleasure and satisfaction are at the bottom of this work. And nobody will maintain that the administration of the school and the attitude of the teachers does not have an influence upon the molding of the psychological foundation for pupils.

To me the worst thing seems to be for a school principally to work with methods of fear, force and artificial authority. Such treatment destroys the sound sentiments, the sincerity and the self-confidence of the pupil. It produces the submissive subject. It is no wonder that such schools are the rule in Germany and Russia. I know that the schools in this country are free from this worst evil; this also is so in Switzerland and probably in all democratically governed countries. It is comparatively simple to keep the school free from this worst of all evils. Give into the power of the teacher the fewest possible coercive measures, so that the only source of the pupil's respect for the teacher is the human and intellectual qualities of the latter.

The second-named motive, ambition or, in milder terms, the aiming at recognition and consideration, lies firmly fixed in human nature. With absence of mental stimulus of this kind, human cooperation would be entirely impossible; the desire for the approval of one's fellowman certainly is one of the most important binding powers of society. In this complex of feelings, constructive and destructive forces lie closely together. Desire for approval and recognition is a healthy motive; but the desire to be acknowledged as better, stronger or more intelligent than a fellow being or fellow scholar easily leads to an excessively egoistic psychological adjustment, which may become injurious for the individual and for the community. Therefore the school and the teacher must guard against employing the easy method of creating individual ambition, in order to induce the pupils to diligent work.

Darwin's theory of the struggle for existence and the selectivity connected with it has by many people been cited as authorization of the encouragement of the spirit of competition. Some people also in such a way have tried to prove pseudo-scientifically the necessity of the destructive economic struggle of competition between individuals. But this is wrong, because man owes his strength in the struggle for existence to the fact that he is a socially living animal. As little as a battle between single ants of an ant hill is essential for survival, just so little is this the case with the individual members of a human community.

Therefore one should guard against preaching to the young man success in the customary sense as the aim of life. For a successful man is he who receives a great deal from his fellowmen, usually incomparably more than corresponds to his

OUT OF MY LATER YEARS

service to them. The value of a man, however, should be seen in what he gives and not in what he is able to receive.

The most important motive for work in the school and in life is the pleasure in work, pleasure in its result and the knowledge of the value of the result to the community. In the awakening and strengthening of these psychological forces in the young man, I see the most important task given by the school. Such a psychological foundation alone leads to a joyous desire for the highest possessions of men, knowledge and artistlike workmanship.

The awakening of these productive psychological powers is certainly less easy than the practice of force or the awakening of individual ambition but is the more valuable for it. The point is to develop the childlike inclination for play and the childlike desire for recognition and to guide the child over to important fields for society; it is that education which in the main is founded upon the desire for successful activity and acknowledgment. If the school succeeds in working successfully from such points of view, it will be highly honored by the rising generation and the tasks given by the school will be submitted to as a sort of gift. I have known children who preferred schooltime to vacation.

Such a school demands from the teacher that he be a kind of artist in his province. What can be done that this spirit be gained in the school? For this there is just as little a universal remedy as there is for an individual to remain well. But there are certain necessary conditions which can be met. First, teachers should grow up in such schools. Second, the teacher should be given extensive liberty in the selection of the material to be taught and the methods of teaching employed by him. For it is true also of him that pleasure in the shaping of his work is killed by force and exterior pressure.

If you have followed attentively my meditations up to this point, you will probably wonder about one thing. I have spoken fully about in what spirit, according to my opinion, youth should be instructed. But I have said nothing yet about the choice of subjects for instruction, nor about the method of teaching. Should language predominate or technical education in science?

To this I answer: In my opinion all this is of secondary importance. If a young man has trained his muscles and physical endurance by gymnastics and walking, he will later be fitted for every physical work. This is also analogous to the training of the mind and the exercising of the mental and manual skill. Thus the wit was not wrong who defined education in this way: "Education is that which remains, if one has forgotten everything he learned in school." For this reason I am not at all anxious to take sides in the struggle between the followers of the classical philologic-historical education and the education more devoted to natural science.

On the other hand, I want to oppose the idea that the school has to teach directly that special knowledge and those accomplishments which one has to use later directly in life. The demands of life are much too manifold to let such a specialized training in school appear possible. Apart from that, it seems to me, moreover, objectionable to treat the individual like a dead tool. The school should always have as its aim that the young man leave it as a harmonious personality, not as a specialist. This in my opinion is true in a certain sense even for technical schools, whose students will devote themselves to a quite definite profession. The development of general ability for independent thinking and judgment should always be placed foremost, not the acquisition of special knowledge. If a person masters the fundamentals of his subject and has learned to think and work independently, he will surely find his way and besides will better be able to adapt himself to progress and changes than the person whose training principally consists in the acquiring of detailed knowledge.

Finally, I wish to emphasize once more that what has been said here in a somewhat categorical form does not claim to mean more than the personal opinion of a man, which is founded upon *nothing but* his own personal experience, which he has gathered as a student and as a teacher.

Science

10

THE THEORY OF RELATIVITY

MATHEMATICS DEALS exclusively with the relations of concepts to each other without consideration of their relation to experience. Physics too deals with mathematical concepts; however, these concepts attain physical content only by the clear determination of their relation to the objects of experience. This in particular is the case for the concepts of motion, space, time.

The theory of relativity is that physical theory which is based on a consistent physical interpretation of these three concepts. The name "theory of relativity" is connected with the fact that motion from the point of view of possible experience always appears as the *relative* motion of one object with respect to another (e.g., of a car with respect to the ground, or the earth with respect to the sun and the fixed stars). Motion is never observable as "motion with respect to space" or, as it has been expressed, as "absolute motion." The "principle of relativity" in its widest sense is contained in the statement: The totality of physical phenomena is of such a character that it gives no basis for the introduction of the concept of "absolute motion"; or shorter but less precise: There is no absolute motion.

It might seem that our insight would gain little from such a negative statement. In reality, however, it is a strong restriction for the (conceivable) laws of nature. In this sense there exists an analogy between the theory of relativity and thermodynamics. The latter too is based on a negative statement: "There exists no perpetuum mobile."

The development of the theory of relativity proceeded in two steps, "special theory of relativity" and "general theory of relativity." The latter presumes the validity of the former as a limiting case and is its consistent continuation.

A. *Special theory of relativity.*

Physical interpretation of space and time in classical mechanics.

Geometry, from a physical standpoint, is the totality of laws according to which rigid bodies mutually at rest can be placed with respect to each other (e.g., a triangle consists of three rods whose ends touch permanently). It is assumed that with such an interpretation the Euclidean laws are valid. "Space" in this interpretation is in principle an infinite rigid body (or skeleton) to which the position of all other bodies is related (body of reference). Analytic geometry (Descartes) uses as the body of reference, which represents space, three mutually perpendicular rigid rods on which the "coordinates" (x, y, z) of space points are measured in the known manner as perpendicular projections (with the aid of a rigid unit-measure).

Physics deals with "events" in space and time. To each event belongs, besides its place coordinates x, y, z, a time value t. The latter was considered measurable by a clock (ideal periodic process) of negligible spatial extent. This clock C is to be considered at rest at one point of the coordinate system, e.g., at the coordinate origin (x = y = z = O). The time of an event taking place at a point P(x, y, z) is then defined as the time shown on the clock C simultaneously with the event. Here the concept "simultaneous" was assumed as physically meaningful without special definition. This is a lack of exactness which seems harmless only since with the help of light (whose velocity is practically infinite from the point of view of daily experience) the simultaneity of spatially distant events can apparently be decided immediately.

The special theory of relativity removes this lack of precision by defining simultaneity physically with the use of light signals. The time t of the event in P is the reading of the clock C at the time of arrival of a light signal emitted from the event, corrected with respect to the time needed for the light signal to travel the distance. This correction presumes (postulates) that the velocity of light is constant.

This definition reduces the concept of simultaneity of spatially distant events to that of the simultaneity of events happening at the same place (coincidence), namely the arrival of the light signal at C and the reading of C.

Classical mechanics is based on Galileo's principle: A body is in rectilinear and uniform motion as long as other bodies do not act on it. This statement cannot be valid for arbitrary moving systems of coordinates. It can claim validity only for so-called "inertial systems". Inertial systems are in rectilinear and uniform motion with respect to each other. In classical physics laws claim validity only with respect to all inertial systems (special principle of relativity).

It is now easy to understand the dilemma which has led to the special theory of relativity. Experience and theory have gradually led to the conviction that light in empty space always travels with the same velocity c independent of its color and the state of motion of the source of light (principle of the constancy of the velocity of light—in the following referred to as "L-principle"). Now elementary intuitive considerations seem to show that the same light ray *cannot* move with respect to all inertial systems with the same velocity c. The L-principle seems to contradict the special principle of relativity.

It turns out, however, that this contradiction is only an apparent one which is based essentially on the prejudice about the absolute character of time or rather of the simultaneity of distant events. We just saw that x, y, z and t of an event can, for the moment, be defined only with respect to a certain chosen system of coordinates (inertial system). The transformation of the x, y, z, t of events which has to be carried out with the passage from one inertial system to another (coordinate transformation), is a problem which cannot be solved without special physical assumptions. However, the following postulate is exactly sufficient for a solution: *The L-principle holds for all inertial systems* (application of the special principle of relativity to the L-principle). The transformations thus defined, which are linear in x, y, z, t, are called Lorentz transformations. Lorentz transformations are formally characterized by the demand that the expression

$$dx^2 + dy^2 + dz^2 - c^2dt^2,$$

which is formed from the coordinate differences dx, dy, dz, dt of two infinitely close events, be invariant (i.e., that through the transformation it goes over into the *same* expression formed from the coordinate differences in the new system).

With the help of the Lorentz transformations the special principle of relativity can be expressed thus: The laws of nature are invariant with respect to Lorentz-transformations (i.e., a law of nature does not change its form if one introduces into it a new inertial system with the help of a Lorentz-transformation on x, y, z, t).

The special theory of relativity has led to a clear understanding of the physical concepts of space and time and in connection with this to a recognition of the behavior of moving measuring rods and clocks. It has in principle removed the concept of absolute simultaneity and thereby also that of instantaneous action at a distance in the sense of Newton. It has shown how the law of motion must be modified in dealing with motions that are not negligibly small as compared with the velocity of light. It has led to a formal clarification of Maxwell's equations of the electromagnetic field; in particular it has led to an understanding of the essential oneness of the electric and the magnetic field. It has unified the laws of conservation of momentum and of energy into one single law and has demonstrated the equivalence of mass and energy. From a formal point of view one may characterize the achievement of the special theory of relativity thus: it has shown generally the role which the universal constant c (velocity of light) plays in the laws of nature and has demonstrated that there exists a close connection between the form in which time on the one hand and the spatial coordinates on the other hand enter into the laws of nature.

B. *General theory of relativity.*

The special theory of relativity retained the basis of classical mechanics in one fundamental point, namely the statement: The laws of nature are valid only with respect to inertial systems. The "permissible" transformations for the coordinates (i.e., those which leave the form of the laws unchanged) are *exclusively* the (linear) Lorentz-transformations. Is this restriction really founded in physical facts? The following argument convincingly denies it.

Principle of equivalence. A body has an inertial mass (resistance to acceleration) and a heavy mass (which determines the weight of the body in a given gravitational field, e.g., that at the surface of the earth). These two quantities, so different according to their definition, are according to experience measured by one and the same number. There must be a deeper reason for this. The fact can also be described thus: In a gravitational field different masses receive the same acceleration. Finally, it can also be expressed thus: Bodies in a gravitational field behave as in the absence of a gravitational field if, in the latter case, the system of reference used is a uniformly accelerated coordinate system (instead of an inertial system).

There seems, therefore, to be no reason to ban the following interpretation of the latter case. One considers the system as being "at rest" and considers the "apparent" gravitational field which exists with respect to it as a "real" one. This gravitational field "generated" by the acceleration of the coordinate system would of course be of unlimited extent in such a way that it could not be caused by gravitational masses in a finite region; however, if we are looking for a field-like theory, this fact need not deter us. With this interpretation the inertial system loses its meaning and one has an "explanation" for the equality of heavy and inertial mass (the same property of matter appears as weight or as inertia depending on the mode of description).

Considered formally, the admission of a coordinate system which is accelerated with respect to the original "inertial" coordinates means the admission of non-linear coordinate transformations, hence a mighty enlargement of the idea of invariance, i.e., the principle of relativity.

First, a penetrating discussion, using the results of the special theory of relativity, shows that with such a generalization the coordinates can no longer be interpreted directly as the results of measurements. Only the coordinate difference together with the field quantities which describe the gravitational field determine measurable distances between events. After one has found oneself forced to admit non-linear coordinate transformations as transformations between equivalent coordinate systems, the simplest demand appears to admit all continuous coordinate transformations (which form a group), i.e., to admit arbitrary curvilinear coordinate systems in which the fields are described by regular functions (general principle of relativity).

Now it is not difficult to understand why the general principle of relativity (*on the basis of the equivalence principle*) has led to a theory of gravitation. There is a special kind of space whose physical structure (field) we can presume as precisely known on the basis of the special theory of relativity. This is empty space without electromagnetic field and without matter. It is completely determined by its "metric" property: Let dx_0, dy_0, dz_0, dt_0 be the coordinate differences of two infinitesimally near points (events); then

$$(1) \qquad ds^2 = dx_0{}^2 + dy_0{}^2 + dz_0{}^2 - c^2 dt_0{}^2$$

is a measurable quantity which is independent of the special choice of the inertial system. If one introduces in this space the new coordinates x_1, x_2, x_3, x_4 through a general transformation of coordinates, then the quantity ds^2 for the same pair of points has an expression of the form

$$(2) \quad ds^2 = \Sigma g_{ik} dx^i dx^k \text{ (summed for i and k from 1 to 4)}$$

where $g_{ik} = g_{ki}$. The g_{ik} which form a "symmetric tensor" and are continuous functions of x_1, . . . x_4 then describe according to the "principle of equivalence" a gravitational field of a special kind (namely one which can be retransformed to the form (1)). From Riemann's investigations on metric spaces the mathematical properties of this g_{ik} field can be given exactly ("Riemann-condition"). However, what we are looking for are the equations satisfied by "general" gravitational fields. It is natural to assume that they too can be described as tensor-fields of the type g_{ik}, which in general do *not* admit a transformation to the form (1), i.e., which do not satisfy the "Riemann condition," but weaker conditions, which, just as the Riemann condition, are independent of the choice of coordinates (i.e., are generally invariant). A simple formal consideration leads to weaker conditions which are closely connected with the Riemann condition. These conditions are the very equations of the pure gravitational field (on the outside of matter and at the absence of an electromagnetic field).

These equations yield Newton's equations of gravitational mechanics as an approximate law and in addition certain small effects which have been confirmed by observation (deflection of light by the gravitational field of a star, influence of the gravitational potential on the frequency of emitted light, slow rotation of the elliptic circuits of planets—perihelion motion of the planet Mercury). They further yield an explanation for the expanding motion of galactic systems, which is manifested by the red-shift of the light omitted from these systems.

The general theory of relativity is as yet incomplete insofar as it has been able to apply the general principle of relativity satisfactorily only to gravitational fields, but not to the total field. We do not yet know with certainty, by what mathematical mechanism the total field in space is to be described and what the general invariant laws are to which this total field is subject. One thing, however, seems certain: namely, that the general principle of relativity will prove a necessary and effective tool for the solution of the problem of the total field.

11

E = M C²

Iɴ ᴏʀᴅᴇʀ ᴛᴏ ᴜɴᴅᴇʀsᴛᴀɴᴅ the law of the equivalence of mass and energy, we must go back to two conservation or "balance" principles which, independent of each other, held a high place in pre-relativity physics. These were the principle of the conservation of energy and the principle of the conservation of mass. The first of these, advanced by Leibnitz as long ago as the seventeenth century, was developed in the nineteenth century essentially as a corollary of a principle of mechanics.

Drawing from Dr. Einstein's manuscript.

Consider, for example, a pendulum whose mass swings back and forth between the points A and B. At these points the mass m is higher by the amount h than it is at C, the lowest point of the path (see drawing). At C, on the other hand, the lifting height has disappeared and instead of it the mass has a velocity v. It is as though the lifting height could be converted entirely into velocity, and vice versa. The exact relation would be expressed as $mgh = \frac{m}{2} v^2$, with g representing the acceleration of gravity. What is interesting here is that this relation is independent of both the length of the pendulum and the form of the path through which the mass moves.

The significance is that something remains constant throughout the process, and that something is energy. At A and at B it is an energy of position, or "potential" energy; at C it is an energy of motion, or "kinetic" energy. If this concept is correct, then the sum $mgh + m\frac{v^2}{2}$ must have the same value for any position of the pendulum, if h is understood to represent the height above C, and v the velocity at that point in the pendulum's path. And such is found to be actually the case. The generalization of this principle gives us the law of the conservation of mechanical energy. But what happens when friction stops the pendulum?

The answer to that was found in the study of heat phenomena. This study, based on the assumption that heat is an indestructible substance which flows from a warmer to a colder object, seemed to give us a principle of the "conservation of heat." On the other hand, from time immemorial it has been known that heat could be produced by friction, as in the fire-making drills of the Indians. The physicists were for long unable to account for this kind of heat "production." Their difficulties were overcome only when it was successfully established that, for any given amount of heat produced by friction, an exactly proportional amount of energy had to be expended. Thus did we arrive at a principle of the "equivalence of work and heat." With our pendulum, for example, mechanical energy is gradually converted by friction into heat.

In such fashion the principles of the conservation of mechanical and thermal energies were merged into one. The physicists were thereupon persuaded that the conservation principle could be further extended to take in chemical and electromagnetic processes—in short, could be applied to all fields. It appeared that in our physical system there was a sum total of energies that remained constant through all changes that might occur.

Now for the principle of the conservation of mass. Mass is defined by the resistance that a body opposes to its acceleration (inert mass). It is also measured by the weight of the body (heavy mass). That these two radically different definitions lead to the same value for the mass of a body is, in itself, an astonishing fact. According to the principle—namely, that masses remain unchanged under any physical or chemical changes—the mass appeared to be the essential (because unvarying) quality of matter. Heating, melting, vaporization, or combining into chemical compounds would not change the total mass.

Physicists accepted this principle up to a few decades ago. But it proved inadequate in the face of the special theory of relativity. It was therefore merged with the energy principle —just as, about 60 years before, the principle of the conservation of mechanical energy had been combined with the principle of the conservation of heat. We might say that the principle of the conservation of energy, having previously swallowed up that of the conservation of heat, now proceeded to swallow that of the conservation of mass—and holds the field alone.

It is customary to express the equivalence of mass and energy (though somewhat inexactly) by the formula $E = mc^2$, in which c represents the velocity of light, about 186,000 miles per second. E is the energy that is contained in a stationary body; m is its mass. The energy that belongs to the mass m is equal to this mass, multiplied by the square of the enormous speed of light—which is to say, a vast amount of energy for every unit of mass.

But if every gram of material contains this tremendous energy, why did it go so long unnoticed? The answer is simple enough: so long as none of the energy is given off externally, it cannot be observed. It is as though a man who is fabulously rich should never spend or give away a cent; no one could tell how rich he was.

Now we can reverse the relation and say that an increase of E in the amount of energy must be accompanied by an increase of $\frac{E}{c^2}$ in the mass. I can easily supply energy to the mass—for instance, if I heat it by 10 degrees. So why not measure the mass increase, or weight increase, connected with this change? The trouble here is that in the mass increase the enormous factor c^2 occurs in the denominator of the fraction. In such a case the increase is too small to be measured directly; even with the most sensitive balance.

For a mass increase to be measurable, the change of energy per mass unit must be enormously large. We know of only one sphere in which such amounts of energy per mass unit are released: namely, radioactive disintegration. Schematically, the process goes like this: An atom of the mass M splits into two atoms of the mass M′ and M″, which separate with tremendous kinetic energy. If we imagine these two masses as brought to rest—that is, if we take this energy of motion from them—then, considered together, they are essentially poorer in energy than was the original atom. According to the equivalence principle, the mass sum M′ + M″ of the disintegration products must also be somewhat smaller than the original mass M of the disintegrating atom—in contradiction to the old principle of the conservation of mass. The relative difference of the two is on the order of $\frac{1}{10}$ of one percent.

Now, we cannot actually weigh the atoms individually. However, there are indirect methods for measuring their weights exactly. We can likewise determine the kinetic energies that are transferred to the disintegration products M′ and M″. Thus it has become possible to test and confirm the equivalence formula. Also, the law permits us to calculate in advance, from precisely determined atom weights, just how much energy will be released with any atom disintegration we have in mind. The law says nothing, of course, as to whether—or how—the disintegration reaction can be brought about.

What takes place can be illustrated with the help of our rich man. The atom M is a rich miser who, during his life, gives away no money (*energy*). But in his will he bequeaths his fortune to his sons M′ and M″, on condition that they give to the community a small amount, less than one thousandth of the whole estate (*energy or mass*). The sons together have somewhat less than the father had (*the mass sum M′ + M″ is somewhat smaller than the mass M of the radioactive atom*). But the part given to the community, though relatively small, is still so enormously large (*considered as kinetic energy*) that it brings with it a great threat of evil. Averting that threat has become the most urgent problem of our time.

12

WHAT IS THE THEORY OF RELATIVITY?

I GLADLY accede to the request of your colleague to write something for *The Times* on relativity. After the lamentable breakdown of the old active intercourse between men of learning, I welcome this opportunity of expressing my feelings of joy and gratitude towards the astronomers and physicists of England. It is thoroughly in keeping with the great and proud traditions of scientific work in your country that eminent scientists should have spent much time and trouble, and your scientific institutions have spared no expense, to test the implications of a theory which was perfected and published during the War in the land of your enemies. Even though the investigation of the influence of the gravitational field of the sun on light rays is a purely objective matter, I cannot forbear to express my personal thanks to my English colleagues for their work; for without it I could hardly have lived to see the most important implication of my theory tested.

We can distinguish various kinds of theories in physics. Most of them are constructive. They attempt to build up a picture of the more complex phenomena out of the materials of a relatively simple formal scheme from which they start out. Thus the kinetic theory of gases seeks to reduce mechanical, thermal and diffusional processes to movements of molecules—i.e., to build them up out of the hypothesis of molecular motion. When we say that we have succeeded in understanding a group of natural processes, we invariably mean that a constructive theory has been found which covers the processes in question.

Along with this most important class of theories there exists a second, which I will call "principle-theories." These employ the analytic, not the synthetic, method. The elements which form their basis and starting-point are not hypothetically constructed but empirically discovered ones, general characteristics of natural processes, principles that give rise to mathematically formulated criteria which the separate processes or the theoretical representations of them have to satisfy. Thus the science of thermodynamics seeks by analytical means to deduce necessary connections, which separate events have to satisfy, from the universally experienced fact that perpetual motion is impossible.

The advantages of the constructive theory are completeness, adaptability and clearness, those of the principle theory are logical perfection and security of the foundations.

The theory of relativity belongs to the latter class. In order to grasp its nature, one needs first of all to become acquainted with the principles on which it is based. Before I go into these, however, I must observe that the theory of relativity resembles a building consisting of two separate stories, the special theory and the general theory. The special theory, on which the general theory rests, applies to all physical phenomena with the exception of gravitation; the general theory provides the law of gravitation and its relations to the other forces of nature.

It has, of course, been known since the days of the ancient Greeks that in order to describe the movement of a body, a second body is needed to which the movement of the first is referred. The movement of a vehicle is considered in reference to the earth's surface, that of a planet to the totality of the visible fixed stars. In physics the body to which events are spatially referred is called the co-ordinate system.

The laws of the mechanics of Galileo and Newton, for instance, can only be formulated with the aid of a co-ordinate system.

The state of motion of the co-ordinate system may not, however, be arbitrarily chosen, if the laws of mechanics are to be valid (it must be free from rotation and acceleration). A co-ordinate system which is admitted in mechanics is called an "inertial system." The state of motion of an inertial system is according to mechanics not one that is determined uniquely by nature. On the contrary, the following definition holds good:—a co-ordinate system that is moved uniformly and in a straight line relatively to an inertial system is likewise an inertial system. By the "special principle of relativity" is meant the generalization of this definition to include any natural event whatever: thus, every universal law of nature which is valid in relation to a co-ordinate system C, must also be valid, as it stands, in relation to a co-ordinate system C', which is in uniform translatory motion relatively to C.

The second principle, on which the special theory of relativity rests, is the "principle of the constant velocity of light in vacuo." This principle asserts that light in vacuo always has a definite velocity of propagation (independent of the state of motion of the observer or of the source of the light). The confidence which physicists place in this principle springs from the successes achieved by the electro-dynamics of Clerk Maxwell and Lorentz.

Both the above-mentioned principles are powerfully supported by experience, but appear not to be logically reconcilable. The special theory of relativity finally succeeded in reconciling them logically by a modification of kinematics— i.e., of the doctrine of the laws relating to space and time (from the point of view of physics). It became clear that to speak of the simultaneity of two events had no meaning except in relation to a given co-ordinate system, and that the shape of measuring devices and the speed at which clocks move depend on their state of motion with respect to the co-ordinate system.

But the old physics, including the laws of motion of Galileo and Newton, did not fit in with the suggested relativist kinematics. From the latter, general mathematical conditions issued, to which natural laws had to conform, if the above-mentioned two principles were really to apply. To these, physics had to be adapted. In particular, scientists arrived at a new law of motion for (rapidly moving) mass points, which was admirably confirmed in the case of electrically charged particles. The most important upshot of the special theory of relativity concerned the inert mass of corporeal systems. It turned out that the inertia of a system necessarily depends on its energy-content, and this led straight to the notion that inert mass is simply latent energy. The principle of the conservation of mass lost its independence and became fused with that of the conservation of energy.

The special theory of relativity, which was simply a systematic development of the electro-dynamics of Clerk Maxwell and Lorentz, pointed beyond itself, however. Should the independence of physical laws of the state of motion of the co-ordinate system be restricted to the uniform translatory motion of co-ordinate systems in respect to each other? What has nature to do with our co-ordinate systems and their state of motion? If it is necessary for the purpose of describing nature, to make use of a co-ordinate system arbitrarily introduced by us, then the choice of its state of motion ought to be subject to no restriction; the laws ought to be entirely independent of this choice (general principle of relativity).

The establishment of this general principle of relativity is made easier by a fact of experience that has long been known, namely that the weight and the inertia of a body are controlled by the same constant. (Equality of inertial and gravitational mass.) Imagine a co-ordinate system which is rotating uniformly with respect to an inertial system in the Newtonian manner. The centrifugal forces which manifest themselves in relation to this system must, according to Newton's teaching, be regarded as effects of inertia. But these centrifugal forces are, exactly like the forces of gravity, proportional to the masses of the bodies. Ought it not to be possible in this case to regard the co-ordinate system as stationary and the centrifugal forces as gravitational forces? This seems the obvious view, but classical mechanics forbid it.

This hasty consideration suggests that a general theory of relativity must supply the laws of gravitation, and the consistent following up of the idea has justified our hopes.

But the path was thornier than one might suppose, because it demanded the abandonment of Euclidean geometry. This is to say, the laws according to which fixed bodies may be arranged in space, do not completely accord with the spatial laws attributed to bodies by Euclidean geometry. This is what we mean when we talk of the "curvature of space." The fundamental concepts of the "straight line," the "plane," etc., thereby lose their precise significance in physics.

In the general theory of relativity the doctrine of space and time, or kinematics, no longer figures as a fundamental independent of the rest of physics. The geometrical behavior of bodies and the motion of clocks rather depend on gravitational fields, which in their turn are produced by matter.

The new theory of gravitation diverges considerably, as regards principles, from Newton's theory. But its practical results agree so nearly with those of Newton's theory that it is difficult to find criteria for distinguishing them which are accessible to experience. Such have been discovered so far:—

(1) In the revolution of the ellipses of the planetary orbits round the sun (confirmed in the case of Mercury).

(2) In the curving of light rays by the action of gravitational fields (confirmed by the English photographs of eclipses).

(3) In a displacement of the spectral lines towards the red end of the spectrum in the case of light transmitted to us from stars of considerable magnitude (unconfirmed so far).[1]

The chief attraction of the theory lies in its logical completeness. If a single one of the conclusions drawn from it proves wrong, it must be given up; to modify it without destroying the whole structure seems to be impossible.

Let no one suppose, however, that the mighty work of Newton can really be superseded by this or any other theory. His great and lucid ideas will retain their unique significance for all time as the foundation of our whole modern conceptual structure in the sphere of natural philosophy.

NOTE: Some of the statements in your paper concerning my life and person owe their origin to the lively imagination of the writer. Here is yet another application of the principle of relativity for the delectation of the reader:—Today I am described in Germany as a "German savant," and in England as a "Swiss Jew." Should it ever be my fate to be represented as a *bête noire*, I should, on the contrary, become a "Swiss Jew" for the Germans and a "German savant" for the English.

[1] Editor's Note: This criterion has also been confirmed in the meantime.

13

PHYSICS AND REALITY

---

§ 1. GENERAL CONSIDERATION CONCERNING THE METHOD OF SCIENCE

IT HAS OFTEN BEEN SAID, and certainly not without justification, that the man of science is a poor philosopher. Why then should it not be the right thing for the physicist to let the philosopher do the philosophizing? Such might indeed be the right thing at a time when the physicist believes he has at his disposal a rigid system of fundamental concepts and fundamental laws which are so well established that waves of doubt can not reach them; but, it can not be right at a time when the very foundations of physics itself have become problematic as they are now. At a time like the present, when experience forces us to seek a newer and more solid foundation, the physicist cannot simply surrender to the philosopher the critical contemplation of the theoretical foundations; for, he himself knows best, and feels more surely where the shoe pinches. In looking for a new foundation, he must try to make clear in his own mind just how far the concepts which he uses are justified, and are necessities.

The whole of science is nothing more than a refinement of every day thinking. It is for this reason that the critical thinking of the physicist cannot possibly be restricted to the examination of the concepts of his own specific field. He cannot proceed without considering critically a much more difficult problem, the problem of analyzing the nature of everyday thinking.

On the stage of our subconscious mind appear in colorful succession sense experiences, memory pictures of them, representations and feelings. In contrast to psychology, physics treats directly only of sense experiences and of the "understanding" of their connection. But even the concept of the "real external world" of everyday thinking rests exclusively on sense impressions.

Now we must first remark that the differentiation between sense impressions and representations is not possible; or, at least it is not possible with absolute certainty. With the discussion of this problem, which affects also the notion of reality, we will not concern ourselves but we shall take the existence of sense experiences as given, that is to say as psychic experiences of special kind.

I believe that the first step in the setting of a "real external world" is the formation of the concept of bodily objects and of bodily objects of various kinds. Out of the multitude of our sense experiences we take, mentally and arbitrarily, certain repeatedly occurring complexes of sense impression (partly in conjunction with sense impressions which are interpreted as signs for sense experiences of others), and we attribute to them a meaning—the meaning of the bodily object. Considered logically this concept is not identical with the totality of sense impressions referred to; but it is an arbitrary creation of the human (or animal) mind. On the other hand, the concept owes its meaning and its justification exclusively to the totality of the sense impressions which we associate with it.

The second step is to be found in the fact that, in our thinking (which determines our expectation), we attribute to this concept of the bodily object a significance, which is to a high degree independent of the sense impression which originally gives rise to it. This is what we mean when we attribute to the bodily object "a real existence." The justification of such a setting rests exclusively on the fact that, by means of such concepts and mental relations between them, we are able to orient ourselves in the labyrinth of sense impressions. These notions and relations, although free statements of our thoughts, appear to us as stronger and more unalterable than the individual sense experience itself, the character of which as anything other than the result of an illusion or hallucination is never completely guaranteed. On the other hand, these concepts and relations, and indeed the setting of real objects and, generally speaking, the existence of "the real world," have justification only in so far as they are connected with sense impressions between which they form a mental connection.

The very fact that the totality of our sense experiences is such that by means of thinking (operations with concepts, and the creation and use of definite functional relations between them, and the coordination of sense experiences to these concepts) it can be put in order, this fact is one which leaves us in awe, but which we shall never understand. One may say "the eternal mystery of the world is its comprehensibility." It is one of the great realizations of Immanuel Kant that the setting up of a real external world would be senseless without this comprehensibility.

In speaking here concerning "comprehensibility," the expression is used in its most modest sense. It implies: the production of some sort of order among sense impressions, this order being produced by the creation of general concepts, relations between these concepts, and by relations between the concepts and sense experience, these relations being determined in any possible manner. It is in this sense that the world of our sense experiences is comprehensible. The fact that it is comprehensible is a miracle.

In my opinion, nothing can be said concerning the manner in which the concepts are to be made and connected, and how we are to coordinate them to the experiences. In guiding us in the creation of such an order of sense experiences, success in the result is alone the determining factor. All that is necessary is *the statement* of a set of rules, since without such rules the acquisition of knowledge in the desired sense would be impossible. One may compare these rules with the rules of a game in which, while the rules themselves are arbitrary, it is their rigidity alone which makes the game possible. However, the fixation will never be final. It will have validity only for a special field of application (i.e. there are no final categories in the sense of Kant).

The connection of the elementary concepts of every day thinking with complexes of sense experiences can only be comprehended intuitively and it is unadaptable to scientifically logical fixation. The totality of these connections—none of which is expressible in notional terms—is the only thing which differentiates the great building which is science from a logical but empty scheme of concepts. By means of these connections, the purely notional theorems of science become statements about complexes of sense experiences.

We shall call "primary concepts" such concepts as are directly and intuitively connected with typical complexes of sense experiences. All other notions are—from the physical point of view—possessed of meaning, only in so far as they are connected, by theorems, with the primary notions. These theorems are partially definitions of the concepts (and of the statements derived logically from them) and partially theorems not derivable from the definitions, which express at least indirect relations between the "primary concepts," and in this way between sense experiences. Theorems of the latter kind are "statements about reality" or laws of nature, i.e. theorems which have to show their usefulness when applied to sense experiences comprehended by primary concepts. The question as to which of the theorems shall be considered as definitions and which as natural laws will depend largely upon the chosen representation. It really becomes absolutely necessary to make this differentiation only when one examines the degree to which the whole system of concepts considered is not empty from the physical point of view.

STRATIFICATION OF THE SCIENTIFIC SYSTEM

The aim of science is, on the one hand, a comprehension, as *complete* as possible, of the connection between the sense experiences in their totality, and, on the other hand, the accomplishment of this aim *by the use of a minimum of primary concepts and relations.* (Seeking, as far as possible, logical unity in the world picture, i.e. paucity in logical elements.)

Science concerns the totality of the primary concepts, i.e. concepts directly connected with sense experiences, and theorems connecting them. In its first stage of development, science does not contain anything else. Our everyday thinking is satisfied on the whole with this level. Such a state of affairs cannot, however, satisfy a spirit which is really scientifically minded; because, the totality of concepts and relations obtained in this manner is utterly lacking in logical unity. In order to supplement this deficiency, one invents a system poorer in concepts and relations, a system retaining the primary concepts and relations of the "first layer" as logically derived concepts and relations. This new "secondary system" pays for its higher logical unity by having, as its own elementary concepts (concepts of the second layer), only those which are no longer directly connected with complexes of sense experiences. Further striving for logical unity brings us to a tertiary system, still poorer in concepts and relations, for the deduction of the concepts and relations of the secondary (and so indirectly of the primary) layer. Thus the story goes on until we have arrived at a system of the greatest conceivable unity, and of the greatest poverty of concepts of the logical foundations, which are still compatible with the observation made by our senses. We do not know whether or not this ambition will ever result in a definite system. If one is asked for his opinion, he is inclined to answer no. While wrestling with the problems, however, one will never give up the hope that this greatest of all aims can really be attained to a very high degree.

An adherent to the theory of abstraction or induction might call our layers "degrees of abstraction"; but, I do not consider it justifiable to veil the logical independence of the concept from the sense experiences. The relation is not analogous to that of soup to beef but rather of wardrobe number to overcoat.

The layers are furthermore not clearly separated. It is not even absolutely clear which concepts belong to the primary layer. As a matter of fact, we are dealing with freely formed concepts, which, with a certainty sufficient for practical use, are intuitively connected with complexes of sense experiences in such a manner that, in any given case of experience, there is no uncertainty as to the applicability or non-applicability of the statement. The essential thing is the aim to represent the multitude of concepts and theorems, close to experience, as theorems, logically deduced and belonging to a basis, as narrow as possible, of fundamental concepts and fundamental relations which themselves can be chosen freely (axioms). The liberty of choice, however, is of a special kind; it is not in any way similar to the liberty of a writer of fiction. Rather, it is similar to that of a man engaged in solving a well designed word puzzle. He may, it is true, propose any word as the solution; but, there is only *one* word which really solves the puzzle in all its forms. It is an outcome of faith that nature —as she is perceptible to our five senses—takes the character of such a well formulated puzzle. The successes reaped up to now by science do, it is true, give a certain encouragement for this faith.

The multitude of layers discussed above corresponds to the several stages of progress which have resulted from the struggle for unity in the course of development. As regards the final aim, intermediary layers are only of temporary nature. They must eventually disappear as irrelevant. We have to deal, however, with the science of today, in which these strata represent problematic partial successes which support one another but which also threaten one another, because today's systems of concepts contain deep seated incongruities which we shall meet later on.

It will be the aim of the following lines to demonstrate what paths the constructive human mind has entered, in order to arrive at a basis of physics which is logically as uniform as possible.

§ 2. Mechanics and the Attempts to Base All Physics upon It

An important property of our sense experiences, and, more generally, of all of our experience, is its time-like order. This kind of order leads to the mental conception of a subjective time, an ordinating scheme for our experience. The subjective time leads then through the concept of the bodily object and of space, to the concept of objective time, as we shall see later on.

Ahead of the notion of objective time there is, however, the concept of space; and, ahead of the latter we find the concept of the bodily object. The latter is directly connected with complexes of sense experiences. It has been pointed out that one property which is characteristic of the notion "bodily object" is the property which provides that we coordinate to it an existence, independent of (subjective) time, and independent of the fact that it is perceived by our senses. We do this in spite of the fact that we perceive temporal alterations in it. Poincaré has justly emphasized the fact that we distinguish two kinds of alterations of the bodily object, "changes of state" and "changes of position." The latter, he remarked, are alterations which we can reverse by arbitrary motions of our bodies.

That there are bodily objects to which we have to ascribe,

within a certain sphere of perception, no alteration of state, but only alterations of position, is a fact of fundamental importance for the formation of the concept of space (in a certain degree even for the justification of the notion of the bodily object itself). Let us call such an object "practically rigid."

If, as the object of our perception, we consider simultaneously (i.e. as a single unit) two practically rigid bodies, then there exist for this ensemble such alterations as can *not* possibly be considered as changes of position of the whole, notwithstanding the fact that this is the case for each one of the two constituents. This leads to the notion of "change of relative position" of the two objects; and, in this way, also to the notion of "relative position" of the two objects. It is found moreover that among the relative positions, there is one of a specific kind which we designate as "Contact." [1] Permanent contact of two bodies in three or more "points" means that they are united as a quasi rigid compound body. It is permissible to say that the second body forms then a (quasi rigid) continuation on the first body and may, in its turn, be continued quasi rigidly. The possibility of the quasi rigid continuation of a body is unlimited. The real essence of the conceivable quasi rigid continuation of a body B_0 is the infinite "space" determined by it.

In my opinion, the fact that every bodily object situated in any arbitrary manner can be put into contact with the quasi rigid continuation of a predetermined and chosen body B_0 (body of relation), this fact is the empirical basis of our conception of space. In pre-scientific thinking, the solid earth's crust plays the role of B_0 and its continuation. The very name geometry indicates that the concept of space is

[1] It is in the nature of things that we are able to talk about these objects only by means of concepts of our own creation, concepts which themselves are not subject to definition. It is essential, however, that we make use only of such concepts concerning whose coordination to our experience we feel no doubt.

psychologically connected with the earth as an assigned body.

The bold notion of "space" which preceded all scientific geometry transformed our mental concept of the relations of positions of bodily objects into the notion of the position of these bodily objects in "space." This, of itself, represents a great formal simplification. Through this concept of space one reaches, moreover, an attitude in which any description of position is admittedly a description of contact; the statement that a point of a bodily object is located at a point P of space means that the object touches the point P of the standard body of reference B_0 (supposed appropriately continued) at the point considered.

In the geometry of the Greeks, space plays only a qualitative role, since the position of bodies in relation to space is considered as given, it is true, but is not described by means of numbers. Descartes was the first to introduce this method. In his language, the whole content of Euclidian geometry can axiomatically be founded upon the following statements: (1) Two specified points of a rigid body determine a distance. (2) We may coordinate triplets of numbers X_1, X_2, X_3, to points of space in such a manner that for every distance $P' - P''$ under consideration, the coordinates of whose end points are X_1', X_2', X_3'; X_1'', X_2'', X_3'', the expression

$$S^2 = (X_1'' - X_1')^2 + (X_2'' - X_2')^2 + (X_3'' - X_3')^2$$

is independent of the position of the body, and of the positions of any and all other bodies.

The (positive) number S means the length of the stretch, or the distance between the two points P' and P'' of space (which are coincident with the points P' and P'' of the stretch).

The formulation is chosen, intentionally, in such a way that it expresses clearly, not only the logical and axiomatic, but also the empirical content of Euclidian geometry. The purely logical (axiomatic) representation of Euclidian geometry has, it is true, the advantage of greater simplicity and clarity. It pays for this, however, by renouncing representation of the connection between the notional construction and the sense experience upon which connection, alone, the significance of geometry for physics rests. The fatal error that the necessity of thinking, preceding all experience, was at the basis of Euclidian geometry and the concept of space belonging to it, this fatal error arose from the fact that the empirical basis, on which the axiomatic construction of Euclidian geometry rests, had fallen into oblivion.

In so far as one can speak of the existence of rigid bodies in nature, Euclidian geometry is a physical science, the usefulness of which must be shown by application to sense experiences. It relates to the totality of laws which must hold for the relative positions of rigid bodies independently of time. As one may see, the physical notion of space also, as originally used in physics, is tied to the existence of rigid bodies.

From the physicist's point of view, the central importance of Euclidian geometry rests in the fact that its laws are independent of the specific nature of the bodies whose relative positions it discusses. Its formal simplicity is characterized by the properties of homogeneity and isotropy (and the existence of similar entities).

The concept of space is, it is true, useful, but not indispensable for geometry proper, i.e. for the formulation of rules about the relative positions of rigid bodies. In opposition to this, the concept of objective time, without which the formulation of the fundamentals of classical mechanics is impossible, is linked with the concept of the spacial continuum.

The introduction of objective time involves two statements which are independent of each other.

(1) The introduction of the objective local time by connecting the temporal sequence of experiences with the indications of a "clock," i.e. of a closed system with periodical occurrence.

(2) The introduction of the notion of objective time for the happenings in the whole space, by which notion alone the idea of local time is enlarged to the idea of time in physics.

Note concerning (1). As I see it, it does not mean a "petitio principii" if one puts the concept of periodical occurrence ahead of the concept of time, while one is concerned with the clarification of the origin and of the empirical content of the concept of time. Such a conception corresponds exactly to the precedence of the concept of the rigid (or quasi rigid) body in the interpretation of the concept of space.

Further discussion of (2). The illusion which prevailed prior to the enunciation of the theory of relativity—that, from the point of view of experience the meaning of simultaneity in relation to happenings distant in space and consequently that the meaning of time in physics is a priori clear—this illusion had its origin in the fact that in our everyday experience, we can neglect the time of propagation of light. We are accustomed on this account to fail to differentiate between "simultaneously seen" and "simultaneously happening"; and, as a result the difference between time and local time fades away.

The lack of definiteness which, from the point of view of empirical importance, adheres to the notion of time in classical mechanics was veiled by the axiomatic representation of space and time as things given independently of our senses. Such a use of notions—independent of the empirical basis, to which they owe their existence—does not necessarily damage science. One may however easily be led into the error of believing that these notions, whose origin is forgotten, are necessary and unalterable accompaniments to our thinking, and this error may constitute a serious danger to the progress of science.

It was fortunate for the development of mechanics and hence also for the development of physics in general, that the lack of definiteness in the concept of objective time remained obscured from the earlier philosophers as regards its empirical interpretation. Full of confidence in the real meaning of the space-time construction they developed the foundations of mechanics which we shall characterize, schematically, as follows:

(a) Concept of a material point: a bodily object which—as regards its position and motion—can be described with sufficient exactness as a point with coordinates X_1, X_2, X_3. Description of its motion (in relation to the "space" B_0) by giving X_1, X_2, X_3, as functions of the time.

(b) Law of inertia: the disappearance of the components of acceleration for the material point which is sufficiently far away from all other points.

(c) Law of motion (for the material point): Force = mass × acceleration.

(d) Laws of force (actions and reactions between material points).

In this (b) is nothing more than an important special case of (c). A real theory exists only when the laws of force are given. The forces must in the first place only obey the law of equality of action and reaction in order that a system of points —permanently connected to each other—may behave like *one* material point.

These fundamental laws, together with Newton's law for gravitational force, form the basis of the mechanics of celestial bodies. In this mechanics of Newton, and in contrast to the above conceptions of space derived from rigid bodies, the space B_0 enters in a form which contains a new idea; it is not for every B_0 that validity is required (for a given law of force) by (b) and (c), but only for a B_0 in the appropriate condition of motion (inertial system). On account of this fact, the coordinate space acquired an independent physical property which is not contained in the purely geometrical notion of space, a circumstance which gave Newton considerable food for thought (pail-experiment).[2]

Classical mechanics is only a general scheme; it becomes a theory only by explicit indication of the force laws (d) as was done so very successfully by Newton for celestial mechanics. From the point of view of the aim of the greatest logical simplicity of the foundations, this theoretical method is deficient in so far as the laws of force cannot be obtained by logical and formal considerations, so that their choice is *a priori* to a large extent arbitrary. Also Newton's gravitation law of force is distinguished from other conceivable laws of force exclusively by its *success*.

In spite of the fact that, today, we know positively that classical mechanics fails as a foundation dominating all physics, it still occupies the center of all of our thinking in physics. The reason for this lies in the fact that, regardless of important progress reached since the time of Newton, we have not yet arrived at a new foundation of physics concerning which we may be certain that the whole complexity of investigated phenomena, and of partial theoretical systems of a successful kind, could be deduced logically from it. In the following lines I shall try to describe briefly how the matter stands.

First we try to get clearly in our minds how far the system of classical mechanics has shown itself adequate to serve as a basis for the whole of physics. Since we are dealing here only with the foundations of physics and with its development, we need not concern ourselves with the purely *formal* progresses of mechanics (equation of Lagrange, canonical

[2] This defect of the theory could only be eliminated by such a formulation of mechanics as would command validity for all B_0. This is one of the steps which lead to the general theory of relativity. A second defect, also eliminated only by the introduction of the general theory of relativity, lies in the fact that there is no reason given by mechanics itself for the equality of the gravitational and inertial mass of the material point.

equations, etc.). *One* remark, however, appears indispensable. The notion "material point" is fundamental for mechanics. If now we seek the mechanics of a bodily object which itself can *not* be treated as a material point—and strictly speaking every object "perceptible to our senses" is of this category—then the question arises: How shall we imagine the object to be built up out of material points, and what forces must we assume as acting between them? The formulation of this question is indispensable, if mechanics is to pretend to describe the object *completely*.

It is natural to the tendency of mechanics to assume these material points, and the laws of forces acting between them, as invariable, since time alterations would lie outside of the scope of mechanical explanation. From this we can see that classical mechanics must lead us to an atomistic construction of matter. We now realize, with special clarity, how much in error are those theorists who believe that theory comes inductively from experience. Even the great Newton could not free himself from this error ("Hypotheses non fingo").*

In order to save itself from becoming hopelessly lost in this line of thought (atomistic), science proceeded first in the following manner. The mechanics of a system is determined if its potential energy is given as a function of its configuration. Now, if the acting forces are of such a kind as to guarantee maintenance of certain qualities of order of the system's configuration, then the configuration may be described with sufficient accuracy by a relatively small number of configuration variables q_r; the potential energy is considered only insofar as it is dependent upon *these* variables (for instance, description of the configuration of a practically rigid body by six variables).

A second method of application of mechanics, which avoids the consideration of a subdivision of matter down to "real" material points, is the mechanics of so-called continuous

* "I make no hypotheses."

media. This mechanics is characterized by the fiction that the density of matter and speed of matter is dependent in a continuous manner upon coordinates and time, and that the part of the interactions not explicitly given can be considered as surface forces (pressure forces) which again are continuous functions of location. Herein we find the hydrodynamic theory, and the theory of elasticity of solid bodies. These theories avoid the explicit introduction of material points by fictions which, in the light of the foundation of classical mechanics, can only have an approximate significance.

In addition to their great *practical* significance, these categories of science have—by enlargement of the mathematical world of ideas—created those formal auxiliary instruments (partial differential equations) which have been necessary for the subsequent attempts at formulating the total scheme of physics in a manner which is new as compared with that of Newton.

These two modes of application of mechanics belong to the so-called "phenomenological" physics. It is characteristic of this kind of physics that it makes as much use as possible of concepts which are close to experience but which, for this reason, have to give up, to a large degree, unity in the foundations. Heat, electricity and light are described by special variables of state and constants of matter other than the mechanical state; and to determine all of these variables in their relative dependence was a rather empirical task. Many contemporaries of Maxwell saw in such a manner of presentation the ultimate aim of physics, which they thought could be obtained purely inductively from experience on account of the relative closeness of the concepts used to the experience. From the point of view of theories of knowledge St. Mill and E. Mach took their stand approximately on this ground.

According to my belief, the greatest achievement of Newton's mechanics lies in the fact that its consistent application has led beyond this phenomenological representation, particularly in the field of heat phenomena. This occurred in the kinetic theory of gases and, in a general way, in statistical mechanics. The former connected the equation of state of the ideal gases, viscosity, diffusion and heat conductivity of gases and radiometric phenomena of gases, and gave the logical connection of phenomena which, from the point of view of direct experience, had nothing whatever to do with one another. The latter gave a mechanical interpretation of the thermodynamic ideas and laws as well as the discovery of the limit of applicability of the notions and laws to the classical theory of heat. This kinetic theory which surpassed, by far, the phenomenological physics as regards the logical unity of its foundations, produced moreover definite values for the true magnitudes of atoms and molecules which resulted from several independent methods and were thus placed beyond the realm of reasonable doubt. These decisive progresses were paid for by the coordination of atomistic entities to the material points, the constructively speculative character of which entities being obvious. Nobody could hope ever to "perceive directly" an atom. Laws concerning variables connected more directly with experimental facts (for example: temperature, pressure, speed) were deduced from the fundamental ideas by means of complicated calculations. In this manner physics (at least part of it), originally more phenomenologically constructed, was reduced, by being founded upon Newton's mechanics for atoms and molecules, to a basis further removed from direct experiment, but more uniform in character.

§ 3. THE FIELD CONCEPT

In explaining optical and electrical phenomena Newton's mechanics has been far less successful than it had been in the fields cited above. It is true that Newton tried to reduce light to the motion of material points in his corpuscular theory of light. Later on, however, as the phenomena of polarization, diffraction and interference of light forced upon his theory

more and more unnatural modifications, Huyghens' undulatory theory of light, prevailed. Probably this theory owes its
origin essentially to the phenomena of crystallographic optics
and to the theory of sound, which was then already elaborated to a certain degree. It must be admitted that Huyghens'
theory also was based in the first instance upon classical mechanics; but, the all-penetrating ether had to be assumed as
the carrier of the waves and the structure of the ether, formed
from material points, could not be explained by any known
phenomenon. One could never get a clear picture of the
interior forces governing the ether, nor of the forces acting
between the ether and the "ponderable" matter. The foundations of this theory remained, therefore, eternally in the dark.
The true basis was a partial differential equation, the reduc-
tion of which to mechanical elements remained always
problematic.

For the theoretical conception of electric and magnetic
phenomena one introduced, again, masses of a special kind,
and between these masses one assumed the existence of forces
acting at a distance, similar to Newton's gravitational forces.
This special kind of matter, however, appeared to be lacking
in the fundamental property of inertia; and, the forces acting
between these masses and the ponderable matter remained
obscure. To these difficulties there had to be added the polar
character of these kinds of matter which did not fit into the
scheme of classical mechanics. The basis of the theory became still more unsatisfactory when electrodynamic phenomena became known, notwithstanding the fact that these
phenomena brought the physicist to the explanation of magnetic phenomena through electrodynamic phenomena and,
in this way, made the assumption of magnetic masses superfluous. This progress had, indeed, to be paid for by increasing
the complexity of the forces of interaction which had to be
assumed as existing between electrical masses in motion.

The escape from this unsatisfactory situation by the electric field theory of Faraday and Maxwell represents probably the most profound transformation which has been experienced by the foundations of physics since Newton's time. Again, it has been a step in the direction of constructive speculation which has increased the distance between the foundation of the theory and what can be experienced by means of our five senses. The existence of the field manifests itself, indeed, only when electrically charged bodies are introduced into it. The differential equations of Maxwell connect the spacial and temporal differential coefficients of the electric and magnetic fields. The electric masses are nothing more than places of non-disappearing divergency of the electric field. Light waves appear as undulatory electromagnetic field processes in space.

To be sure, Maxwell still tried to interpret his field theory mechanically by means of mechanical ether models. But these attempts receded gradually to the background following the representation—purged of any unnecessary additions —by Heinrich Hertz, so that, in this theory the field finally took the fundamental position which had been occupied in Newton's mechanics by the material points. At first, however, this applies only for electromagnetic fields in empty space.

In its initial stage the theory was yet quite unsatisfactory for the interior of matter, because there, two electric vectors had to be introduced, which were connected by relations dependent on the nature of the medium, these relations being inaccessible to any theoretical analysis. An analogous situation arose in connection with the magnetic field, as well as in the relation between electric current density and the field.

Here H. A. Lorentz found an escape which showed, at the same time, the way to an electrodynamic theory of bodies in motion, a theory which was more or less free of arbitrary assumption. His theory was built on the following fundamental hypothesis:

Everywhere (including the interior of ponderable bodies)

the seat of the field is the empty space. The participation of matter in electromagnetic phenomena has its origin only in the fact that the elementary particles of matter carry unalterable electric charges, and, on this account are subject on the one hand to the actions of ponderomotive forces and on the other hand possess the property of generating a field. The elementary particles obey Newton's law of motion for the material point.

This is the basis on which H. A. Lorentz obtained his synthesis of Newton's mechanics and Maxwell's field theory. The weakness of this theory lies in the fact that it tried to determine the phenomena by a combination of partial differential equations (Maxwell's field equations for empty space) and total differential equations (equations of motion of points), which procedure was obviously unnatural. The unsatisfactory part of the theory showed up externally by the necessity of assuming finite dimensions for the particles in order to prevent the electromagnetic field existing at their surfaces from becoming infinitely great. The theory failed moreover to give any explanation concerning the tremendous forces which hold the electric charges on the individual particles. H. A. Lorentz accepted these weaknesses of his theory, which were well known to him, in order to explain the phenomena correctly at least as regards their general lines.

Furthermore, there was one consideration which reached beyond the frame of Lorentz's theory. In the environment of an electrically charged body there is a magnetic field which furnishes an (apparent) contribution to its inertia. Should it not be possible to explain the *total* inertia of the particles electromagnetically? It is clear that this problem could be worked out satisfactorily only if the particles could be interpreted as regular solutions of the electromagnetic partial differential equations. The Maxwell equations in their original form do not, however, allow such a description of particles, because their corresponding solutions contain a singularity.

Theoretical physicists have tried for a long time, therefore, to reach the goal by a modification of Maxwell's equations. These attempts have, however, not been crowned with success. Thus it happened that the goal of erecting a pure electromagnetic field theory of matter remained unattained for the time being, although in principle no objection could be raised against the possibility of reaching such a goal. The thing which deterred one in any further attempt in this direction was the lack of any systematic method leading to the solution. What appears certain to me, however, is that, in the foundations of any consistent field theory, there shall not be, in addition to the concept of field, any concept concerning particles. The whole theory must be based solely on partia differential equations and their singularity-free solutions.

§ 4. The Theory of Relativity

There is no inductive method which could lead to the fundamental concepts of physics. Failure to understand this fact constituted the basic philosophical error of so many investigators of the nineteenth century. It was probably the reason why the molecular theory, and Maxwell's theory were able to establish themselves only at a relatively late date. Logical thinking is necessarily deductive; it is based upon hypothetical concepts and axioms. How can we hope to choose the latter in such a manner as to justify us in expecting success as a consequence?

The most satisfactory situation is evidently to be found in cases where the new fundamental hypotheses are suggested by the world of experience itself. The hypothesis of the non-existence of perpetual motion as a basis for thermodynamics affords such an example of a fundamental hypothesis suggested by experience; the same thing holds for the principle of inertia of Galileo. In the same category, moreover, we find the fundamental hypotheses of the theory of relativity, which theory has led to an unexpected expansion and broadening of the field theory, and to the superseding of the foundations of classical mechanics.

The successes of the Maxwell-Lorentz theory have given great confidence in the validity of the electromagnetic equations for empty space and hence, in particular, to the statement that light travels "in space" with a certain constant speed c. Is this law of the invariability of light velocity in relation to any desired inertial system valid? If it were not, then one specific inertial system or more accurately, one specific state of motion (of a body of reference), would be distinguished from all others. In opposition to this idea, however, stand all the mechanical and electromagnetic-optical facts of our experience.

For these reasons it was necessary to raise to the degree of a principle, the validity of the law of constancy of light velocity for all inertial systems. From this, it follows that the spacial coordinates X_1, X_2, X_3, and the time X_4, must be transformed according to the "Lorentz-transformation" which is characterized by invariance of the expression

$$ds^2 = dx_1{}^2 + dx_2{}^2 + dx_3{}^2 - dx_4{}^2$$

(if the unit of time is chosen in such a manner that the speed of light $c = 1$).

By this procedure time lost its absolute character, and was included with the "spacial" coordinates as of algebraically (nearly) similar character. The absolute character of time and particularly of simultaneity were destroyed, and the four dimensional description became introduced as the only adequate one.

In order to account, also, for the equivalence of all inertial systems with regard to all the phenomena of nature, it is necessary to postulate invariance of all systems of physical equations which express general laws, with regard to the Lorentzian transformation. The elaboration of this requirement forms the content of the special theory of relativity.

This theory is compatible with the equations of Maxwell; but, it is incompatible with the basis of classical mechanics. It is true that the equations of motion of the material point can be modified (and with them the expressions for momentum and kinetic energy of the material point) in such a manner as to satisfy the theory; but, the concept of the force of interaction, and with it the concept of potential energy of a system, lose their basis, because these concepts rest upon the idea of absolute instantaneousness. The field, as determined by differential equations, takes the place of the force.

Since the foregoing theory allows interaction only by fields, it requires a field theory of gravitation. Indeed, it is not difficult to formulate such a theory in which, as in Newton's theory, the gravitational fields can be reduced to a scalar which is the solution of a partial differential equation. However, the experimental facts expressed in Newton's theory of gravitation lead in another direction, that of the general theory of relativity.

Classical mechanics contains one point which is unsatisfactory in that, in the fundamentals, the same mass constant is met twice over in two different rôles, namely as "inertial mass" in the law of motion, and as "gravitational mass" in the law of gravitation. As a result of this, the acceleration of a body in a pure gravitational field is independent of its material; or, in a coordinate system of *uniform acceleration* (accelerated in relation to an "inertial system") the motions take place as they would in a homogeneous gravitational field (in relation to a "motionless" system of coordinates). If one assumes that the equivalence of these two cases is complete, then one attains an adaptation of our theoretical thinking to the fact that the gravitational and inertial masses are identical.

From this it follows that there is no longer any reason for favoring, as a fundamental principle, the "inertial systems"; and, we must admit as equivalent in their own right, also *non-linear* transformations of the coordinates (x_1, x_2, x_3, x_4). If we make such a transformation of a system of coordinates of the special theory of relativity, then the metric

$$ds^2 = dx_1{}^2 + dx_2{}^2 + dx_3{}^2 - dx_4{}^2$$

goes over to a general (Riemannian) metric of Bane

$$ds^2 = g_{\mu\nu}\, dx_\mu\, dx_\nu \quad \text{(Summed over } \mu \text{ and } \nu)$$

where the $g_{\mu\nu}$, symmetrical in μ and ν, are certain functions of $x_1 \cdots x_4$ which describe both the metric property, and the gravitational field in relation to the new system of coordinates.

The foregoing improvement in the interpretation of the mechanical basis must, however, be paid for in that—as becomes evident on closer scrutiny—the new coordinates could no longer be interpreted, as results of measurements by rigid bodies and clocks, as they could in the original system (an inertial system with vanishing gravitational field).

The passage to the general theory of relativity is realized by the assumption that such a representation of the field properties of space already mentioned, by functions $g_{\mu\nu}$ (that is to say by a Riemann metric), is also justified in the *general* case in which there is no system of coordinates in relation to which the metric takes the simple quasi-Euclidian form of the special theory of relativity.

Now the coordinates, by themselves, no longer express metric relations, but only the "neighborliness" of the things described, whose coordinates differ but little from one another. All transformations of the coordinates have to be admitted so long as these transformations are free from singularities. Only such equations as are covariant in relation to arbitrary transformations in this sense have meaning as expressions of general laws of nature (postulate of general covariancy).

The first aim of the general theory of relativity was a preliminary statement which, by giving up the requirement of constituting a closed thing in itself, could be connected in as simple a manner as possible with the "facts directly observed." Newton's gravitational theory gave an example, by restricting itself to the pure mechanics of gravitation. This preliminary statement may be characterized as follows:

(1) The concept of the material point and of its mass is retained. A law of motion is given for it, this law of motion being the translation of the law of inertia into the language of the general theory of relativity. This law is a system of total differential equations, the system characteristic of the geodetic line.

(2) In place of Newton's law of interaction by gravitation, we shall find the system of the simplest generally covariant differential equations which can be set up for the $g_{\mu\nu}$-tensor. It is formed by equating to zero the once contracted Riemannian curvature tensor $(R_{\mu\nu} = 0)$.

This formulation permits the treatment of the problem of the planets. More accurately speaking, it allows the treatment of the problem of motion of material points of practically negligible mass in the gravitational field produced by a material point which itself is supposed to have no motion (central symmetry). It does not take into account the reaction of the "moved" material points on the gravitational field, nor does it consider how the central mass produces this gravitational field.

Analogy with classical mechanics shows that the following is a way to complete the theory. One sets up as field equation

$$R_{ik} - \tfrac{1}{2}g_{ik}R = -T_{ik}$$

where R represents the scalar of Riemannian curvature, T_{ik} the energy tensor of the matter in a phenomenological representation. The left side of the equation is chosen in such a manner that its divergence disappears identically. The resulting disappearance of the divergence of the right side produces the "equations of motion" of matter, in the form of partial differential equations for the case where T_{ik} introduces, for the description of the matter, only *four* further functions independent of each other (for instance, density, pressure, and velocity components, where there is between the latter an identity, and between pressure and density an equation of condition).

By this formulation one reduces the whole mechanics of gravitation to the solution of a single system of covariant partial differential equations. The theory avoids all internal discrepancies which we have charged against the basis of classical mechanics. It is sufficient—as far as we know—for the representation of the observed facts of celestial mechanics. But, it is similar to a building, one wing of which is made of fine marble (left part of the equation), but the other wing of which is built of low grade wood (right side of equation). The phenomenological representation of matter is, in fact, only a crude substitute for a representation which would correspond to all known properties of matter.

There is no difficulty in connecting Maxwell's theory of the electromagnetic field with the theory of the gravitational field so long as one restricts himself to space, free of ponderable matter and free of electric density. All that is necessary is to put on the right hand side of the above equation for T_{ik}, the energy tensor of the electromagnetic field in empty space and to associate with the so modified system of equations the Maxwell field equation for empty space, written in general covariant form. Under these conditions there will exist, between all these equations, a sufficient number of the differential identities to guarantee their consistency. We may add that this necessary formal property of the total system of equations leaves arbitrary the choice of the sign of the member T_{ik}, a fact which was later shown to be important.

The desire to have, for the foundations of the theory, the greatest possible unity has resulted in several attempts to include the gravitational field and the electromagnetic field in one formal but homogeneous picture. Here we must mention particularly the five-dimensional theory of Kaluza and Klein. Having considered this possibility very carefully I feel that it is more desirable to accept the lack of internal uniformity of the original theory, because I do not consider that the totality of the hypothetical basis of the five-dimensional theory contains less of an arbitrary nature than does the original theory. The same statement may be made for the projective variety of the theory, which has been elaborated with great care, in particular, by v. Dantzig and by Pauli.

The foregoing considerations concern, exclusively, the theory of the field, free of matter. How are we to proceed from this point in order to obtain a complete theory of atomically constructed matter? In such a theory, singularities must certainly be excluded, since without such exclusion the differential equations do not completely determine the total field. Here, in the field theory of general relativity, we meet the same problem of a theoretical field-representation of matter as was met originally in connection with the pure Maxwell theory.

Here again the attempt to construct particles out of the field theory, leads apparently to singularities. Here also the endeavor has been made to overcome this defect by the introduction of new field variables and by elaborating and extending the system of field equations. Recently, however, I discovered, in collaboration with Dr. Rosen, that the above mentioned simplest combination of the field equations of gravitation and electricity produces centrally symmetrical solutions which can be represented as free of singularity (the well known centrally symmetrical solutions of Schwarzschild for the pure gravitational field, and those of Reissner for the electric field with consideration of its gravitational action). We shall refer to this shortly in the paragraph next but one. In this way it seems possible to get for matter and its interactions a pure field theory free of additional hypotheses, one moreover whose test by submission to facts of experience does not result in difficulties other than purely mathematical ones, which difficulties, however, are very serious.

§ 5. QUANTUM THEORY AND THE FUNDAMENTALS OF PHYSICS

The theoretical physicists of our generation are expecting the erection of a new theoretical basis for physics which would make use of fundamental concepts greatly different from those of the field theory considered up to now. The reason is that it has been found necessary to use—for the mathematical representation of the so-called quantum phenomena—new sorts of methods of consideration.

While the failure of classical mechanics, as revealed by the theory of relativity, is connected with the finite speed of light (its avoidance of being ∞), it was discovered at the beginning of our century that there were other kinds of inconsistencies between deductions from mechanics and experimental facts, which inconsistencies are connected with the finite magnitude (the avoidance of being zero) of Planck's constant h. In particular, while molecular mechanics requires that both, heat content and (monochromatic) radiation density, of solid bodies should decrease *in proportion* to the decreasing absolute temperature, experience has shown that they decrease much more rapidly than the absolute temperature. For a theoretical explanation of this behavior it was necessary to assume that the energy of a mechanical system cannot assume any sort of value, but only certain discrete values whose mathematical expressions were always dependent upon Planck's constant h. Moreover, this conception was essential for the theory of the atom (Bohr's theory). For the transitions of these states into one another—with or without emission or absorption of radiation—no causal laws could be given, but only statistical ones; and, a similar conclusion holds for the radioactive decomposition of atoms, which decomposition was carefully investigated about the same time. For more than two decades physicists tried vainly to find a uniform interpretation of this "quantum character" of systems and phenomena. Such an attempt was successful about ten years ago, through the agency of two entirely different theoretical methods of attack. We owe one of these to Heisenberg and Dirac, and the other to de Broglie and Schrödinger. The mathematical equivalence of the two methods was soon recognized by Schrödinger. I shall try here to sketch the line of thought of de Broglie and Schrödinger, which lies closer to the physicist's method of thinking, and shall accompany the description with certain general considerations.

The question is first: How can one assign a discrete succession of energy value H_σ to a system specified in the sense of classical mechanics (the energy function is a given function of the coordinates q_r and the corresponding momenta p_r)? Planck's constant h relates the frequency H_σ/h to the energy values H_σ. It is therefore sufficient to give to the system a succession of discrete *frequency* values. This reminds us of the fact that in acoustics, a series of discrete frequency values is coordinated to a linear partial differential equation (if boundary values are given) namely the sinusoidal periodic solutions. In corresponding manner, Schrödinger set himself the task of coordinating a partial differential equation for a scalar function ψ to the given energy function $\mathcal{E}(q_r, p_r)$, where the q_r and the time t are independent variables. In this he succeeded (for a complex function ψ) in such a manner that the theoretical values of the energy H_σ, as required by the statistical theory, actually resulted in a satisfactory manner from the periodic solution of the equation.

To be sure, it did not happen to be possible to associate a definite movement, in the sense of mechanics of material points, with a definite solution $\psi(q_r, t)$ of the Schrödinger equation. This means that the ψ function does not determine, at any rate *exactly*, the story of the q_r as functions of the time t. According to Born, however, an interpretation of the physical meaning of the ψ functions was shown to be possible in the following manner: $\psi\psi$ (the square of the absolute value of the complex function ψ) is the probability density at the point under consideration in the configuration-space of the q_r, at the time t. It is therefore possible to characterize the content of the Schrödinger equation in a manner, easy to be understood, but not quite accurate, as follows: it determines how the probability density of a statistical ensemble of systems varies in the configuration-space with the time. Briefly: the Schrödinger equation determines the alteration of the function ψ of the q_r with the time.

It must be mentioned that the result of this theory contains —as limiting values—the result of the particle mechanics if the wave-length encountered during the solution of the Schrödinger problem is everywhere so small that the potential energy varies by a practically infinitely small amount for a change of one wave-length in the configuration-space. Under these conditions the following can in fact be shown: We choose a region G_0 in the configuration-space which, although large (in every dimension) in relation to the wave length, is small in relation to the practical dimensions of the configuration-space. Under these conditions it is possible to choose a function of ψ for an initial time t_0 in such a manner that it vanishes outside of the region G_0, and behaves, according to the Schrödinger equation, in such a manner that it retains this property—approximately at least—also for a later time, but with the region G_0 having passed at that time t into another region G. In this manner one can, with a certain degree of approximation, speak of the motion of the region G as a whole, and one can approximate this motion by the motion of a point in the configuration-space. This motion then coincides with the motion which is required by the equations of classical mechanics.

Experiments on interference made with particle rays have given a brilliant proof that the wave character of phenomena of motion as assumed by the theory does, really, correspond to the facts. In addition to this, the theory succeeded, easily, in demonstrating the statistical laws of the transition of a system from one quantum condition to another under the action of external forces, which, from the standpoint of classical mechanics, appears as a miracle. The external forces were here represented by small additions of the potential energy as functions of the time. Now, while in classical mechanics, such additions can produce only correspondingly small alterations of the system, in the quantum mechanics they produce alterations of any magnitude however large, but with correspondingly small probability, a consequence in perfect harmony with experience. Even an understanding of the laws of radioactive decomposition, at least in their broad lines, was provided by the theory.

Probably never before has a theory been evolved which has given a key to the interpretation and calculation of such a heterogeneous group of phenomena of experience as has the quantum theory. In spite of this, however, I believe that the theory is apt to beguile us into error in our search for a uniform basis for physics, because, in my belief, it is an *incomplete* representation of real things, although it is the only one which can be built out of the fundamental concepts of force and material points (quantum corrections to classical mechanics). The incompleteness of the representation is the outcome of the statistical nature (incompleteness) of the laws. I will now justify this opinion.

I ask first: How far does the ψ function describe a real condition of a mechanical system? Let us assume the ψ_r to be the periodic solutions (put in the order of increasing energy values) of the Schrödinger equation. I shall leave open, for the time being, the question as to how far the individual ψ_r are *complete* descriptions of physical conditions. A system is first in the condition ψ_1 of lowest energy $\mathcal{E}_1$. Then during a finite time a small disturbing force acts upon the system. At a later instant one obtains then from the Schrödinger equation a ψ function of the form

$$\psi = \Sigma \, c_r \psi_r$$

where the c_r are (complex) constants. If the ψ_r are "normalized," then $|c_1|$ is nearly equal to 1, $|c_2|$ etc. is small compared with 1. One may now ask: Does ψ describe a real condition of the system? If the answer is yes, then we can hardly do otherwise than ascribe [3] to this condition a definite energy $\mathcal{E}$, and, in particular, such an energy as exceeds $\mathcal{E}_1$ by a small amount (in any case $\mathcal{E}_1 < \mathcal{E} < \mathcal{E}_2$). Such an assumption is, however, at variance with the experiments on electron impact such as have been made by J. Franck and G. Hertz, if, in addition to this, one accepts Millikan's demonstration of the discrete nature of electricity. As a matter of fact, these experiments lead to the conclusion that energy values of a state lying between the quantum values do not exist. From this it follows that our function ψ does not in any way describe a homogeneous condition of the body, but represents rather a statistical description in which the c_r represent probabilities of the individual energy values. It seems to be clear, therefore, that the Born statistical interpretation of the quantum theory is the only possible one. The ψ function does not in any way describe a condition which could be that of a single system; it relates rather to many systems, to "an ensemble of systems" in the sense of statistical mechanics. If, except for certain special cases, the ψ function furnishes only *statistical* data concerning measurable magnitudes, the reason lies not only in the fact that the *operation of measuring* introduces unknown elements, which can be grasped only statistically, but because of the very fact that the ψ function

---

[3] Because, according to a well established consequence of the relativity theory, the energy of a complete system (at rest) is equal to its inertia (as a whole). This, however, must have a well defined value.

does not, in any sense, describe the condition of *one* single system. The Schrödinger equation determines the time variations which are experienced by the ensemble of systems which may exist with or without external action on the single system.

Such an interpretation eliminates also the paradox recently demonstrated by myself and two collaborators, and which relates to the following problem.

Consider a mechanical system constituted of two partial systems *A* and *B* which have interaction with each other only during limited time. Let the ψ function before their interaction be given. Then the Schrödinger equation will furnish the ψ function after the interaction has taken place. Let us now determine the physical condition of the partial system *A* as completely as possible by measurements. Then the quantum mechanics allows us to determine the ψ function of the partial system *B* from the measurements made, and from the ψ function of the total system. This determination, however, gives a result which depends upon *which* of the determining magnitudes specifying the condition of *A* has been measured (for instance coordinates *or* momenta). Since there can be only *one* physical condition of *B* after the interaction and which can reasonably not be considered as dependent on the particular measurement we perform on the system *A* separated from *B* it may be concluded that the ψ function is *not* unambiguously coordinated with the physical condition. This coordination of several ψ functions with the same physical condition of system *B* shows again that the ψ function cannot be interpreted as a (complete) description of a physical condition of a unit system. Here also the coordination of the ψ function to an ensemble of systems eliminates every difficulty.[4]

[4] The operation of measuring *A*, for example, thus involves a transition to a narrower ensemble of systems. The latter (hence also its ψ function) depends upon the point of view according to which this narrowing of the ensemble of systems is made.

The fact that quantum mechanics affords, in such a simple manner, statements concerning (apparently) discontinuous transitions from one total condition to another without actually giving a representation of the specific process, this fact is connected with another, namely the fact that the theory, in reality, does not operate with the single system, but with a totality of systems. The coefficients c_r of our first example are really altered very little under the action of the external force. With this interpretation of quantum mechanics one can understand why this theory can easily account for the fact that weak disturbing forces are able to produce alterations of any magnitude in the physical condition of a system. Such disturbing forces produce, indeed, only correspondingly small alterations of the *statistical density* in the ensemble of systems, and hence only infinitely weak alterations of the ψ functions, the mathematical description of which offers far less difficulty than would be involved in the mathematical representation of finite alterations experienced by part of the single systems. What happens to the single system remains, it is true, entirely unclarified by this mode of consideration; this enigmatic happening is entirely eliminated from the representation by the statistical manner of consideration.

But now I ask: Is there really any physicist who believes that we shall never get any inside view of these important alterations in the single systems, in their structure and their causal connections, and this regardless of the fact that these single happenings have been brought so close to us, thanks to the marvelous inventions of the Wilson chamber and the Geiger counter? To believe this is logically possible without contradiction; but, it is so very contrary to my scientific instinct that I cannot forego the search for a more complete conception.

To these considerations we should add those of another kind which also voice their plea against the idea that the methods introduced by quantum mechanics are likely to give a useful basis for the whole of physics. In the Schrödinger equation, absolute time, and also the potential energy, play a decisive role, while these two concepts have been recognized by the theory of relativity as inadmissible in principle. If one wishes to escape from this difficulty he must found the theory upon field and field laws instead of upon forces of interaction. This leads us to transpose the statistical methods of quantum mechanics to fields, that is to systems of infinitely many degrees of freedom. Although the attempts so far made are restricted to linear equations, which, as we know from the results of the general theory of relativity, are insufficient, the complications met up to now by the very ingenious attempts are already terrifying. They certainly will rise sky high if one wishes to obey the requirements of the general theory of relativity, the justification of which in principle nobody doubts.

To be sure, it has been pointed out that the introduction of a space-time continuum may be considered as contrary to nature in view of the molecular structure of everything which happens on a small scale. It is maintained that perhaps the success of the Heisenberg method points to a purely algebraical method of description of nature, that is to the elimination of continuous functions from physics. Then, however, we must also give up, by principle, the space-time continuum. It is not unimaginable that human ingenuity will some day find methods which will make it possible to proceed along such a path. At the present time, however, such a program looks like an attempt to breathe in empty space.

There is no doubt that quantum mechanics has seized hold of a beautiful element of truth, and that it will be a test stone for any future theoretical basis, in that it must be deducible as a limiting case from that basis, just as electrostatics is deducible from the Maxwell equations of the electromagnetic field or as thermodynamics is deducible from classical mechanics. However, I do not believe that quantum mechanics will be the *starting point* in the search for this basis, just as, vice versa, one could not go from thermodynamics (resp. statistical mechanics) to the foundations of mechanics.

In view of this situation, it seems to be entirely justifiable seriously to consider the question as to whether the basis of field physics cannot by *any* means be put into harmony with the facts of the quantum theory. Is this not the only basis which, consistently with today's possibility of mathematical expression, can be adapted to the requirements of the general theory of relativity? The belief, prevailing among the physicists of today, that such an attempt would be hopeless, may have its root in the unjustifiable idea that such a theory should lead, as a first approximation, to the equations of classical mechanics for the motion of corpuscles, or at least to total differential equations. As a matter of fact up to now we have never succeeded in representing corpuscles theoretically by fields free of singularities, and we can, a priori, say nothing about the behavior of such entities. *One thing*, however, is certain: if a field theory results in a representation of corpuscles free of singularities, then the behavior of these corpuscles with time is determined solely by the differential equations of the field.

§ 6. Relativity Theory and Corpuscles

I shall now show that, according to the general theory of relativity, there exist singularity-free solutions of field equations which can be interpreted as representing corpuscles. I restrict myself here to neutral particles because, in another recent publication in collaboration with Dr. Rosen, I have treated this question in a detailed manner, and because the essentials of the problem can be completely shown by this case.

The gravitational field is entirely described by the tensor $g_{\mu\nu}$. In the three-index symbols $\Gamma_{\mu\nu}{}^{\sigma}$, there appear also the contravariants $g^{\mu\nu}$ which are defined as the minors of the $g_{\mu\nu}$ divided by the determinant $g(=|g_{\alpha\beta}|)$. In order that the R_{ik} shall be defined and finite, it is not sufficient that there shall be, for the environment of every part of the continuum, a system of coordinates in which the $g_{\mu\nu}$ and their first differential quotients are continuous and differentiable, but it is also necessary that the determinant g shall nowhere vanish. This last restriction is, however, eliminated if one replaces the differential equations $R_{ik} = 0$ by $g^2 R_{ik} = 0$, the left hand sides of which are *whole* rational functions of the g_{ik} and of their derivatives.

These equations have the centrally symmetrical solutions indicated by Schwarzschild

$$ds^2 = -\frac{1}{1-2m/r}dr^2 - r^2(d\theta^2 + \sin^2\theta d\varphi^2) + \left(1-\frac{2m}{r}\right)dt^2$$

This solution has a singularity at $r = 2m$, since the coefficient of dr^2 (i.e. g_{11}), becomes infinite on this hypersurface. If, however, we replace the variable r by ρ defined by the equation

$$\rho^2 = r - 2m$$

we obtain

$$ds^2 = -4(2m+\rho^2)d\rho^2 - (2m+\rho^2)^2(d\theta^2 + \sin^2\theta d\varphi^2)$$
$$+ \frac{\rho^2}{2m+\rho^2}dt^2$$

This solution behaves regularly for all values of ρ. The vanishing of the coefficient of dt^2 i.e. (g_{44}) for $\rho = 0$ results, it is true, in the consequence that the determinant g vanishes for this value; but, with the methods of writing the field equations actually adopted, this does not constitute a singularity.

If ρ extends from $-\infty$ to $+\infty$, then r runs from $+\infty$ to $r = 2m$ and then back to $+\infty$, while for such values of r as correspond to $r < 2m$ there are no corresponding real values of ρ. Hence the Schwarzschild solution becomes a regular solution by representation of the physical space as consisting of two identical "shells" neighboring upon the hypersurface $\rho = 0$, that is $r = 2m$, while for this hypersurface the determinant g vanishes. Let us call such a connection between the two (identical) shells a "bridge." Hence the existence of such a bridge between the two shells in the finite realm corresponds to the existence of a material neutral particle which is described in a manner free from singularities.

The solution of the problem of the motion of neutral particles evidently amounts to the discovery of such solutions of the gravitational equations (written free of denominators), as contain several bridges.

The conception sketched above corresponds, a priori, to the atomistic structure of matter insofar as the "bridge" is by its nature a discrete element. Moreover, we see that the mass constant m of the neutral particles must necessarily be positive, since no solution free of singularities can correspond to the Schwarzschild solution for a negative value of m. Only the examination of the several-bridge-problem, can show whether or not this theoretical method furnishes an explanation of the empirically demonstrated equality of the masses of the particles found in nature, and whether it takes into account the facts which the quantum mechanics has so wonderfully comprehended.

In an analogous manner, it is possible to demonstrate that the combined equations of gravitation and electricity (with appropriate choice of the sign of the electrical member in the gravitational equations) produce a singularity-free bridge-representation of the electric corpuscle. The simplest solution of this kind is that for an electrical particle without gravitational mass.

So long as the important mathematical difficulties concerned with the solution of the several-bridge-problem, are not overcome, nothing can be said concerning the usefulness of the theory from the physicist's point of view. However, it constitutes, as a matter of fact, the first attempt towards the consistent elaboration of a field theory which presents a possibility of explaining the properties of matter. In favor of this attempt one should also add that it is based on the simplest possible relativistic field equations known today.

Summary

Physics constitutes a logical system of thought which is in a state of evolution, and whose basis cannot be obtained through distillation by any inductive method from the experiences lived through, but which can only be attained by free invention. The justification (truth content) of the system rests in the proof of usefulness of the resulting theorems on the basis of sense experiences, where the relations of the latter to the former can only be comprehended intuitively. Evolution is going on in the direction of increasing simplicity of the logical basis. In order further to approach this goal, we must make up our mind to accept the fact that the logical basis departs more and more from the facts of experience, and that the path of our thought from the fundamental basis to these resulting theorems, which correlate with sense experiences, becomes continually harder and longer.

Our aim has been to sketch, as briefly as possible, the development of the fundamental concepts in their dependence upon the facts of experience and upon the strife towards the goal of internal perfection of the system. Today's state of affairs had to be illuminated by these considerations, as they appear to me. (It is unavoidable that historic schematic representation is of a personal color.)

I try to demonstrate how the concepts of bodily objects, space, subjective and objective time, are connected with one another and with the nature of the experience. In classical mechanics the concepts of space and time become independent. The concept of the bodily object is replaced in the foundations by the concept of the material point, by which means mechanics becomes fundamentally atomistic. Light and electricity produce insurmountable difficulties when one attempts to make mechanics the basis of all physics. We are thus led to the field theory of electricity, and, later on to the attempt to base physics entirely upon the concept of the field (after an attempted compromise with classical mechanics). This attempt leads to the theory of relativity (evolution of the notion of space and time into that of the continuum with metric structure).

I try to demonstrate, furthermore, why in my opinion the quantum theory does not seem likely to be able to produce a usable foundation for physics: one becomes involved in contradictions if one tries to consider the theoretical quantum description as a *complete* description of the individual physical system or happening.

On the other hand, up to the present time, the field theory is unable to give an explanation of the molecular structure of matter and of quantum phenomena. It is shown, however, that the conviction to the effect that the field theory is unable to give, by its methods, a solution of these problems rests upon prejudice.

14

THE FUNDAMENTS OF
THEORETICAL PHYSICS

SCIENCE IS THE ATTEMPT to make the chaotic diversity of our sense-experience correspond to a logically uniform system of thought. In this system single experiences must be correlated with the theoretic structure in such a way that the resulting coordination is unique and convincing.

The sense-experiences are the given subject-matter. But the theory that shall interpret them is man-made. It is the result of an extremely laborious process of adaptation: hypothetical, never completely final, always subject to question and doubt.

The scientific way of forming concepts differs from that which we use in our daily life, not basically, but merely in the more precise definition of concepts and conclusions; more painstaking and systematic choice of experimental material; and greater logical economy. By this last we mean the effort to reduce all concepts and correlations to as few as possible logically independent basic concepts and axioms.

What we call physics comprises that group of natural sciences which base their concepts on measurements; and whose concepts and propositions lend themselves to mathematical formulation. Its realm is accordingly defined as that part of the sum total of our knowledge which is capable of being expressed in mathematical terms. With the progress of science, the realm of physics has so expanded that it seems to be limited only by the limitations of the method itself.

The larger part of physical research is devoted to the development of the various branches of physics, in each of which the object is the theoretical understanding of more or less restricted fields of experience, and in each of which the laws and concepts remain as closely as possible related to experience. It is this department of science, with its ever-growing specialization, which has revolutionized practical life in the last centuries, and given birth to the possibility that man may at last be freed from the burden of physical toil.

On the other hand, from the very beginning there has always been present the attempt to find a unifying theoretical basis for all these single sciences, consisting of a minimum of concepts and fundamental relationships, from which all the concepts and relationships of the single disciplines might be derived by logical process. This is what we mean by the search for a foundation of the whole of physics. The confident belief that this ultimate goal may be reached is the chief source of the passionate devotion which has always animated the researcher. It is in this sense that the following observations are devoted to the foundations of physics.

From what has been said it is clear that the word foundations in this connection does not mean something analogous in all respects to the foundations of a building. Logically considered, of course, the various single laws of physics rest upon this foundation. But whereas a building may be seriously damaged by a heavy storm or spring flood, yet its foundations remain intact, in science the logical foundation is always in greater peril from new experiences or new knowledge than are the branch disciplines with their closer experimental contacts. In the connection of the foundation with all the single parts lies its great significance, but likewise its greatest danger in face of any new factor. When we realize this, we are led to wonder why the so-called revolutionary epochs of the science of physics have not more often and more completely changed its foundation than has actually been the case.

The first attempt to lay a uniform theoretical foundation was the work of Newton. In his system everything is reduced to the following concepts: (1) Mass points with invariable mass; (2) action at a distance between any pair of mass points; (3) law of motion for the mass point. There was not, strictly speaking, any all-embracing foundation, because an explicit law was formulated only for the actions-at-a-distance of gravitation; while for other actions-at-a-distance nothing was established *a priori* except the law of equality of *actio* and *reactio*. Moreover, Newton himself fully realized that time and space were essential elements, as physically effective factors, of his system, if only by implication.

This Newtonian basis proved eminently fruitful and was regarded as final up to the end of the nineteenth century. It not only gave results for the movements of the heavenly bodies, down to the most minute details, but also furnished a theory of the mechanics of discrete and continuous masses, a simple explanation of the principle of the conservation of energy and a complete and brilliant theory of heat. The explanation of the facts of electrodynamics within the Newtonian system was more forced; least convincing of all, from the very beginning, was the theory of light.

It is not surprising that Newton would not listen to a wave theory of light; for such a theory was most unsuited to his theoretical foundation. The assumption that space was filled with a medium consisting of material points that propagated light waves without exhibiting any other mechanical properties must have seemed to him quite artificial. The strongest empirical arguments for the wave nature of light, fixed speeds of propagation, interference, diffraction, polarization, were either unknown or else not known in any well-ordered synthesis. He was justified in sticking to his corpuscular theory of light.

During the nineteenth century the dispute was settled in favor of the wave theory. Yet no serious doubt of the mechanical foundation of physics arose, in the first place because nobody knew where to find a foundation of another sort. Only slowly, under the irresistible pressure of facts, there developed a new foundation of physics, field-physics.

From Newton's time on, the theory of action-at-a-distance was constantly found artificial. Efforts were not lacking to explain gravitation by a kinetic theory, that is, on the basis of collision forces of hypothetical mass particles. But the attempts were superficial and bore no fruit. The strange part played by space (or the inertial system) within the mechanical foundation was also clearly recognized, and criticized with especial clarity by Ernst Mach.

The great change was brought about by Faraday, Maxwell and Hertz—as a matter of fact half-unconsciously and against their will. All three of them, throughout their lives, considered themselves adherents of the mechanical theory. Hertz had found the simplest form of the equations of the electromagnetic field, and declared that any theory leading to these equations was Maxwellian theory. Yet toward the end of his short life he wrote a paper in which he presented as the foundation of physics a mechanical theory freed from the force-concept.

For us, who took in Faraday's ideas so to speak with our mother's milk, it is hard to appreciate their greatness and audacity. Faraday must have grasped with unerring instinct the artificial nature of all attempts to refer electromagnetic phenomena to actions-at-a-distance between electric particles reacting on each other. How was each single iron filing among a lot scattered on a piece of paper to know of the single electric particles running round in a nearby conductor? All these electric particles together seemed to create in the surrounding space a condition which in turn produced a certain order in the filings. These spatial states, to-day called fields, if their geometrical structure and interdependent action were once rightly grasped, would, he was convinced,

furnish the clue to the mysterious electromagnetic interactions. He conceived these fields as states of mechanical
stress in a space-filling medium, similar to the states of stress
in an elastically distended body. For at that time this was
the only way one could conceive of states that were apparently continuously distributed in space. The peculiar type of
mechanical interpretation of these fields remained in the
background—a sort of placation of the scientific conscience in
view of the mechanical tradition of Faraday's time. With the
help of these new field concepts Faraday succeeded in forming a qualitative concept of the whole complex of electromagnetic effects discovered by him and his predecessors. The
precise formulation of the time-space laws of those fields was
the work of Maxwell. Imagine his feelings when the differential equations he had formulated proved to him that electromagnetic fields spread in the form of polarized waves and
with the speed of light! To few men in the world has such an
experience been vouchsafed. At that thrilling moment he
surely never guessed that the riddling nature of light, apparently so completely solved, would continue to baffle succeeding generations. Meantime, it took physicists some decades
to grasp the full significance of Maxwell's discovery, so bold
was the leap that his genius forced upon the conceptions of
his fellow-workers. Only after Hertz had demonstrated experimentally the existence of Maxwell's electromagnetic
waves, did resistance to the new theory break down.

But if the electromagnetic field could exist as a wave independent of the material source, then the electrostatic interaction could no longer be explained as action-at-a-distance.
And what was true for electrical action could not be denied
for gravitation. Everywhere Newton's actions-at-a-distance
gave way to fields spreading with finite velocity.

Of Newton's foundation there now remained only the material mass points subject to the law of motion. But J. J. Thom-
son pointed out that an electrically charged body in motion

must, according to Maxwell's theory, possess a magnetic field whose energy acted precisely as does an increase of kinetic energy to the body. If, then, a part of kinetic energy consists of field energy, might that not then be true of the whole of the kinetic energy? Perhaps the basic property of matter, its inertia, could be explained within the field theory? The question led to the problem of an interpretation of matter in terms of field theory, the solution of which would furnish an explanation of the atomic structure of matter. It was soon realized that Maxwell's theory could not accomplish such a program. Since then many scientists have zealously sought to complete the field theory by some generalization that should comprise a theory of matter; but so far such efforts have not been crowned with success. In order to construct a theory, it is not enough to have a clear conception of the goal. One must also have a formal point of view which will sufficiently restrict the unlimited variety of possibilities. So far this has not been found; accordingly the field theory has not succeeded in furnishing a foundation for the whole of physics.

For several decades most physicists clung to the conviction that a mechanical substructure would be found for Maxwell's theory. But the unsatisfactory results of their efforts led to gradual acceptance of the new field concepts as irreducible fundamentals—in other words, physicists resigned themselves to giving up the idea of a mechanical foundation.

Thus physicists held to a field-theory program. But it could not be called a foundation, since nobody could tell whether a consistent field theory could ever explain on the one hand gravitation, on the other hand the elementary components of matter. In this state of affairs it was necessary to think of material particles as mass points subject to Newton's laws of motion. This was the procedure of Lorentz in creating his electron theory and the theory of the electromagnetic phenomena of moving bodies.

Such was the point at which fundamental conceptions had

arrived at the turn of the century. Immense progress was made in the theoretical penetration and understanding of whole groups of new phenomena; but the establishment of a unified foundation for physics seemed remote indeed. And this state of things has even been aggravated by subsequent developments. The development during the present century is characterized by two theoretical systems essentially independent of each other: the theory of relativity and the quantum theory. The two systems do not directly contradict each other; but they seem little adapted to fusion into one unified theory. We must briefly discuss the basic idea of these two systems.

The theory of relativity arose out of efforts to improve, with reference to logical economy, the foundation of physics as it existed at the turn of the century. The so-called special or restricted relativity theory is based on the fact that Maxwell's equations (and thus the law of propagation of light in empty space) are converted into equations of the same form, when they undergo Lorentz transformation. This formal property of the Maxwell equations is supplemented by our fairly secure empirical knowledge that the laws of physics are the same with respect to all inertial systems. This leads to the result that the Lorentz transformation—applied to space and time coordinates—must govern the transition from one inertial system to any other. The content of the restricted relativity theory can accordingly be summarized in one sentence: all natural laws must be so conditioned that they are covariant with respect to Lorentz transformations. From this it follows that the simultaneity of two distant events is not an invariant concept and that the dimensions of rigid bodies and the speed of clocks depend upon their state of motion. A further consequence was a modification of Newton's law of motion in cases where the speed of a given body was not small compared with the speed of light. There followed also the principle of the equivalence of mass and energy, with the laws of conservation of mass and energy becoming one and the same. Once it was shown that simultaneity was relative and depended on the frame of reference, every possibility of retaining actions-at-a-distance within the foundation of physics disappeared, since that concept presupposed the absolute character of simultaneity (it must be possible to state the location of the two interacting mass points "at the same time").

The general theory of relativity owes its origin to the attempt to explain a fact known since Galileo's and Newton's time but hitherto eluding all theoretical interpretation: the inertia and the weight of a body, in themselves two entirely distinct things, are measured by one and the same constant, the mass. From this correspondence follows that it is impossible to discover by experiment whether a given system of coordinates is accelerated, or whether its motion is straight and uniform and the observed effects are due to a gravitational field (this is the equivalence principle of the general relativity theory). It shatters the concepts of the inertial system, as soon as gravitation enters in. It may be remarked here that the inertial system is a weak point of the Galilean-Newtonian mechanics. For there is presupposed a mysterious property of physical space, conditioning the kind of coordination-systems for which the law of inertia and the Newtonian law of motion hold good.

These difficulties can be avoided by the following postulate: natural laws are to be formulated in such a way that their form is identical for coordinate systems of any kind of states of motion. To accomplish this is the task of the general theory of relativity. On the other hand, we deduce from the restricted theory the existence of a Riemannian metric within the time-space continuum, which, according to the equivalence principle, describes both the gravitational field and the metric properties of space. Assuming that the field equations of gravitation are of the second differential order, the field law is clearly determined.

Aside from this result, the theory frees field physics from the disability it suffered from, in common with the Newtonian mechanics, of ascribing to space those independent physical properties which heretofore had been concealed by the use of an inertial system. But it can not be claimed that those parts of the general relativity theory which can to-day be regarded as final have furnished physics with a complete and satisfactory foundation. In the first place, the total field appears in it to be composed of two logically unconnected parts, the gravitational and the electromagnetic. And in the second place, this theory, like the earlier field theories, has not up till now supplied an explanation of the atomistic structure of matter. This failure has probably some connection with the fact that so far it has contributed nothing to the understanding of quantum phenomena. To take in these phenomena, physicists have been driven to the adoption of entirely new methods, the basic characteristics of which we shall now discuss.

In the year nineteen hundred, in the course of a purely theoretic investigation, Max Planck made a very remarkable discovery: the law of radiation of bodies as a function of temperature could not be derived solely from the laws of Maxwellian electrodynamics. To arrive at results consistent with the relevant experiments, radiation of a given frequency had to be treated as though it consisted of energy atoms of the individual energy h.v., where h is Planck's universal constant. During the years following it was shown that light was everywhere produced and absorbed in such energy quanta. In particular Niels Bohr was able largely to understand the structure of the atom, on the assumption that atoms can have only discrete energy values, and that the discontinuous transitions between them are connected with the emission or absorption of such an energy quantum. This threw some light on the fact that in their gaseous state elements and their compounds radiate and absorb only light of certain sharply defined frequencies. All this was quite inexplicable within the frame of the hitherto existing theories. It was clear that at least in the field of atomistic phenomena the character of everything that happens is determined by discrete states and by apparently discontinuous transitions between them, Planck's constant h playing a decisive role.

The next step was taken by De Broglie. He asked himself how the discrete states could be understood by the aid of the current concepts, and hit on a parallel with stationary waves, as for instance in the case of the proper frequencies of organ pipes and strings in acoustics. True, wave actions of the kind here required were unknown; but they could be constructed, and their mathematical laws formulated, employing Planck's constant h. De Broglie conceived an electron revolving about the atomic nucleus as being connected with such a hypothetical wave train, and made intelligible to some extent the discrete character of Bohr's "permitted" paths by the stationary character of the corresponding waves.

Now in mechanics the motion of material points is determined by the forces or fields of force acting upon them. Hence it was to be expected that those fields of force would also influence De Broglie's wave fields in an analogous way. Erwin Schrödinger showed how this influence was to be taken into account, re-interpreting by an ingenious method certain formulations of classical mechanics. He even succeeded in expanding the wave mechanical theory to a point where without the introduction of any additional hypotheses, it became applicable to any mechanical system consisting of an arbitrary number of mass points, that is to say possessing an arbitrary number of degrees of freedom. This was possible because a mechanical system consisting of n mass points is mathematically equivalent to a considerable degree, to one single mass point moving in a space of 3 n dimensions.

On the basis of this theory there was obtained a surprisingly good representation of an immense variety of facts which otherwise appeared entirely incomprehensible. But on one point, curiously enough, there was failure: it proved impossible to associate with these Schrödinger waves definite motions of the mass points—and that, after all, had been the original purpose of the whole construction.

The difficulty appeared insurmountable, until it was overcome by Born in a way as simple as it was unexpected. The De Broglie-Schrödinger wave fields were not to be interpreted as a mathematical description of how an event actually takes place in time and space, though, of course, they have reference to such an event. Rather they are a mathematical description of what we can actually know about the system. They serve only to make statistical statements and predictions of the results of all measurements which we can carry out upon the system.

Let me illustrate these general features of quantum mechanics by means of a simple example: we shall consider a mass point kept inside a restricted region G by forces of finite strength. If the kinetic energy of the mass point is below a certain limit, then the mass point, according to classical mechanics, can never leave the region G. But according to quantum mechanics, the mass point, after a period not immediately predictable, is able to leave the region G, in an unpredictable direction, and escape into surrounding space. This case, according to Gamow, is a simplified model of radioactive disintegration.

The quantum theoretical treatment of this case is as follows: at the time t_0 we have a Schrödinger wave system entirely inside G. But from the time t_0 onwards, the waves leave the interior of G in all directions, in such a way that the amplitude of the outgoing wave is small compared to the initial amplitude of the wave system inside G. The further these outside waves spread, the more the amplitude of the waves inside G diminishes, and correspondingly the intensity of the later waves issuing from G. Only after infinite time has passed is the wave supply inside G exhausted, while the outside wave has spread over an ever-increasing space.

But what has this wave process to do with the first object of our interest, the particle originally enclosed in G? To answer this question, we must imagine some arrangement which will permit us to carry out measurements on the particle. For instance, let us imagine somewhere in the surrounding space a screen so made that the particle sticks to it on coming into contact with it. Then from the intensity of the waves hitting the screen at some point, we draw conclusions as to the probability of the particle hitting the screen there at that time. As soon as the particle has hit any particular point of the screen, the whole wave field loses all its physical meaning; its only purpose was to make probability predictions as to the place and time of the particle hitting the screen (or, for instance, its momentum at the time when it hits the screen).

All other cases are analogous. The aim of the theory is to determine the probability of the results of measurement upon a system at a given time. On the other hand, it makes no attempt to give a mathematical representation of what is actually present or goes on in space and time. On this point the quantum theory of to-day differs fundamentally from all previous theories of physics, mechanistic as well as field theories. Instead of a model description of actual space-time events, it gives the probability distributions for possible measurements as functions of time.

It must be admitted that the new theoretical conception owes its origin not to any flight of fancy but to the compelling force of the facts of experience. All attempts to represent the particle and wave features displayed in the phenomena of light and matter, by direct course to a space-time model, have so far ended in failure. And Heisenberg has convincingly shown, from an empirical point of view, any decision as to a rigorously deterministic structure of nature is definitely ruled out, because of the atomistic structure of our experimental apparatus. Thus it is probably out of the question that any future knowledge can compel physics again to relinquish our present statistical theoretical foundation in favor of a deterministic one which would deal directly with physical reality. Logically the problem seems to offer two possibilities, between which we are in principle given a choice. In the end the choice will be made according to which kind of description yields the formulation of the simplest foundation, logically speaking. At the present, we are quite without any deterministic theory directly describing the events themselves and in consonance with the facts.

For the time being, we have to admit that we do not possess any general theoretical basis for physics, which can be regarded as its logical foundation. The field theory, so far, has failed in the molecular sphere. It is agreed on all hands that the only principle which could serve as the basis of quantum theory would be one that constituted a translation of the field theory into the scheme of quantum statistics. Whether this will actually come about in a satisfactory manner, nobody can venture to say.

Some physicists, among them myself, can not believe that we must abandon, actually and forever, the idea of direct representation of physical reality in space and time; or that we must accept the view that events in nature are analogous to a game of chance. It is open to every man to choose the direction of his striving; and also every man may draw comfort from Lessing's fine saying, that the search for truth is more precious than its possession.

15

THE COMMON LANGUAGE OF SCIENCE

THE FIRST STEP towards language was to link acoustically or otherwise commutable signs to sense-impressions. Most likely all sociable animals have arrived at this primitive kind of communication—at least to a certain degree. A higher development is reached when further signs are introduced and understood which establish relations between those other signs designating sense-impression. At this stage it is already possible to report somewhat complex series of impressions; we can say that language has come to existence. If language is to lead at all to understanding, there must be rules concerning the relations between the signs on the one hand and on the other hand there must be a stable correspondence between signs and impressions. In their childhood individuals connected by the same language grasp these rules and relations mainly by intuition. When man becomes conscious of the rules concerning the relations between signs the so-called grammar of language is established.

In an early stage the words may correspond directly to impressions. At a later stage this direct connection is lost insofar as some words convey relations to perceptions only if used in connection with other words (for instance such words as: "is," "or," "thing"). Then word-groups rather than single words refer to perceptions. When language becomes thus partially independent from the background of impressions a greater inner coherence is gained.

Only at this further development where frequent use is

made of so-called abstract concepts, language becomes an instrument of reasoning in the true sense of the word. But it is also this development which turns language into a dangerous source of error and deception. Everything depends on the degree to which words and word-combinations correspond to the world of impression.

What is it that brings about such an intimate connection between language and thinking? Is there no thinking without the use of language, namely in concepts and concept-combinations for which words need not necessarily come to mind? Has not everyone of us struggled for words although the connection between "things" was already clear?

We might be inclined to attribute to the act of thinking complete independence from language if the individual formed or were able to form his concepts without the verbal guidance of his environment. Yet most likely the mental shape of an individual, growing up under such conditions, would be very poor. Thus we may conclude that the mental development of the individual and his way of forming concepts depend to a high degree upon language. This makes us realize to what extent the same language means the same mentality. In this sense thinking and language are linked together.

What distinguishes the language of science from language as we ordinarily understand the word? How is it that scientific language is international? What science strives for is an utmost acuteness and clarity of concepts as regards their mutual relation and their correspondence to sensory data. As an illustration let us take the language of Euclidian geometry and Algebra. They manipulate with a small number of independently introduced concepts, respectively symbols, such as the integral number, the straight line, the point, as well as with signs which designate the fundamental operations, that is the connections between those fundamental concepts. This is the basis for the construction, respectively definition of all other statements and concepts. The connection between concepts and statements on the one hand and the sensory data on the other hand is established through acts of counting and measuring whose performance is sufficiently well determined.

The super-national character of scientific concepts and scientific language is due to the fact that they have been set up by the best brains of all countries and all times. In solitude and yet in cooperative effort as regards the final effect they created the spiritual tools for the technical revolutions which have transformed the life of mankind in the last centuries. Their system of concepts have served as a guide in the bewildering chaos of perceptions so that we learned to grasp general truths from particular observations.

What hopes and fears does the scientific method imply for mankind? I do not think that this is the right way to put the question. Whatever this tool in the hand of man will produce depends entirely on the nature of the goals alive in this mankind. Once these goals exist, the scientific method furnishes means to realize them. Yet it cannot furnish the very goals. The scientific method itself would not have led anywhere, it would not even have been born without a passionate striving for clear understanding.

Perfections of means and confusion of goals seem—in my opinion—to characterize our age. If we desire sincerely and passionately the safety, the welfare and the free development of the talents of all men, we shall not be in want of the means to approach such a state. Even if only a small part of mankind strives for such goals, their superiority will prove itself in the long run.

16

THE LAWS OF SCIENCE AND
THE LAWS OF ETHICS

Science searches for relations which are thought to exist independently of the searching individual. This includes the case where man himself is the subject. Or the subject of scientific statements may be concepts created by ourselves, as in mathematics. Such concepts are not necessarily supposed to correspond to any objects in the outside world. However, all scientific statements and laws have one characteristic in common: they are "true or false" (adequate or inadequate). Roughly speaking, our reaction to them is "yes" or "no."

The scientific way of thinking has a further characteristic. The concepts which it uses to build up its coherent systems are not expressing emotions. For the scientist, there is only "being," but no wishing, no valuing, no good, no evil; no goal. As long as we remain within the realm of science proper, we can never meet with a sentence of the type: "Thou shalt not lie." There is something like a Puritan's restraint in the scientist who seeks truth: he keeps away from everything voluntaristic or emotional. Incidentally, this trait is the result of a slow development, peculiar to modern Western thought.

From this it might seem as if logical thinking were irrelevant for ethics. Scientific statements of facts and relations, indeed, cannot produce ethical directives. However, ethical directives can be made rational and coherent by logical thinking and empirical knowledge. If we can agree on some fundamental ethical propositions, then other ethical propositions can be derived from them, provided that the original premises are stated with sufficient precision. Such ethical premises play a similar role in ethics, to that played by axioms in mathematics.

This is why we do not feel at all that it is meaningless to ask such questions as: "Why should we not lie?" We feel that such questions are meaningful because in all discussions of this kind some ethical premises are tacitly taken for granted. We then feel satisfied when we succeed in tracing back the ethical directive in question to these basic premises. In the case of lying this might perhaps be done in some way such as this: Lying destroys confidence in the statements of other people. Without such confidence, social cooperation is made impossible or at least difficult. Such cooperation, however, is essential to make human life possible and tolerable. This means that the rule "Thou shalt not lie" has been traced back to the demands: "Human life shall be preserved" and "Pain and sorrow shall be lessened as much as possible."

But what is the origin of such ethical axioms? Are they arbitrary? Are they based on mere authority? Do they stem from experiences of men and are they conditioned indirectly by such experiences?

For pure logic all axioms are arbitrary, including the axioms of ethics. But they are by no means arbitrary from a psychological and genetic point of view. They are derived from our inborn tendencies to avoid pain and annihilation, and from the accumulated emotional reaction of individuals to the behavior of their neighbors.

It is the privilege of man's moral genius, impersonated by inspired individuals, to advance ethical axioms which are so comprehensive and so well founded that men will accept them as grounded in the vast mass of their individual emotional experiences. Ethical axioms are found and tested not very differently from the axioms of science. Truth is what stands the test of experience.

17

AN ELEMENTARY DERIVATION OF THE EQUIVALENCE OF MASS AND ENERGY

THE FOLLOWING DERIVATION of the law of equivalence, which has not been published before, has two advantages. Although it makes use of the principle of special relativity, it does not presume the formal machinery of the theory but uses only three previously known laws:

(1) The law of the conservation of momentum.
(2) The expression for the pressure of radiation; that is, the momentum of a complex of radiation moving in a fixed direction.
(3) The well known expression for the aberration of light (influence of the motion of the earth on the apparent location of the fixed stars—Bradley).

We now consider the following system. Let the body B rest

freely in space with respect to the system K_0. Two complexes of radiation S, S' each of energy $\frac{E}{2}$ move in the positive and negative x_0 direction respectively and are eventually absorbed by B. With this absorption the energy of B increases by E. The body B stays at rest with respect to K_0 by reasons of symmetry.

Now we consider this same process with respect to the system K, which moves with respect to K_0 with the constant velocity v in the negative Z_0 direction. With respect to K the description of the process is as follows:

The body B moves in the positive Z direction with velocity v. The two complexes of radiation now have directions with respect to K which make an angle α with the x axis. The law of aberration states that in the first approximation $\alpha = \frac{c}{v}$, where c is the velocity of light. From the consideration with respect to K_0 we know that the velocity v of B remains unchanged by the absorption of S and S'.

Now we apply the law of conservation of momentum with respect to the z direction to our system in the coordinate-frame K.

I. *Before the absorption* let M be the mass of B; Mv is then the expression of the momentum of B (according to classical mechanics). Each of the complexes has the energy $\frac{E}{2}$ and hence, by a well known conclusion of Maxwell's theory, it has the momentum $\frac{E}{2c}$. Rigorously speaking this is the momentum of S with respect to K_0. However, when v is small with respect to c, the momentum with respect to K is the same except for a quantity of second order of magnitude ($\frac{v^2}{c^2}$ compared to 1). The z-component of this momentum is $\frac{E}{2c} \sin \alpha$ or with sufficient accuracy (except for quantities of higher order of magnitude) $\frac{E}{2c} \alpha$ or $\frac{E}{2} \cdot \frac{v}{c^2}$. S and S′ together therefore have a momentum $E\frac{v}{c^2}$ in the z direction. The total momentum of the system before absorption is therefore

$$Mv + \frac{E}{c^2} \cdot v$$

II. *After the absorption* let M′ be the mass of B. We anticipate here the possibility that the mass increased with the absorption of the energy E (this is necessary so that the final result of our consideration be consistent). The momentum of the system after absorption is then

$$M'v$$

We now assume the law of the conservation of momentum and apply it with respect to the z direction. This gives the equation

$$Mv + \frac{E}{c^2} v = M'v$$

or

$$M' - M = \frac{E}{c^2}$$

This equation expresses the law of the equivalence of energy and mass. The energy increase E is connected with the mass increase $\frac{E}{c^2}$. Since energy according to the usual definition leaves an additive constant free, we may so choose the latter that

$$E = Mc^2$$

Public Affairs

18
WHY SOCIALISM?

Is it advisable for one who is not an expert on economic and social issues to express views on the subject of socialism? I believe for a number of reasons that it is.

Let us first consider the question from the point of view of scientific knowledge. It might appear that there are no essential methodological differences between astronomy and economics: scientists in both fields attempt to discover laws of general acceptability for a circumscribed group of phenomena in order to make the interconnection of these phenomena as clearly understandable as possible. But in reality such methodological differences do exist. The discovery of general laws in the field of economics is made difficult by the circumstance that observed economic phenomena are often affected by many factors which are very hard to evaluate separately. In addition, the experience which has accumulated since the beginning of the so-called civilized period of human history has—as is well known—been largely influenced and limited by causes which are by no means exclusively economic in nature. For example, most of the major states of history owed their existence to conquest. The conquering peoples established themselves, legally and economically, as the privileged class of the conquered country. They seized for themselves a monopoly of the land ownership and appointed a priesthood from among their own ranks. The priests, in control of education, made the class division of society into a permanent institution and created a system of values by which the people were thenceforth, to a large extent unconsciously, guided in their social behavior.

But historic tradition is, so to speak, of yesterday; nowhere have we really overcome what Thorstein Veblen called "the predatory phase" of human development. The observable economic facts belong to that phase and even such laws as we can derive from them are not applicable to other phases. Since the real purpose of socialism is precisely to overcome and advance beyond the predatory phase of human development, economic science in its present state can throw little light on the socialist society of the future.

Second, socialism is directed towards a social-ethical end. Science, however, cannot create ends and, even less, instill them in human beings; science, at most, can supply the means by which to attain certain ends. But the ends themselves are conceived by personalities with lofty ethical ideals and—if these ends are not stillborn, but vital and vigorous—are adopted and carried forward by those many human beings who, half unconsciously, determine the slow evolution of society.

For these reasons, we should be on our guard not to over-estimate science and scientific methods when it is a question of human problems; and we should not assume that experts are the only ones who have a right to express themselves on questions affecting the organization of society.

Innumerable voices have been asserting for some time now that human society is passing through a crisis, that its stability has been gravely shattered. It is characteristic of such a situation that individuals feel indifferent or even hostile toward the group, small or large, to which they belong. In order to illustrate my meaning, let me record here a personal experience. I recently discussed with an intelligent and well-disposed man the threat of another war, which in my opinion would seriously endanger the existence of mankind, and I remarked that only a supra-national organization would offer protection from that danger. Thereupon my visitor, very calmly and coolly, said to me: "Why are you so deeply opposed to the disappearance of the human race?"

I am sure that as little as a century ago no one would have so lightly made a statement of this kind. It is the statement of a man who has striven in vain to attain an equilibrium within himself and has more or less lost hope of succeeding. It is the expression of a painful solitude and isolation from which so many people are suffering in these days. What is the cause? Is there a way out?

It is easy to raise such questions, but difficult to answer them with any degree of assurance. I must try, however, as best I can, although I am very conscious of the fact that our feelings and strivings are often contradictory and obscure and that they cannot be expressed in easy and simple formulas.

Man is, at one and the same time, a solitary being and a social being. As a solitary being, he attempts to protect his own existence and that of those who are closest to him, to satisfy his personal desires, and to develop his innate abilities. As a social being, he seeks to gain the recognition and affection of his fellow human beings, to share in their pleasures, to comfort them in their sorrows, and to improve their conditions of life. Only the existence of these varied, frequently conflicting, strivings accounts for the special character of a man, and their specific combination determines the extent to which an individual can achieve an inner equilibrium and can contribute to the well-being of society. It is quite possible that the relative strength of these two drives is, in the main, fixed by inheritance. But the personality that finally emerges is largely formed by the environment in which a man happens to find himself during his development, by the structure of the society in which he grows up, by the tradition of that society, and by its appraisal of particular types of behavior. The abstract concept "society" means to the individual human being the sum total of his direct and indirect relations to his contemporaries and to all the people of earlier generations. The individual is able to think, feel, strive, and work by himself; but he depends so much upon society—in his physical, intellectual, and emotional existence—that it is impossible to think of him, or to understand him, outside the framework of society. It is "society" which provides man with food, clothing, a home, the tools of work, language, the forms of thought, and most of the content of thought; his life is made possible through the labor and the accomplishments of the many millions past and present who are all hidden behind the small word "society."

It is evident, therefore, that the dependence of the individual upon society is a fact of nature which cannot be abolished—just as in the case of ants and bees. However, while the whole life process of ants and bees is fixed down to the smallest detail by rigid, hereditary instincts, the social pattern and interrelationships of human beings are very variable and susceptible to change. Memory, the capacity to make new combinations, the gift of oral communication have made possible developments among human beings which are not dictated by biological necessities. Such developments manifest themselves in traditions, institutions, and organizations; in literature; in scientific and engineering accomplishments; in works of art. This explains how it happens that, in a certain sense, man can influence his life through his own conduct, and that in this process conscious thinking and wanting can play a part.

Man acquires at birth, through heredity, a biological constitution which we must consider fixed and unalterable, including the natural urges which are characteristic of the human species. In addition, during his lifetime, he acquires a cultural constitution which he adopts from society through communication and through many other types of influences. It is this cultural constitution which, with the passage of time, is subject to change and which determines to a very large extent the relationship between the individual and society. Modern anthropology has taught us, through comparative investigation of so-called primitive cultures, that the social behavior of human beings may differ greatly, depending upon prevailing cultural patterns and the types of organization which predominate in society. It is on this that those who are striving to improve the lot of man may ground their hopes: human beings are *not* condemned, because of their biological constitution, to annihilate each other or to be at the mercy of a cruel, self-inflicted fate.

If we ask ourselves how the structure of society and the cultural attitude of man should be changed in order to make human life as satisfying as possible, we should constantly be conscious of the fact that there are certain conditions which we are unable to modify. As mentioned before, the biological nature of man is, for all practical purposes, not subject to change. Furthermore, technological and demographic developments of the last few centuries have created conditions which are here to stay. In relatively densely settled populations with the goods which are indispensable to their continued existence, an extreme division of labor and a highly-centralized productive apparatus are absolutely necessary. The time—which, looking back, seems so idyllic—is gone forever when individuals or relatively small groups could be completely self-sufficient. It is only a slight exaggeration to say that mankind constitutes even now a planetary community of production and consumption.

I have now reached the point where I may indicate briefly what to me constitutes the essence of the crisis of our time. It concerns the relationship of the individual to society. The individual has become more conscious than ever of his dependence upon society. But he does not experience this dependence as a positive asset, as an organic tie, as a protective force, but rather as a threat to his natural rights, or even to his economic existence. Moreover, his position in society is such that the egotistical drives of his make-up are constantly being accentuated, while his social drives, which are by nature weaker, progressively deteriorate. All human beings, whatever their position in society, are suffering from this process of deterioration. Unknowingly prisoners of their own egotism, they feel insecure, lonely, and deprived of the naive, simple, and unsophisticated enjoyment of life. Man can find meaning in life, short and perilous as it is, only through devoting himself to society.

The economic anarchy of capitalist society as it exists today is, in my opinion, the real source of the evil. We see before us a huge community of producers the members of which are unceasingly striving to deprive each other of the fruits of their collective labor—not by force, but on the whole in faithful compliance with legally established rules. In this respect, it is important to realize that the means of production—that is to say, the entire productive capacity that is needed for producing consumer goods as well as additional capital goods —may legally be, and for the most part are, the private property of individuals.

For the sake of simplicity, in the discussion that follows I shall call "workers" all those who do not share in the ownership of the means of production—although this does not quite correspond to the customary use of the term. The owner of the means of production is in a position to purchase the labor power of the worker. By using the means of production, the worker produces new goods which become the property of the capitalist. The essential point about this process is the relation between what the worker produces and what he is paid, both measured in terms of real value. Insofar as the labor contract is "free," what the worker receives is determined not by the real value of the goods he produces, but by his minimum needs and by the capitalists' requirements for labor power in relation to the number of workers competing for jobs. It is important to understand that even in theory the payment of the worker is not determined by the value of his product.

Private capital tends to become concentrated in few hands, partly because of competition among the capitalists, and partly because technological development and the increasing division of labor encourage the formation of larger units of production at the expense of the smaller ones. The result of these developments is an oligarchy of private capital the enormous power of which cannot be effectively checked even by a democratically organized political society. This is true since the members of legislative bodies are selected by political parties, largely financed or otherwise influenced by private capitalists who, for all practical purposes, separate the electorate from the legislature. The consequence is that the representatives of the people do not in fact sufficiently protect the interests of the underprivileged sections of the population. Moreover, under existing conditions, private capitalists inevitably control, directly or indirectly, the main sources of information (press, radio, education). It is thus extremely difficult, and indeed in most cases quite impossible, for the individual citizen to come to objective conclusions and to make intelligent use of his political rights.

The situation prevailing in an economy based on the private ownership of capital is thus characterized by two main principles: first, means of production (capital) are privately owned and the owners dispose of them as they see fit; second, the labor contract is free. Of course, there is no such thing as a *pure* capitalist society in this sense. In particular, it should be noted that the workers, through long and bitter political struggles, have succeeded in securing a somewhat improved form of the "free labor contract" for certain categories of workers. But taken as a whole, the present day economy does not differ much from "pure" capitalism.

Production is carried on for profit, not for use. There is no provision that all those able and willing to work will always be in a position to find employment; an "army of unemployed" almost always exists. The worker is constantly in fear of losing his job. Since unemployed and poorly paid workers do not provide a profitable market, the production of consumers' goods is restricted, and great hardship is the consequence. Technological progress frequently results in more unemployment rather than in an easing of the burden of work for all. The profit motive, in conjunction with competition among capitalists, is responsible for an instability in the accumulation and utilization of capital which leads to increasingly severe depressions. Unlimited competition leads to a huge waste of labor, and to that crippling of the social consciousness of individuals which I mentioned before.

This crippling of individuals I consider the worst evil of capitalism. Our whole educational system suffers from this evil. An exaggerated competitive attitude is inculcated into the student, who is trained to worship acquisitive success as a preparation for his future career.

I am convinced there is only *one* way to eliminate these grave evils, namely through the establishment of a socialist economy, accompanied by an educational system which would be oriented toward social goals. In such an economy, the means of production are owned by society itself and are utilized in a planned fashion. A planned economy, which adjusts production to the needs of the community, would distribute the work to be done among all those able to work and would guarantee a livelihood to every man, woman, and child. The education of the individual, in addition to promoting his own innate abilities, would attempt to develop in him a sense of responsibility for his fellow men in place of the glorification of power and success in our present society.

Nevertheless, it is necessary to remember that a planned economy is not yet socialism. A planned economy as such may be accompanied by the complete enslavement of the individual. The achievement of socialism requires the solution of some extremely difficult socio-political problems: how is it possible, in view of the far-reaching centralization of political and economic power, to prevent bureaucracy from becoming all-powerful and overweening? How can the rights of the individual be protected and therewith a democratic counterweight to the power of bureaucracy be assured?

19

THE NEGRO QUESTION

I AM WRITING AS ONE who has lived among you in America only a little more than ten years. And I am writing seriously and warningly. Many readers may ask: "What right has he to speak out about things which concern us alone, and which no newcomer should touch?"

I do not think such a standpoint is justified. One who has grown up in an environment takes much for granted. On the other hand, one who has come to this country as a mature person may have a keen eye for everything peculiar and characteristic. I believe he should speak out freely on what he sees and feels, for by so doing he may perhaps prove himself useful.

What soon makes the new arrival devoted to this country is the democratic trait among the people. I am not thinking here so much of the democratic political constitution of this country, however highly it must be praised. I am thinking of the relationship between individual people and of the attitude they maintain toward one another.

In the United States everyone feels assured of his worth as an individual. No one humbles himself before another person or class. Even the great difference in wealth, the superior power of a few, cannot undermine this healthy self-confidence and natural respect for the dignity of one's fellow-man.

There is, however, a somber point in the social outlook of Americans. Their sense of equality and human dignity is mainly limited to men of white skins. Even among these there are prejudices of which I as a Jew am clearly conscious; but they are unimportant in comparison with the attitude of the "Whites" toward their fellow-citizens of darker complexion, particularly toward Negroes. The more I feel an American, the more this situation pains me. I can escape the feeling of complicity in it only by speaking out.

Many a sincere person will answer me: "Our attitude towards Negroes is the result of unfavorable experiences which we have had by living side by side with Negroes in this country. They are not our equals in intelligence, sense of responsibility, reliability."

I am firmly convinced that whoever believes this suffers from a fatal misconception. Your ancestors dragged these black people from their homes by force; and in the white man's quest for wealth and an easy life they have been ruthlessly suppressed and exploited, degraded into slavery. The modern prejudice against Negroes is the result of the desire to maintain this unworthy condition.

The ancient Greeks also had slaves. They were not Negroes but white men who had been taken captive in war. There could be no talk of racial differences. And yet Aristotle, one of the great Greek philosophers, declared slaves inferior beings who were justly subdued and deprived of their liberty. It is clear that he was enmeshed in a traditional prejudice from which, despite his extraordinary intellect, he could not free himself.

A large part of our attitude toward things is conditioned by opinions and emotions which we unconsciously absorb as children from our environment. In other words, it is tradition —besides inherited aptitudes and qualities—which makes us what we are. We but rarely reflect how relatively small as compared with the powerful influence of tradition is the influence of our conscious thought upon our conduct and convictions.

It would be foolish to despise tradition. But with our growing self-consciousness and increasing intelligence we must begin to control tradition and assume a critical attitude toward it, if human relations are ever to change for the better. We must try to recognize what in our accepted tradition is damaging to our fate and dignity—and shape our lives accordingly.

I believe that whoever tries to think things through honestly will soon recognize how unworthy and even fatal is the traditional bias against Negroes.

What, however, can the man of good will do to combat this deeply rooted prejudice? He must have the courage to set an example by word and deed, and must watch lest his children become influenced by this racial bias.

I do not believe there is a way in which this deeply entrenched evil can be quickly healed. But until this goal is reached there is no greater satisfaction for a just and well-meaning person than the knowledge that he has devoted his best energies to the service of the good cause.

20

SCIENCE AND SOCIETY

There are two ways in which science affects human affairs. The first is familiar to everyone: Directly, and to an even greater extent indirectly, science produces aids that have completely transformed human existence. The second way is educational in character—it works on the mind. Although it may appear less obvious to cursory examination, it is no less incisive than the first.

The most conspicuous practical effect of science is that it makes possible the contriving of things that enrich life, though they complicate it at the same time—inventions such as the steam engine, the railway, electric power and light, the telegraph, radio, automobile, airplane, dynamite, etc. To these must be added the life-preserving achievements of biology and medicine, especially the production of pain relievers and preservative methods of storing food. The greatest practical benefit which all these inventions confer on man I see in the fact that they liberate him from the excessive muscular drudgery that was once indispensable for the preservation of bare existence. Insofar as we may at all claim that slavery has been abolished today, we owe its abolition to the practical consequences of science.

On the other hand, technology—or applied science—has confronted mankind with problems of profound gravity. The very survival of mankind depends on a satisfactory solution of these problems. It is a matter of creating the kind of social institutions and traditions without which the new tools must inevitably bring disaster of the worst kind.

323

Mechanical means of production in an unorganized economy have had the result that a substantial proportion of mankind is no longer needed for the production of goods and is thus excluded from the process of economic circulation. The immediate consequences are the weakening of purchasing power and the devaluation of labor because of excessive competition, and these give rise, at ever shortening intervals, to a grave paralysis in the production of goods. Ownership of the means of production, on the other hand, carries a power to which the traditional safeguards of our political institutions are unequal. Mankind is caught up in a struggle for adaptation to these new conditions—a struggle that may bring true liberation, if our generation shows itself equal to the task.

Technology has also shortened distances and created new and extraordinarily effective means of destruction which, in the hands of nations claiming unrestricted freedom of action, become threats to the security and very survival of mankind. This situation requires a single judicial and executive power for the entire planet, and the creation of such a central authority is desperately opposed by national traditions. Here too we are in the midst of a struggle whose issue will decide the fate of all of us.

Means of communication, finally—reproduction processes for the printed word, and the radio—when combined with modern weapons, have made it possible to place body and soul under bondage to a central authority—and here is a third source of danger to mankind. Modern tyrannies and their destructive effects show plainly how far we are from exploiting these achievements organizationally for the benefit of mankind. Here too circumstances require an international solution, with the psychological foundation for such a solution not yet laid.

Let us now turn to the intellectual effects that proceed from science. In prescientific times it was not possible by means of thought alone to attain results that all mankind could have accepted as certain and necessary. Still less was there a conviction that all that happens in nature is subject to inexorable laws. The fragmentary character of natural law, as seen by the primitive observer, was such as to foster a belief in ghosts and spirits. Hence even today primitive man lives in constant fear that supernatural and arbitrary forces will intervene in his destiny.

It stands to the everlasting credit of science that by acting on the human mind it has overcome man's insecurity before himself and before nature. In creating elementary mathematics the Greeks for the first time wrought a system of thought whose conclusions no one could escape. The scientists of the Renaissance then devised the combination of systematic experiment with mathematical method. This union made possible such precision in the formulation of natural laws and such certainty in checking them by experience that as a result there was no longer room for basic differences of opinion in natural science. Since that time each generation has built up the heritage of knowledge and understanding, without the slightest danger of a crisis that might jeopardize the whole structure.

The general public may be able to follow the details of scientific research to only a modest degree; but it can register at least one great and important gain: confidence that human thought is dependable and natural law universal.

21
TOWARDS A WORLD
GOVERNMENT

A CONVERSATION I HAD with three students of the University of Chicago has made a strong impression on me. It showed me that a sense of responsibility and initiative is at work in the young generation of this country. These students are aware of the fact that the destiny of the new generation will be decided in these few years. They are determined to influence the pace of events within the framework of their possibilities.

What is the situation? The development of technology and of the implements of war has brought about something akin to a shrinking of our planet. Economic interlinking has made the destinies of nations interdependent to a degree far greater than in previous years. The available weapons of destruction are of a kind such that no place on earth is safeguarded against sudden total destruction. The only hope for protection lies in the securing of peace in a supranational way. A world government must be created which is able to solve conflicts between nations by judicial decision. This government must be based on a clearcut constitution which is approved by the governments and the nations and which gives it the sole disposition of offensive weapons. A person or a nation can be considered peace loving only if it is ready to cede its military force to the international authorities and to renounce every attempt or even the means, of achieving its interests abroad by the use of force.

326

It is apparent that the development of political relations in the year which has elapsed since the conclusion of the second world war, has brought us in no way nearer to the achievement of this goal. The U. N. as it stands today has neither the military force nor the legal basis to bring about a state of international security. Nor does it take account of the actual distribution of power. Real power is at present in the hands of few. It is no exaggeration to say that the solution of the real problem is linked solely to an agreement on a grand scale between this country and Russia. For, if such an agreement would be achieved then these two powers alone would be able to cause the other nations to give up their sovereignty to the degree necessary for the establishment of military security for all.

Now many will say that fundamental agreement with Russia is impossible under the present circumstances. Such a statement would be justified if the United States had made a serious attempt in this direction during the past year. I find, however, that the opposite has happened. There was no need to accept fascist Argentina into the U. N. against Russia's opposition. There was no need to manufacture new atomic bombs without letup and to appropriate twelve billion dollars for defense in a year in which no military threat was to be expected for the nearest future. Nor was it necessary to delay the proposed measures against Franco-Spain. It is senseless to recount here the details which all show that nothing has been done in order to alleviate Russia's distrust, a distrust which can very well be understood in the light of the events of the last decades and to whose origin we have contributed no little.

A permanent peace cannot be prepared by threats but only by the honest attempt to create mutual trust. One should think that the wish to create a decent form of life on this planet and to avert the danger of unspeakable destruction would tame the passions of responsible men. You cannot rely on that, my young friends. May you succeed in activating the young generation in this sense, so that it will strive for a policy of peace on a grand scale. Thus you can not only defend yourself successfully but you can serve your country and your descendants in a degree as was not given to any previous generation.

22

THE WAY OUT

THE CONSTRUCTION of the atom bomb has brought about the effect that all the people living in cities are threatened, everywhere and constantly, with sudden destruction. There is no doubt that this condition has to be abolished if man is to prove himself worthy, at least to some extent, of the self-chosen name of *homo sapiens*. However, there still exist widely divergent opinions concerning the degree to which traditional social and political forms, historically developed, will have to be sacrificed in order to achieve the desired security.

After the First World War, we were confronted with a paradoxical situation regarding the solution of international conflicts. An international court of justice had been established for a peaceful solution of these conflicts on the basis of international law. Furthermore, a political instrument for securing peace by means of international negotiation in a sort of world parliament had been created in the form of the League of Nations. The nations united in the League had further outlawed as criminal the method of solving conflicts by means of war.

Thus the nations were imbued with an illusion of security that led inevitably to bitter disappointment. For the best court of justice is meaningless unless it is backed by the authority and power to execute its decisions, and exactly the same thing is true of a world parliament. An individual state with sufficient military and economic power can easily resort to violence and voluntarily destroy the entire structure of supranational security built on nothing but words and documents. Moral authority alone is an inadequate means of securing the peace.

The United Nations Organization is now in the process of being tested. It may eventually emerge as the agency of "security without illusion" that we so badly need. But it has not as yet gone beyond the area of moral authority as, in my opinion, it must.

Our situation is rendered more acute by other circumstances, only two of which will be presented here. So long as the individual state, despite its official condemnation of war, has to consider the possibility of engaging in war, it must influence and educate its citizens—and its youth in particular—in such a way that they can easily be converted into efficient soldiers in the event of war. Therefore it is compelled not only to cultivate a technical-military training and type of thinking but also to implant a spirit of national vanity in its people in order to secure their inner readiness for the outbreak of war. Of course, this kind of education counteracts all endeavors to establish moral authority for any supranational security organization.

The danger of war in our time is further heightened by another technical factor. Modern weapons, in particular the atom bomb, have led to a considerable advantage in the means of offense or attack over those of defense. And this could well bring about the result that even responsible statesmen might find themselves compelled to wage a preventive war.

In view of these evident facts there is, in my opinion, only *one* way out.

It is necessary that conditions be established that guarantee the individual state the right to solve its conflicts with other states on a legal basis and under international jurisdiction.

It is necessary that the individual state be prevented from

making war by a supranational organization supported by a military power that is exclusively under its control.

Only when these two conditions have been fully met can we have some assurance that we shall not vanish into the atmosphere, dissolved into atoms, one of these days.

From the viewpoint of the political mentality prevailing at present, it may seem illusory, even fantastic, to hope for the realization of such conditions within a period of a few years. Yet their realization cannot wait for a gradual historical development to take its course. For, so long as we do not achieve supranational military security, the above-mentioned factors can always and forcibly lead us into war. Even more than the will for power, the fear of sudden attack will prove to be disastrous for us if we do not openly and decisively meet the problem of depriving national spheres of power of their military strength, turning such power over to a supranational authority.

With due consideration for the difficulties involved in this task, I have no doubt about *one* point. *We shall be able to solve the problem when it will be clearly evident to all that there is no other, no cheaper way out of the present situation.*

Now I feel it my obligation to say something about the individual steps which might lead to a solution of the security problem.

1. Mutual inspection by the leading military powers of methods and installations used for the production of offensive weapons, combined with an interchange of pertinent technical and scientific discoveries, would diminish fear and distrust, at least for the time being. In the breathing spell thus provided we would have to prepare more thorough measures. For this preliminary step should be taken with conscious awareness that the ultimate goal is the denationalization of military power altogether.

This first step is necessary to make any successive moves possible. However, we should be wary of believing that its execution would immediately result in security. There still would remain the possibility of an armament race with regard to a possible future war, and there always exists the temptation to resort once more, by "underground" methods, to the military secret, that is, keeping secret the knowledge about methods and means of and actual preparations for warfare. Real security is tied to the denationalization of military power.

2. This denationalization can be prepared through a steadily increasing interchange of military and scientific-technical personnel among the armies of the different nations. The interchange should follow a carefully elaborated plan, aimed at converting the national armies systematically into a supranational military force. A national army, one might say, is the last place where national feeling may be expected to weaken. Even so, the nationalism can be progressively immunized at a rate proportionate at least to the building of the supranational army; and the whole process can be facilitated by integrating it with the recruiting and training of the latter. The process of interchanging personnel would further lessen the danger of surprise attacks and in itself would lay the psychological foundation for internationalization of military resources.

Simultaneously the strongest military powers could draft the working papers for a supranational security organization and for an arbitration committee, as well as the legal basis for, and the precise stipulation of, obligations, competencies, and restrictions of the latter with respect to the individual nations. They could further decide upon the terms of election for establishing and maintaining these bodies.

When an agreement on these points shall have been reached, a guarantee against wars of world-wide dimensions can be assured.

3. The above-named bodies can now begin to function. The vestiges of national armies can then be either disbanded

or placed under the high command of the supranational authority.

4. After the cooperation of the nations of highest military importance has been secured, the attempt should be made to incorporate, if possible, all nations into the supranational organization, provided that it is their voluntary decision to join.

This outline may perhaps create the impression that the presently prevailing military powers are to be assigned too dominant a role. I have tried, however, to present the problem with a view to a sufficiently swift realization that will allow us to avoid difficulties greater than those already inherent in the nature of such a task. It may be simpler, of course, to reach preliminary agreement among the strongest military powers than among *all* nations, big and small, for a body of representatives of all nations is a hopelessly clumsy instrument for the speedy achievement of even preliminary results. Even so, the task confronting us requires of all concerned the utmost sagacity and tolerance, which can be achieved only through awareness of the harsh necessity we have to face.

23

ON RECEIVING THE ONE
WORLD AWARD

I AM GREATLY TOUCHED by the signal honor which you have wished to confer upon me. In the course of my long life I have received from my fellow-men far more recognition than I deserve, and I confess that my sense of shame has always outweighed my pleasure therein. But never, on any previous occasion, has the pain so far outweighed the pleasure as now. For all of us who are concerned for peace and the triumph of reason and justice must today be keenly aware how small an influence reason and honest good will exert upon events in the political field. But however that may be, and whatever fate may have in store for us, yet we may rest assured that without the tireless efforts of those who are concerned with the welfare of humanity as a whole, the lot of mankind would be still worse than in fact it even now is.

In this time of decisions so heavy with fate what we must say to our fellow-citizens seems above all to be this: where belief in the omnipotence of physical force gets the upper hand in political life this force takes on a life of its own, and proves stronger than the men who think to use force as a tool. The proposed militarization of the nation not only immediately threatens us with war; it will also slowly but surely destroy the democratic spirit and the dignity of the individual in our land. The assertion that events abroad force us to arm is wrong, we must combat it with all our strength. Actually, our own rearmament, through the reaction of other nations to it, will bring about that very situation on which its advocates seek to base their proposals.

There is only *one* path to peace and security: the path of supra-national organization. One-sided armament on a national basis only heightens the general uncertainty and confusion without being an effective protection.

24

SCIENCE AND CIVILIZATION

IT IS IN TIMES of economic distress such as we experience everywhere today, one sees very clearly the strength of the moral forces that live in a people. Let us hope that a historian delivering judgment in some future period when Europe is politically and economically united, will be able to say that in our days the liberty and honour of this Continent was saved by its Western nations, which stood fast in hard times against the temptations of hatred and oppression; and that Western Europe defended successfully the liberty of the individual which has brought us every advance of knowledge and invention—liberty without which life to a self-respecting man is not worth living.

It cannot be my task today to act as judge of the conduct of a nation which for many years has considered me as her own; perhaps it is an idle task to judge in times when action counts.

Today, the questions which concern us are: how can we save mankind and its spiritual acquisitions of which we are the heirs? How can one save Europe from a new disaster?

It cannot be doubted that the world crisis and the suffering and privations of the people resulting from the crisis are in some measure responsible for the dangerous upheavals of which we are the witness. In such periods discontent breeds hatred, and hatred leads to acts of violence and revolution, and often even to war. Thus distress and evil produce new distress and new evil. Again the leading statesmen are burdened with tremendous responsibilities just the same as twenty years ago. May they succeed through timely agreement to establish a condition of unity and clarity of international obligations in Europe, so that for every State a warlike adventure must appear as utterly hopeless. But the work of statesmen can succeed only if they are backed by the serious and determined will of the people.

We are concerned not merely with the technical problem of securing and maintaining peace, but also with the important task of education and enlightenment. If we want to resist the powers which threaten to suppress intellectual and individual freedom we must keep clearly before us what is at stake, and what we owe to that freedom which our ancestors have won for us after hard struggles.

Without such freedom there would have been no Shakespeare, no Goethe, no Newton, no Faraday, no Pasteur and no Lister. There would be no comfortable houses for the mass of the people, no railway, no wireless, no protection against epidemics, no cheap books, no culture and no enjoyment of art for all. There would be no machines to relieve the people from the arduous labor needed for the production of the essential necessities of life. Most people would lead a dull life of slavery just as under the ancient despotisms of Asia. It is only men who are free, who create the inventions and intellectual works which to us moderns make life worth while.

Without doubt the present economic difficulties will eventually bring us to the point where the balance between supply of labor and demand of labor, between production and consumption, will be enforced by law. But even this problem we shall solve as free men and we shall not allow ourselves for its sake to be driven into a slavery, which ultimately would bring with it stagnation of every healthy development.

In this connection I should like to give expression to an idea which has occurred to me recently. I lived in solitude in the country and noticed how the monotony of a quiet life stimulates the creative mind. There are certain callings in our modern organization which entail such an isolated life without making a great claim on bodily and intellectual effort. I think of such occupations as the service in lighthouses and lightships. Would it not be possible to fill such places with young people who wish to think out scientific problems, especially of a mathematical or philosophical nature? Very few of such people have the opportunity during the most productive period of their lives to devote themselves undisturbed for any length of time to scientific problems. Even if a young person is lucky enough to obtain a scholarship for a short period he must endeavor to arrive as quickly as possible at definite conclusions. That cannot be of advantage in the pursuit of pure science. The young scientist who carries on an ordinary practical profession which maintains him is in a much better position—assuming of course that this profession leaves him with sufficient spare time and energy. In this way perhaps a greater number of creative individuals could be given an opportunity for mental development than is possible at present. In these times of economic depression and political upheaval such considerations seem to be worth attention.

Shall we worry over the fact that we are living in a time of danger and want? I think not. Man like every other animal is by nature indolent. If nothing spurs him on, then he will hardly think, and will behave from habit like an automaton. I am no longer young and can, therefore, say, that as a child and as a young man I experienced that phase—when a young man thinks only about the trivialities of personal existence, and talks like his fellows and behaves like them. Only with difficulty can one see what is really behind such a conventional mask. For owing to habit and speech his real personality is, as it were wrapped in cotton wool.

How different it is today! In the lightning flashes of our tempestuous times one sees human beings and things in their nakedness. Every nation and every human being reveal clearly their aims, powers and weaknesses, and also their passions. Routine becomes of no avail under the swift change of conditions; conventions fall away like dry husks.

Men in their distress begin to think about the failure of economic practice and about the necessity of political combinations which are supernational. Only through perils and upheavals can Nations be brought to further developments. May the present upheavals lead to a better world.

Above and beyond this valuation of our time we have this further duty, the care for what is eternal and highest amongst our possessions, that which gives to life its import and which we wish to hand on to our children purer and richer than we received it from our forebears.

25

A MESSAGE
TO INTELLECTUALS *

W E MEET TODAY, as intellectuals and scholars of many nationalities, with a deep and historic responsibility placed upon us. We have every reason to be grateful to our French and Polish colleagues whose initiative has assembled us here for a momentous objective: to use the influence of wise men in promoting peace and security throughout the world. This is the age-old problem with which Plato, as one of the first, struggled so hard: to apply reason and prudence to the solution of man's problems instead of yielding to atavist instincts and passions.

By painful experience we have learnt that rational thinking does not suffice to solve the problems of our social life. Penetrating research and keen scientific work have often had tragic implications for mankind, producing, on the one hand, inventions which liberated man from exhausting physical labor, making his life easier and richer; but on the other hand, introducing a grave restlessness into his life, making him a slave to his technological environment, and—most catastrophic of all—creating the means for his own mass destruction. This, indeed, is a tragedy of overwhelming poignancy!

However poignant that tragedy is, it is perhaps even more tragic that, while mankind has produced many scholars so

* The following address was objected to by the Organizing Committee of the Intellectuals' Conference for Peace. The message was subsequently released to the press on August 29, 1948.

extremely successful in the field of science and technology, we have been for a long time so inefficient in finding adequate solutions to the many political conflicts and economic tensions which beset us. No doubt, the antagonism of economic interests within and among nations is largely responsible to a great extent for the dangerous and threatening condition in the world today. Man has not succeeded in developing political and economic forms of organization which would guarantee the peaceful coexistence of the nations of the world. He has not succeeded in building the kind of system which would eliminate the possibility of war and banish forever the murderous instruments of mass destruction.

We scientists, whose tragic destination has been to help in making the methods of annihilation more gruesome and more effective, must consider it our solemn and transcendent duty to do all in our power in preventing these weapons from being used for the brutal purpose for which they were invented. What task could possibly be more important for us? What social aim could be closer to our hearts? That is why this Congress has such a vital mission. We are here to take counsel with each other. We must build spiritual and scientific bridges linking the nations of the world. We must overcome the horrible obstacles of national frontiers.

In the smaller entities of community life, man has made some progress toward breaking down anti-social sovereignties. This is true, for example, of life within cities and, to a certain degree, even of society within individual states. In such communities tradition and education have had a moderating influence and have brought about tolerable relations among the peoples living within those confines. But in relations among separate states complete anarchy still prevails. I do not believe that we have made any genuine advance in this area during the last few thousand years. All too frequently conflicts among nations are still being decided by brutal power, by war. The unlimited desire for ever greater power seeks to become active and aggressive wherever and whenever the physical possibility offers itself.

Throughout the ages, this state of anarchy in international affairs has inflicted indescribable suffering and destruction upon mankind; again and again it has depraved the development of men, their souls and their well-being. For given time it has almost annihilated whole areas.

However, the desire of nations to be constantly prepared for warfare has, however, still other repercussions upon the lives of men. The power of every state over its citizens has grown steadily during the last few hundred years, no less in countries where the power of the state has been exercised wisely, than in those where it has been used for brutal tyranny. The function of the state to maintain peaceful and ordered relations among and between its citizens has become increasingly complicated and extensive largely because of the concentration and centralization of the modern industrial apparatus. In order to protect its citizens from attacks from without a modern state requires a formidable, expanding military establishment. In addition, the state considers it necessary to educate its citizens for the possibilities of war, an "education" not only corrupting to the soul and spirit of the young, but also adversely affecting the mentality of adults. No country can avoid this corruption. It pervades the citizenry even in countries which do not harbor outspoken aggressive tendencies. The state has thus become a modern idol whose suggestive power few men are able to escape.

Education for war, however, is a delusion. The technological developments of the last few years have created a completely new military situation. Horrible weapons have been invented, capable of destroying in a few seconds huge masses of human beings and tremendous areas of territory. Since science has not yet found protection from these weapons, the modern state is no longer in a position to prepare adequately for the safety of its citizens.

How, then, shall we be saved?

Mankind can only gain protection against the danger of unimaginable destruction and wanton annihilation if a supranational organization has alone the authority to produce or possess these weapons. It is unthinkable, however, that nations under existing conditions would hand over such authority to a supranational organization unless the organization would have the legal right and duty to solve all the conflicts which in the past have led to war. The functions of individual states would be to concentrate more or less upon internal affairs; in their relation with other states they would deal only with issues and problems which are in no way conducive to endangering international security.

Unfortunately, there are no indications that governments yet realize that the situation in which mankind finds itself makes the adoption of revolutionary measures a compelling necessity. Our situation is not comparable to anything in the past. It is impossible, therefore, to apply methods and measures which at an earlier age might have been sufficient. We must revolutionize our thinking, revolutionize our actions, and must have the courage to revolutionize relations among the nations of the world. Clichés of yesterday will no longer do today, and will, no doubt, be hopelessly out of date tomorrow. To bring this home to men all over the world is the most important and most fateful social function intellectuals have ever had to shoulder. Will they have enough courage to overcome their own national ties to the extent that is necessary to induce the peoples of the world to change their deep-rooted national traditions in a most radical fashion?

A tremendous effort is indispensable. If it fails now, the supranational organization will be built later, but then it will have to be built upon the ruins of a large part of the now existing world. Let us hope that the abolition of the existing international anarchy will not need to be bought by a self-inflicted world catastrophe the dimensions of which none of us can possibly imagine. The time is terribly short. We must act now if we are to act at all.

26

OPEN LETTER TO THE GENERAL ASSEMBLY OF THE UNITED NATIONS

W E ARE CAUGHT IN A SITUATION in which every citizen of every country, his children, and his life's work, are threatened by the terrible insecurity which reigns in our world today. The progress of technological development has not increased the stability and the welfare of humanity. Because of our inability to solve the problem of international organization, it has actually contributed to the dangers which threaten peace and the very existence of mankind.

The delegates of fifty-five governments, meeting in the second General Assembly of the United Nations, undoubtedly will be aware of the fact that during the last two years—since the victory over the Axis powers—no appreciable progress has been made either toward the prevention of war or toward agreement in specific fields such as control of atomic energy and economic cooperation in the reconstruction of war-devastated areas.

The UN cannot be blamed for these failures. No international organization can be stronger than the constitutional powers given it, or than its component parts want it to be. As a matter of fact, the United Nations is an extremely important and useful institution *provided* the peoples and governments of the world realize that it is merely a transitional system toward the final goal, which is the establishment of a supranational authority vested with sufficient legislative and executive powers to keep the peace. The present impasse lies in the fact that there is no sufficient, reliable supranational authority. Thus the responsible leaders of all governments are obliged to act on the assumption of eventual war. Every step motivated by that assumption contributes to the general fear and distrust and hastens the final catastrophe. However strong national armaments may be, they do not create military security for any nation nor do they guarantee the maintenance of peace.

There can never be complete agreement on international control and the administration of atomic energy or on general disarmament until there is a modification of the traditional concept of national sovereignty. For as long as atomic energy and armaments are considered a vital part of national security no nation will give more than lip service to international treaties. Security is indivisible. It can be reached only when necessary guarantees of law and enforcement obtain everywhere, so that military security is no longer the problem of any single state. There is no compromise possible between preparation for war, on the one hand, and preparation of a world society based on law and order on the other.

Every citizen must make up his mind. If he accepts the premise of war, he must reconcile himself to the maintenance of troops in strategic areas like Austria and Korea; to the sending of troops to Greece and Bulgaria; to the accumulation of stockpiles of uranium by whatever means; to universal military training, to the progressive limitation of civil liberties. Above all, he must endure the consequences of military secrecy which is one of the worst scourges of our time and one of the greatest obstacles to cultural betterment.

If on the other hand every citizen realizes that the only guarantee for security and peace in this atomic age is the constant development of a supranational government, then he will do everything in his power to strengthen the United Nations. It seems to me that every reasonable and responsible citizen in the world must know where his choice lies.

Yet the world at large finds itself in a vicious circle since the UN powers seem to be incapable of making up their minds on this score. The Eastern and Western blocs each attempt frantically to strengthen their respective power positions. Universal military training, Russian troops in Eastern Europe, United States control over the Pacific Islands, even the stiffening colonial policies of the Netherlands, Great Britain and France, atomic and military secrecy—are all part of the old familiar jockeying for position.

The time has come for the UN to strengthen its moral authority by bold decisions. First, the authority of the General Assembly must be increased so that the Security Council as well as all other bodies of the UN will be subordinated to it. As long as there is a conflict of authority between the Assembly and the Security Council, the effectiveness of the whole institution will remain necessarily impaired.

Second, the method of representation at the UN should be considerably modified. The present method of selection by government appointment does not leave any real freedom to the appointee. Furthermore, selection by governments cannot give the peoples of the world the feeling of being fairly and proportionately represented. The moral authority of the UN would be considerably enhanced if the delegates were elected directly by the people. Were they responsible to an electorate, they would have much more freedom to follow their consciences. Thus we could hope for more statesmen and fewer diplomats.

Third, the General Assembly should remain in session throughout the critical period of transition. By staying constantly on the job, the Assembly could fulfill two major tasks: first, it could take the initiative toward the establishment of a supranational order; second, it could take quick and effective steps in all those danger areas (such as currently exist on the Greek border) where peace is threatened.

The Assembly, in view of these high tasks, should not delegate its powers to the Security Council, especially while that body is paralyzed by the shortcomings of the veto provisions. As the only body competent to take the initiative boldly and resolutely, the UN must act with utmost speed to create the necessary conditions for international security by laying the foundations for a real world government.

Of course there will be opposition. It is by no means certain that the U.S.S.R.—which is often represented as the main antagonist to the idea of world government—would maintain its opposition if an equitable offer providing for real security were made. Even assuming that Russia is now opposed to the idea of world government, once she becomes convinced that world government is nonetheless in the making her whole attitude may change. She may then insist on only the necessary guarantees of equality before the law so as to avoid finding herself in perennial minority as in the present Security Council.

Nevertheless, we must assume that despite all efforts Russia and her allies may still find it advisable to stay out of such a world government. In that case—and only after all efforts have been made in utmost sincerity to obtain the cooperation of Russia and her allies—the other countries would have to proceed alone. It is of the utmost importance that this partial world government be very strong, comprising at least two-thirds of the major industrial and economic areas of the world. Such strength in itself would make it possible for the partial world government to abandon military secrecy and all the other practices born of insecurity.

Such a partial world government should make it clear from the beginning that its doors remain wide open to any non-member—particularly Russia—for participation on the basis of complete equality. In my opinion, the partial world government should accept the presence of observers from non-member governments at all its meetings and constitutional conventions.

In order to achieve the final aim—which is one world, and not two hostile worlds—such a partial world government must never act as an alliance against the rest of the world. The only real step toward world government is world government itself.

In a world government the ideological differences between the various component parts are of no grave consequence. I am convinced that the present difficulties between the U.S.A. and the U.S.S.R. are not due primarily to ideological differences. Of course, these ideological differences are a contributing element in an already serious tension. But I am convinced that even if the U.S.A. and Russia were both capitalist countries—or communist, or monarchist, for that matter—their rivalries, conflicting interests, and jealousies would result in strains similar to those existing between the two countries today.

The UN now and world government eventually must serve one single goal—the guarantee of the security, tranquillity, and the welfare of all mankind.

27

DR. EINSTEIN'S MISTAKEN NOTIONS

An Open Letter from Sergei Vavilov, A. N. Frumkin, A. F. Joffe, and N. N. Semyonov [*]

THE CELEBRATED PHYSICIST, Albert Einstein, is famed not only for his scientific discoveries; of late years he has paid much attention to social and political problems. He speaks over the radio and writes in the press. He is associated with a number of public organizations. Time and again he raised his voice in protest against the Nazi barbarians. He is an advocate of enduring peace, and has spoken against the threat of a new war, and against the ambition of the militarists to bring American science completely under their control.

Soviet scientists, and the Soviet people in general, are appreciative of the humanitarian spirit which prompts these activities of the scientist, although his position has not always been as consistent and clear-cut as might be desired. However, in some of Einstein's more recent utterances there have been aspects which seem to us not only mistaken, but positively prejudicial to the cause of peace which Einstein so warmly espouses.

[*] Biographical Note: Sergei Vavilov, a physicist specializing in the field of fluorescence, is President of the Academy of Sciences of the USSR. A. N. Frumkin, a colloid chemist of note, is Director of the Colloid-Electrochemical Institute of the Academy of Sciences in Moscow. A. F. Joffe is well known for his work on the behavior of crystals under water, and is Director of the Physico-Chemical Institute of the Academy in Leningrad. N. N. Semyonov, an authority on chemical kinetics, is Director of the Institute of Chemical Physics of the Academy in Moscow.

We feel it our duty to draw attention to this, in order to clarify so important a question as to how most effectively to work for peace. It is from this point of view that the idea of a "world government" which Dr. Einstein has of late been sponsoring must be considered.

In the motley company of proponents of this idea, besides out-and-out imperialists who are using it as a screen for unlimited expansion, there are quite a number of intellectuals in the capitalist countries who are captivated by the plausibility of the idea, and who do not realize its actual implications. These pacifist and liberal-minded individuals believe that a "world government" would be an effective panacea against the world's evils and a guardian of enduring peace.

The advocates of a "world government" make wide use of the seemingly radical argument that in this atomic age state sovereignty is a relic of the past, that it is, as Spaak, the Belgian delegate, said in the UN General Assembly, an "old-fashioned" and even "reactionary" idea. It would be hard to imagine an allegation that is farther from the truth.

In the first place, the idea of a "world government" and "superstate" are by no means products of the atomic age. They are much older than that. They were mooted, for instance, at the time the League of Nations was formed.

Further, these ideas have never been progressive in these modern times. They are a reflection of the fact that the capitalist monopolies, which dominate the major industrial countries, find their own national boundaries too narrow. They need a world-wide market, world-wide sources of raw materials, and world-wide spheres of capital investment. Thanks to their domination in political and administrative affairs, the monopoly interests of the big powers are in a position to utilize the machinery of government in their struggle for spheres of influence and their efforts economically and politically to subjugate other countries, to play the master in these countries as freely as in their own.

We know this very well from the past experience of our own country. Under tsarism, Russia, with her reactionary regime, which was servilely accommodating to the interests of capital, with her low-paid labor and vast natural resources, was an alluring morsel to foreign capitalists. French, British, Belgian and German firms battened on our country like birds of prey, earning profits which would have been inconceivable in their own countries. They chained tsarist Russia to the capitalist West with extortionate loans. Supported by funds obtained from foreign banks, the tsarist government brutally repressed the revolutionary movement, retarded the development of Russian science and culture, and instigated Jewish pogroms.

The Great October Socialist Revolution smashed the chains of economic and political dependence that bound our country to the world capitalist monopolies. The Soviet Government made our country for the first time a really free and independent state, promoted the progress of our Socialist economy, technology, science and culture at a speed hitherto unwitnessed in history, and turned our country into a reliable bulwark of international peace and security. Our people upheld their country's independence in the civil war, in the struggle against the intervention of a bloc of imperialist states, and in the great battles of the war against the Nazi invaders.

And now the proponents of a "world super-state" are asking us voluntarily to surrender this independence for the sake of a "world government," which is nothing but a flamboyant signboard for the world supremacy of the capitalist monopolies.

It is obviously preposterous to ask of us anything like that. And it is not only with regard to the Soviet Union that such a demand is absurd. After World War II, a number of countries succeeded in breaking away from the imperialist system of oppression and slavery. The peoples of these countries are working to consolidate their economic and political independence, debarring alien interference in their domestic affairs. Further, the rapid spread of the movement for national independence in the colonies and dependencies has awakened the national consciousness of hundreds of millions of people, who do not desire to remain in the status of slaves any longer.

The monopolies of the imperialist countries, having lost a number of profitable spheres of exploitation, and running the risk of losing more, are doing their utmost to deprive the nations that have escaped from their mastery of the state independence which they, the monopolies, find so irksome, and to prevent the genuine liberation of the colonies. With this purpose, the imperialists are resorting to the most diverse methods of military, political, economic and ideological warfare.

It is in accordance with this social behest that the ideologians of imperialism are endeavoring to discredit the very idea of national sovereignty. One of the methods they resort to is the advocacy of pretentious plans for a "world state," which will allegedly do away with imperialism, wars and national enmity, ensure the triumph of universal law, and so on.

The predatory appetites of the imperialist forces that are striving for world supremacy are thus disguised under the garb of a pseudo-progressive idea which appeals to certain intellectuals—scientists, writers and others—in the capitalist countries.

In an open letter which he addressed last September to the United Nations delegations, Dr. Einstein suggested a new scheme for limiting national sovereignty. He recommends that the General Assembly be reconstructed and converted into a permanently functioning world parliament endowed with greater authority than the Security Council, which, Einstein declares (repeating what the henchmen of American diplomacy are asserting day in and day out), is paralyzed by the veto right. The General Assembly, reconstructed in accordance with Dr. Einstein's plan, is to have final powers of decision, and the principle of the unanimity of the Great Powers is to be abandoned.

Einstein suggests that the delegates to the United Nations should be chosen by popular election and not appointed by their governments, as at present. At a first glance, this proposal may seem progressive and even radical. Actually, it will in no way improve the existing situation.

Let us picture to ourselves what elections to such a "world parliament" would mean in practice.

A large part of humanity still lives in colonial and dependent countries dominated by the governors, the troops, and the financial and industrial monopolies of a few imperialist powers. "Popular election" in such countries would in practice mean the appointment of delegates by the colonial administration or the military authorities. One does not have to go far for examples; one need only recall the parody of a referendum in Greece, which was carried out by her royalist-fascist rulers under the protection of British bayonets.

But things would be not much better in the countries where universal suffrage formally exists. In the bourgeois-democratic countries, where capital dominates, the latter resorts to thousands of tricks and devices to turn universal suffrage and freedom of ballot into a farce. Einstein surely knows that in the last Congressional elections in the United States only 39 per cent of the electorate went to the polls; he surely knows that millions of Negroes in the Southern states are virtually deprived of the franchise, or are forced, not infrequently under threat of lynching, to vote for their bitterest enemies, such as the late arch-reactionary and Negrophobe, Senator Bilbo.

Poll taxes, special tests and other devices are employed to rob millions of immigrants, migrant workers and poor farmers of the vote. We will not mention the widespread practice of purchasing votes, the role of the reactionary press, that powerful instrument for influencing the masses wielded by millionaire newspaper proprietors, and so forth.

All this shows what popular elections to a world parliament, as suggested by Einstein, would amount to under existing conditions in the capitalist world. Its composition would be no better than the present composition of the General Assembly. It would be a distorted reflection of the real sentiments of the masses, of their desire and hope for lasting peace.

As we know, in the General Assembly and the UN committees, the American delegation has a regular voting machine at its disposal, thanks to the fact that the overwhelming majority of the members of the UN are dependent on the United States and are compelled to adapt their foreign policy to the requirements of Washington. A number of Latin-American countries, for instance, countries with single-crop agricultural systems, are bound hand and foot to the American monopolies, which determine the prices of their produce. Such being the case, it is not surprising that, under pressure of the American delegation, a mechanical majority has arisen in the General Assembly which votes in obedience to the orders of its virtual masters.

There are cases when American diplomacy finds it preferable to realize certain measures, not through the State Department, but under the flag of the United Nations. Witness the notorious Balkan committee or the commission appointed to observe the elections in Korea. It is with the object of converting the UN into a branch of the State Department that the American delegation is forcing through the project for a "Little Assembly," which would in practice replace the Security Council, with its principle of unanimity of the Great Powers that is proving such an obstacle to the realization of imperialist schemes.

Einstein's suggestion would lead to the same result, and thus, far from promoting lasting peace and international co-operation, would only serve as a screen for an offensive against nations which have established regimes that prevent foreign capital from extorting its customary profits. It would further the unbridled expansion of American imperialism, and ideologically disarm the nations which insist upon maintaining their independence.

By the irony of fate, Einstein has virtually become a supporter of the schemes and ambitions of the bitterest foes of peace and international cooperation. He has gone so far in this direction as to declare in advance in his open letter that if the Soviet Union refuses to join his newfangled organization, other countries would have every right to go ahead without it, while leaving the door open for eventual Soviet participation in the organization as a member or as an "observer."

Essentially this proposal differs very little from the suggestions of frank advocates of American imperialism, however remote Dr. Einstein may be from them in reality. The sum and substance of these suggestions is that if UN cannot be converted into a weapon of United States policy, into a screen for imperialist schemes and designs, that organization should be wrecked and a new "international" organization formed in its place, without the Soviet Union and the new democracies.

Does Einstein not realize how fatal such plans would be to international security and international cooperation?

We believe that Dr. Einstein has entered a false and dangerous path; he is chasing the mirage of a "world state" in a world where different social, political and economic systems exist. Of course there is no reason why states with different social and economic structures should not cooperate economically and politically, provided that these differences are soberly faced. But Einstein is sponsoring a political fad which plays into the hands of the sworn enemies of sincere international cooperation and enduring peace. The course he is inviting the member states of the United Nations to adopt would lead not to greater international security, but to new international complications. It would benefit only the capitalist monopolies, for whom new international complications hold out the promise of more war contracts and more profits.

It is because we so highly esteem Einstein as an eminent scientist and as a man of public spirit who is striving to the best of his ability to promote the cause of peace, that we consider it our duty to speak with utter frankness and without diplomatic adornment.

A REPLY TO THE SOVIET
SCIENTISTS

Four of my Russian colleagues have published a benevolent attack upon me in an open letter carried by the *New Times*. I appreciate the effort they have made and I appreciate even more the fact that they have expressed their point of view so candidly and straightforwardly. To act intelligently in human affairs is only possible if an attempt is made to understand the thoughts, motives, and apprehensions of one's opponent so fully that one can see the world through his eyes. All well-meaning people should try to contribute as much as possible to improving such mutual understanding. It is in this spirit that I should like to ask my Russian colleagues and any other reader to accept the following answer to their letter. It is the reply of a man who anxiously tries to find a feasible solution without having the illusion that he himself knows "the truth" or "the right path" to follow. If in the following I shall express my views somewhat dogmatically, I do it only for the sake of clarity and simplicity.

Although your letter, in the main, is clothed in an attack upon the non-socialistic foreign countries, particularly the United States, I believe that behind the aggressive front there lies a defensive mental attitude which is nothing else but the trend towards an almost unlimited isolationism. The escape into isolationism is not difficult to understand if one realizes what Russia has suffered at the hands of foreign countries during the last three decades—the German invasions with planned mass murder of the civilian population, foreign interventions during the civil war, the systematic campaign of calumnies in the western press, the support of Hitler as an alleged tool to fight Russia. However understandable this desire for isolation may be, it remains no less disastrous to Russia and to all other nations; I shall say more about it later on.

The chief object of your attack against me concerns my support of "world government." I should like to discuss this important problem only after having said a few words about the antagonism between socialism and capitalism; for your attitude on the significance of this antagonism seems to dominate completely your views on international problems. If the socio-economic problem is considered objectively, it appears as follows: technological development has led to increasing centralization of the economic mechanism. It is this development which is also responsible for the fact that economic power in all widely industrialized countries has become concentrated in the hands of relatively few. These people, in capitalist countries, do not need to account for their actions to the public as a whole; they must do so in socialist countries in which they are civil servants similar to those who exercise political power.

I share your view that a socialist economy possesses advantages which definitely counterbalance its disadvantages whenever the management lives up, at least to some extent, to adequate standards. No doubt, the day will come when all nations (as far as such nations still exist) will be grateful to Russia for having demonstrated, for the first time, by vigorous action the practical possibility of planned economy in spite of exceedingly great difficulties. I also believe that capitalism, or, we should say, the system of free enterprise, will prove unable to check unemployment, which will become increasingly chronic because of technological progress, and unable to maintain a healthy balance between production and the purchasing power of the people.

On the other hand we should not make the mistake of

blaming capitalism for all existing social and political evils, and of assuming that the very establishment of socialism would be able to cure all the social and political ills of humanity. The danger of such a belief lies, first, in the fact that it encourages fanatical intolerance on the part of all the "faithful" by making a possible social method into a type of church which brands all those who do not belong to it as traitors or as nasty evildoers. Once this stage has been reached, the ability to understand the convictions and actions of the "unfaithful" vanishes completely. You know, I am sure, from history how much unnecessary suffering such rigid beliefs have inflicted upon mankind.

Any government is in itself an evil insofar as it carries within it the tendency to deteriorate into tyranny. However, except for a very small number of anarchists, everyone of us is convinced that civilized society cannot exist without a government. In a healthy nation there is a kind of dynamic balance between the will of the people and the government, which prevents its degeneration into tyranny. It is obvious that the danger of such deterioration is more acute in a country in which the government has authority not only over the armed forces but also over all the channels of education and information as well as over the economic existence of every single citizen. I say this merely to indicate that socialism as such cannot be considered the solution to all social problems but merely as a framework within which such a solution is possible.

What has surprised me most in your general attitude, expressed in your letter, is the following aspect: You are such passionate opponents of anarchy in the economic sphere, and yet equally passionate advocates of anarchy, e.g., unlimited sovereignty, in the sphere of international politics. The proposition to curtail the sovereignty of individual states appears to you in itself reprehensible, as a kind of violation of a natural right. In addition, you try to prove that behind the idea of curtailing sovereignty the United States is hiding her intention of economic domination and exploitation of the rest of the world without going to war. You attempt to justify this indictment by analyzing in your fashion the individual actions of this government since the end of the last war. You attempt to show that the Assembly of the United Nations is a mere puppet show controlled by the United States and hence the American capitalists.

Such arguments impress me as a kind of mythology; they are not convincing. They make obvious, however, the deep estrangement among the intellectuals of our two countries which is the result of a regrettable and artificial mutual isolation. If a free personal exchange of views should be made possible and should be encouraged, the intellectuals, possibly more than anyone else, could help to create an atmosphere of mutual understanding between the two nations and their problems. Such an atmosphere is a necessary prerequisite for the fruitful development of political cooperation. However, since for the time being we depend upon the cumbersome method of "open letters" I shall want to indicate briefly my reaction to your arguments.

Nobody would want to deny that the influence of the economic oligarchy upon all branches of our public life is very powerful. This influence, however, should not be overestimated. Franklin Delano Roosevelt was elected president in spite of desperate opposition by these very powerful groups and was reelected three times; and this took place at a time when decisions of great consequence had to be made.

Concerning the policies of the American Government since the end of the war, I am neither willing, nor able, nor entitled to justify or explain them. It cannot be denied, however, that the suggestions of the American Government with regard to atomic weapons represented at least an attempt towards the creation of a supranational security organization. If they were not acceptable, they could at least have served as a basis of discussion for a real solution of the problems of international security. It is, indeed, the attitude of the Soviet Government, that was partly negative and partly dilatory, which has made it so difficult for well-meaning people in this country to use their political influence as they would have wanted, and to oppose the "war mongers." With regard to the influence of the United States upon the United Nations Assembly, I wish to say that, in my opinion, it stems not only from the economic and military power of the United States but also from the efforts of the United States and the United Nations to lead toward a genuine solution of the security problem.

Concerning the controversial veto power, I believe that the efforts to eliminate it or to make it ineffective have their primary cause less in specific intentions of the United States than in the manner in which the veto privilege has been abused.

Let me come now to your suggestion that the policy of the United States seeks to obtain economic domination and exploitation of other nations. It is a precarious undertaking to say anything reliable about aims and intentions. Let us rather examine the objective factors involved. The United States is fortunate in producing all the important industrial products and foods in her own country, in sufficient quantities. The country also possesses almost all important raw materials. Because of her tenacious belief in "free enterprise" she cannot succeed in keeping the purchasing power of the people in balance with the productive capacity of the country. For these very same reasons there is a constant danger that unemployment will reach threatening dimensions.

Because of these circumstances the United States is compelled to emphasize her export trade. Without it, she could not permanently keep her total productive machinery fully utilized. These conditions would not be harmful if the exports were balanced by imports of about the same value. Exploitation of foreign nations would then consist in the fact that the labor value of imports would considerably exceed that of exports. However, every effort is being made to avoid this, since almost every import would make a part of the productive machinery idle.

This is why foreign countries are not able to pay for the export commodities of the United States, payment which, in the long run, would indeed be possible only through imports by the latter. This explains why a large portion of all the gold has come to the United States. On the whole, this gold cannot be utilized except for the purchase of foreign commodities, which because of the reasons already stated, is not practicable. There it lies, this gold, carefully protected against theft, a monument to governmental wisdom and to economic science! The reasons which I have just indicated make it difficult for me to take the alleged exploitation of the world by the United States very seriously.

However, the situation just described has a serious political facet. The United States, for the reasons indicated, is compelled to ship part of its production to foreign countries. These exports are financed through loans which the United States is granting foreign countries. It is, indeed, difficult to imagine how these loans will ever be repaid. For all practical purposes, therefore, these loans must be considered gifts which may be used as weapons in the arena of power politics. In view of the existing conditions and in view of the general characteristics of human beings, this, I frankly admit, represents a real danger. Is it not true, however, that we have stumbled into a state of international affairs which tends to make every invention of our minds and every material good into a weapon and, consequently, into a danger for mankind?

This question brings us to the most important matter, in comparison to which everything else appears insignificant indeed. We all know that power politics, sooner or later, necessarily leads to war, and that war, under present circumstances, would mean a mass destruction of human beings and material goods, the dimensions of which are much, much greater than anything that has ever before happened in history.

Is it really unavoidable that, because of our passions and our inherited customs, we should be condemned to annihilate each other so thoroughly that nothing would be left over which would deserve to be conserved? Is it not true that all the controversies and differences of opinion which we have touched upon in our strange exchange of letters are insignificant pettinesses compared to the danger in which we all find ourselves? Should we not do everything in our power to eliminate the danger which threatens all nations alike?

If we hold fast to the concept and practice of unlimited sovereignty of nations it only means that each country reserves the right for itself of pursuing its objectives through warlike means. Under the circumstances, every nation must be prepared for that possibility; this means it must try with all its might to be superior to anyone else. This objective will dominate more and more our entire public life and will poison our youth long before the catastrophe is itself actually upon us. We must not tolerate this, however, as long as we still retain a tiny bit of calm reasoning and human feelings.

This alone is on my mind in supporting the idea of "World Government," without any regard to what other people may have in mind when working for the same objective. I advocate world government because I am convinced that there is no other possible way of eliminating the most terrible danger in which man has ever found himself. The objective of avoiding total destruction must have priority over any other objective.

I am sure you are convinced that this letter is written with all the seriousness and honesty at my command; I trust you will accept it in the same spirit.

Science and Life

28

FOR AN ORGANIZATION OF
INTELLECTUAL WORKERS

I CONSIDER IT IMPORTANT, indeed urgently necessary, for intellectual workers to get together, both to protect their own economic status and also, generally speaking, to secure their influence in the political field.

On the first-mentioned, the economic side, the working class may serve us as a model: they have succeeded, at least to some extent, in protecting their economic interests. We can learn from them too how this problem can be solved by the method of organization. And also, we can learn from them what is our gravest danger, which we ourselves must seek to avoid: the weakening through inner dissensions, which, when things reach that point, make cooperation difficult and result in quarrels between the constituent groups.

But again, we can also learn from the workers that limitation to immediate economic aims, to the exclusion of all political goals and effective action will not suffice either. In this respect, the working classes in this country have only begun their development. It is inevitable, considering the progressive centralization of production, that the economic and the political struggle should become more and more closely interwoven, the political factor continually growing in significance in the process. In the meantime the intellectual worker, due to his lack of organization, is less well protected against arbitrariness and exploitation than a member of any other calling.

But intellectual workers should unite, not only in their own interest but also and no less importantly in the interest of society as a whole. For division among intellectuals has been partly to blame for the fact that the special parts and the experience which are the birthright of these groups have so seldom been made available for political aims. In their room political ambition and desire for profit almost exclusively determine events, instead of professional knowledge and judgment based upon objective thinking.

An organization of intellectual workers can have the greatest significance for society as a whole by influencing public opinion through publicity and education. Indeed it is its proper task to defend academic freedom, without which a healthy development of democracy is impossible.

An outstandingly important task for an organization of intellectual workers at the present moment is to fight for the establishment of a supranational political force as a protection against fresh wars of aggression. It seems to me that the working out with a view to selection of a particular plan for an international government should not, at the present moment, be our chief aim. For if there existed, among the majority of citizens, the firm intention of establishing international security, the technique of giving shape to such an instrument would not present an all-too-difficult problem. What is lacking in the majority is the conviction, founded on clear thinking, that there is no other means of permanently avoiding catastrophes like the present one. In the organization and promotion of enlightenment on this subject, I see the most important service which an organization of intellectual workers can perform at this historic moment. Only by means of setting energetically about such a task can an organization like the one here planned achieve inward strength and outward influence.

29

"WAS EUROPE A SUCCESS?"

THE HUMANITARIAN IDEAL of Europe appears indeed to be unalterably bound up with the free expression of opinion, to some extent with the free-will of the individual, with the effort toward objectivity in thought without consideration of mere utility, and with the encouragement of differences in the realm of mind and taste. These requirements and ideals comprise the nature of the European spirit. One cannot establish with reason the worth of these values and maxims, for they are matters of fundamental principle in the approach to life and are points of departure which can only be affirmed or denied by emotion. I only know that I affirm them with my whole soul, and would find it intolerable to belong to a society which consistently denied them.

I do not share the pessimism of those who believe that full intellectual growth is dependent on the foundation of open or concealed slavery. That may be true for eras of primitive technical development, where the production of the necessaries of life requires physical work by a majority of the people to the point of total exhaustion. In our time of high technical development, with a reasonably equitable division of labor and adequate provisions for all, the individual would have both time and strength to participate receptively and productively in the finest intellectual and artistic efforts his abilities and inclinations allowed. Unfortunately nothing approaching such conditions exist in our society. But everyone devoted to the specific European ideals will do his utmost to achieve aims of whose desirability and practicability an increasing number of right-minded persons are convinced.

Is it justifiable to set aside for a time the principles of individual freedom in deference to the high endeavor to improve economic organization? A fine and shrewd Russian scholar very skilfully defended this point of view to me in comparing the success of compulsion and terror—at least at the outset—in a functioning Russian Communism with the failure of German Social Democracy after the war. He did not convince me. No purpose is so high that unworthy methods in achieving it can be justified in my eyes. Violence sometimes may have cleared away obstructions quickly, but it never has proved itself creative.

30

AT A GATHERING FOR
FREEDOM OF OPINION

W<small>E HAVE COME HERE TODAY</small> to defend the freedom of opinion guaranteed by the Constitution of the United States, and also in defense of the freedom of teaching. By the same token we wish to draw the attention of intellectual workers to the great danger that now menaces these liberties.

How is such a thing possible? Why is the danger more menacing than in years gone by? The centralization of production has brought about a concentration of productive capital in the hands of a relatively small number of the citizens of the land. This small group exerts an overwhelming domination over the institutions for the education of our youth as well as over the great newspapers of the country. At the same time it wields enormous influences on the government. This in itself is already sufficient to constitute a serious menace to the intellectual freedom of the nation. But there is the additional fact that this process of economic concentration has given birth to a problem previously unknown—permanent unemployment for part of those who are able to work. The federal government is endeavoring to solve this problem by systematic control over economic processes—that is to say, by a limitation of the so-called free interplay of the fundamental economic forces of supply and demand.

But circumstances are stronger than men. The dominant economic minority, heretofore autonomous and responsible to no one, has placed itself in opposition to this limitation of

371

its freedom of action, demanded for the good of the whole people. For its defense this minority is resorting to every known legal method at its disposal. We need not, therefore, be surprised that they are using their preponderant influence on the schools and the press to prevent youth from being enlightened on this problem which is so vital to the sound and peaceful development of life in this country.

It is for this reason that of late we have had to witness repeatedly the dismissal of worthy university teachers against the will of their colleagues, actions of which the press has informed the public but inadequately. It is also to the pressure of this economically dominant minority that we owe the unhappy institution of the teacher's oath, which is meant to diminish the freedom of teaching. I need not dwell on the point that freedom of teaching and of opinion in book or press is the foundation for the sound and natural development of any people. The lessons of history—especially the very latest chapters—are all too plain on this score. It is the bounden duty of everyone to stand with every ounce of energy for the preservation and enhancement of these liberties and to exert all possible influence in keeping public opinion aware of the existing danger.

These difficulties can be solved only when our great economic problem is solved in a democratic manner; but the groundwork for such a solution must be prepared by preserving freedom of expression. This, moreover, is also the only method by which the worst damage can be prevented.

Let all of us therefore summon our strength. Let us be tirelessly on guard, lest it be said later of the intellectual elite of this land: Timidly and without a struggle they surrendered the heritage handed down to them by their forefathers—a heritage of which they were not worthy.

31

ATOMIC WAR OR PEACE

I

THE RELEASE OF ATOMIC ENERGY has not created a new problem. It has merely made more urgent the necessity of solving an existing one. One could say that it has affected us quantitatively, not qualitatively. As long as there are sovereign nations possessing great power, war is inevitable. That is not an attempt to say when it will come, but only that it is sure to come. That was true before the atomic bomb was made. What has been changed is the destructiveness of war.

I do not believe that civilization will be wiped out in a war fought with the atomic bomb. Perhaps two-thirds of the people of the earth might be killed. But enough men capable of thinking, and enough books, would be left to start again, and civilization could be restored.

I do not believe that the secret of the bomb should be given to the United Nations Organization. I do not believe it should be given to the Soviet Union. Either course would be like a man with capital, and wishing another man to work with him on some enterprise, starting out by simply giving that man half of his money. The other man might choose to start a rival enterprise, when what is wanted is his cooperation. The secret of the bomb should be committed to a world government, and the United States should immediately announce its readiness to give it to a world government. This government should be founded by the United States, the Soviet Union and Great Britain, the only three powers with great military strength. All three of them should commit to this world government all of their military strength. The fact that there are only three nations with great military power should make it easier, rather than harder, to establish such a government.

Since the United States and Great Britain have the secret of the atomic bomb and the Soviet Union does not, they should invite the Soviet Union to prepare and present the first draft of a constitution of the proposed world government. That will help dispel the distrust of the Russians, which they already feel because the bomb is being kept a secret chiefly to prevent their having it. Obviously the first draft would not be the final one, but the Russians should be made to feel that the world government will assure them their security.

It would be wise if this constitution were to be negotiated by a single American, a single Briton and a single Russian. They would have to have advisers, but these advisers should only advise when asked. I believe three men can succeed in writing a workable constitution acceptable to them all. Six or seven men, or more, probably would fail. After the three great powers have drafted a constitution and adopted it, the smaller nations should be invited to join the world government. They should be free to stay out, and though they should feel perfectly secure in staying out, I am sure they would wish to join. Naturally they should be entitled to propose changes in the constitution as drafted by the Big Three. But the Big Three should go ahead and organize the world government, whether the smaller nations join or not.

The power of this world government would be over all military matters, and there need be only one further power. That is to interfere in countries where a minority is oppressing a majority, and so is creating the kind of instability that leads to war. Conditions such as exist in Argentina and Spain should be dealt with. There must be an end to the concept of non-intervention, for to end it is part of keeping the peace.

The establishment of this world government must not have to wait until the same conditions of freedom are to be found in all three of the great powers. While it is true that in the Soviet Union the minority rules, I do not consider that internal conditions there are of themselves a threat to world peace. One must bear in mind that the people in Russia did not have a long political education, and changes to improve Russian conditions had to be carried through by a minority for the reason that there was no majority capable of doing it. If I had been born a Russian, I believe I could have adjusted myself to this situation.

It should not be necessary, in establishing a world government with a monopoly of military authority, to change the structure of the three great powers. It would be for the three individuals who draft the constitution to devise ways for their different structures to be fitted together for collaboration.

Do I fear the tyranny of a world government? Of course I do. But I fear still more the coming of another war or wars. Any government is certain to be evil to some extent. But a world government is preferable to the far greater evil of wars, particularly with their intensified destructiveness. If such a world government is not established by a process of agreement, I believe it will come anyway, and in a much more dangerous form. For war or wars will end in one power being supreme and dominating the rest of the world by its overwhelming military strength.

Now we have the atomic secret, we must not lose it, and that is what we should risk doing, if we give it to the United Nations Organization or to the Soviet Union. But we must make it clear as quickly as possible that we are not keeping the bomb a secret for the sake of our power, but in the hope of establishing peace through a world government, and we will do our utmost to bring this world government into being.

I appreciate that there are persons who favor a gradual

approach to world government, even though they approve of it as the ultimate objective. The trouble with taking little steps, one at a time, in the hope of reaching the ultimate goal, is that while they are being taken, we continue to keep the bomb without making our reason convincing to those who do not have it. That of itself creates fear and suspicion, with the consequence that the relations of rival sovereignties deteriorate dangerously. So while persons who take only a step at a time may think they are approaching world peace, they actually are contributing by their slow pace to the coming of war. We have no time to spend in this way. If war is to be averted, it must be done quickly.

We shall not have the secret very long. I know it is argued that no other country has money enough to spend on the development of the atomic bomb, which assures us the secret for a long time. It is a mistake often made in this country to measure things by the amount of money they cost. But other countries which have the materials and the men and care to apply them to the work of developing atomic power can do so, for men and materials and the decision to use them, and not money, are all that are needed.

I do not consider myself the father of the release of atomic energy. My part in it was quite indirect. I did not, in fact, foresee that it would be released in my time. I believed only that it was theoretically possible. It became practical through the accidental discovery of chain reaction, and this was not something I could have predicted. It was discovered by Hahn in Berlin, and he himself misinterpreted what he discovered. It was Lize Meitner who provided the correct interpretation, and escaped from Germany to place the information in the hands of Niels Bohr.

I do not believe that a great era of atomic science is to be assured by organizing science, in the way large corporations are organized. One can organize to apply a discovery already made, but not to make one. Only a free individual can make a discovery. There can be a kind of organizing by which scientists are assured their freedom and proper conditions of work. Professors of science in American universities, for instance, should be relieved of some of their teaching so as to have time for more research. Can you imagine an organization of scientists making the discoveries of Charles Darwin?

Nor do I believe that the vast private corporations of the United States are suitable to the needs of these times. If a visitor should come to this country from another planet, would he not find it strange that in this country so much power is permitted to private corporations without their having commensurate responsibility? I say this to stress that the American government must keep the control of atomic energy, not because socialism is necessarily desirable, but because atomic energy was developed by the government, and it would be unthinkable to turn over this property of the people to any individuals or groups of individuals. As to socialism, unless it is international to the extent of producing world government which controls all military power, it might more easily lead to wars than capitalism, because it represents a still greater concentration of power.

To give any estimate when atomic energy can be applied to constructive purposes is impossible. What now is known is only how to use a fairly large quantity of uranium. The use of small quantities, sufficient, say, to operate a car or an airplane, so far is impossible, and one cannot predict when it will be achieved. No doubt, it will be achieved, but nobody can say when. Nor can one predict when materials more common than uranium can be used to supply atomic energy. Presumably all materials used for this purpose will be among the heavier elements of high atomic weight. Those elements are relatively scarce due to their lesser stability. Most of these materials may have already disappeared by radio-active disintegration. So though the release of atomic energy can be, and no doubt will be, a great boon to mankind, that may not be for some time.

I myself do not have the gift of explanation with which I am able to persuade large numbers of people of the urgency of the problems the human race now faces. Hence I should like to commend someone who has this gift of explanation, Emery Reves, whose book, *The Anatomy of the Peace*, is intelligent, clear, brief, and, if I may use the abused term, dynamic on the topic of war and need for world government.

Since I do not foresee that atomic energy is to be a great boon for a long time, I have to say that for the present it is a menace. Perhaps it is well that it should be. It may intimidate the human race to bring order into its international affairs, which, without the pressure of fear, it undoubtedly would not do.

II

Since the completion of the first atomic bomb nothing has been accomplished to make the world more safe from war, while much has been done to increase the destructiveness of war. I am not able to speak from any firsthand knowledge about the development of the atomic bomb, since I do not work in this field. But enough has been said by those who do to indicate that the bomb has been made more effective. Certainly the possibility can be envisaged of building a bomb of far greater size, capable of producing destruction over a larger area. It also is credible that an extensive use could be made of radioactivated gases which would spread over a wide region, causing heavy loss of life without damage to buildings.

I do not believe it is necessary to go on beyond these possibilities to contemplate a vast extension of bacteriological warfare. I am skeptical that this form presents dangers comparable with those of atomic warfare. Nor do I take into account a danger of starting a chain reaction of a scope great enough to destroy part or all of this planet. I dismiss this on the ground that if it could happen from a man-made atomic explosion it would already have happened from the action of the cosmic rays which are continually reaching the earth's surface.

But it is not necessary to imagine the earth being destroyed like a nova by a stellar explosion to understand vividly the growing scope of atomic war and to recognize that unless another war is prevented it is likely to bring destruction on a scale never before held possible and even now hardly conceived, and that little civilization would survive it.

In the first two years of the atomic era another phenomenon is to be noted. The public, having been warned of the horrible nature of atomic warfare, has done nothing about it, and to a large extent has dismissed the warning from its consciousness. A danger that cannot be averted had perhaps better be forgotten; or a danger against which every possible precaution has been taken also had probably better be forgotten. That is, if the United States had dispersed its industries and decentralized its cities, it might be reasonable for people to forget the peril they face.

I should say parenthetically that it is well that this country has not taken these precautions, for to have done so would make atomic war still more probable, since it would convince the rest of the world that we are resigned to it and are preparing for it. But nothing has been done to avert war, while much has been done to make atomic war more horrible; so there is no excuse for ignoring the danger.

I say that nothing has been done to avert war since the completion of the atomic bomb, despite the proposal for supranational control of atomic energy put forward by the United States in the United Nations. This country has made only a conditional proposal, and on conditions which the Soviet Union is now determined not to accept. This makes it possible to blame the failure on the Russians.

But in blaming the Russians the Americans should not ignore the fact that they themselves have not voluntarily renounced the use of the bomb as an ordinary weapon in the time before the achievement of supranational control, or if supranational control is not achieved. Thus they have fed the fear of other countries that they consider the bomb a legitimate part of their arsenal so long as other countries decline to accept their terms for supranational control.

Americans may be convinced of their determination not to launch an aggressive or preventive war. So they may believe it is superfluous to announce publicly that they will not a second time be the first to use the atomic bomb. But this country has been solemnly invited to renounce the use of the bomb—that is, to outlaw it—and has declined to do so unless its terms for supranational control are accepted.

I believe this policy is a mistake. I see a certain military gain from not renouncing the use of the bomb in that this may be deemed to restrain another country from starting a war in which the United States might use it. But what is gained in one way is lost in another. For an understanding over the supranational control of atomic energy has been made more remote. That may be no military drawback so long as the United States has the exclusive use of the bomb. But the moment another country is able to make it in substantial quantities, the United States loses greatly through the absence of an international agreement, because of the vulnerability of its concentrated industries and its highly developed urban life.

In refusing to outlaw the bomb while having the monopoly of it, this country suffers in another respect, in that it fails to return publicly to the ethical standards of warfare formally accepted previous to the last war. It should not be forgotten that the atomic bomb was made in this country as a preventive measure; it was to head off its use by the Germans, if they discovered it. The bombing of civilian centers was initiated by the Germans and adopted by the Japanese. To it the

Allies responded in kind—as it turned out, with greater effectiveness—and they were morally justified in doing so. But now, without any provocation, and without the justification of reprisal or retaliation, a refusal to outlaw the use of the bomb save in reprisal is making a political purpose of its possession. This is hardly pardonable.

I am not saying that the United States should not manufacture and stockpile the bomb, for I believe that it must do so; it must be able to deter another nation from making an atomic attack when it also has the bomb. But deterrence should be the only purpose of the stockpile of bombs. In the same way I believe that the United Nations should have the atomic bomb when it is supplied with its own armed forces and weapons. But it too should have the bomb for the sole purpose of deterring an aggressor or rebellious nations from making an atomic attack. It should not use the atomic bomb on its own initiative any more than the United States or any other power should do so. To keep a stockpile of atomic bombs without promising not to initiate its use is exploiting the possession of the bombs for political ends. It may be that the United States hopes in this way to frighten the Soviet Union into accepting supranational control of atomic energy. But the creation of fear only heightens antagonism and increases the danger of war. I am of the opinion that this policy has detracted from the very real virtue in the offer of supranational control of atomic energy.

We have emerged from a war in which we had to accept the degradingly low ethical standards of the enemy. But instead of feeling liberated from his standards, and set free to restore the sanctity of human life and the safety of noncombatants, we are in effect making the low standards of the enemy in the last war our own for the present. Thus we are starting toward another war degraded by our own choice.

It may be that the public is not fully aware that in another war atomic bombs will be available in large quantities. It may measure the dangers in the terms of the three bombs exploded before the end of the last war. The public also may not appreciate that, in relation to the damage inflicted, atomic bombs already have become the most economical form of destruction that can be used on the offensive. In another war the bombs will be plentiful and they will be comparatively cheap. Unless there is a determination not to use them that is far stronger than can be noted today among American political and military leaders, and on the part of the public itself, atomic warfare will be hard to avoid. Unless Americans come to recognize that they are not stronger in the world because they have the bomb, but weaker because of their vulnerability to atomic attack, they are not likely to conduct their policy at Lake Success or in their relations with Russia in a spirit that furthers the arrival at an understanding.

But I do not suggest that the American failure to outlaw the use of the bomb except in retaliation is the only cause of the absence of an agreement with the Soviet Union over atomic control. The Russians have made it clear that they will do everything in their power to prevent a supranational regime from coming into existence. They not only reject it in the range of atomic energy: they reject it sharply on principle, and thus have spurned in advance any overture to join a limited world government.

Mr. Gromyko has rightly said that the essence of the American atomic proposal is that national sovereignty is not compatible with the atomic era. He declares that the Soviet Union cannot accept this thesis. The reasons he gives are obscure, for they quite obviously are pretexts. But what seems to be true is that the Soviet leaders believe they cannot preserve the social structure of the Soviet state in a supranational regime. The Soviet government is determined to maintain its present social structure, and the leaders of Russia, who hold their great power through the nature of that structure, will spare no effort to prevent a supranational regime from coming into existence, to control atomic energy or anything else.

The Russians may be partly right about the difficulty of retaining their present social structure in a supranational regime, though in time they may be brought to see that this is a far lesser loss than remaining isolated from a world of law. But at present they appear to be guided by their fears, and one must admit that the United States has made ample contributions to these fears, not only as to atomic energy but in many other respects. Indeed this country has conducted its Russian policy as though it were convinced that fear is the greatest of all diplomatic instruments.

That the Russians are striving to prevent the formation of a supranational security system is no reason why the rest of the world should not work to create one. It has been pointed out that the Russians have a way of resisting with all their arts what they do not wish to have happen; but once it happens, they can be flexible and accommodate themselves to it. So it would be well for the United States and other powers not to permit the Russians to veto an attempt to create supranational security. They can proceed with some hope that once the Russians see they cannot prevent such a regime they may join it.

So far the United States has shown no interest in preserving the security of the Soviet Union. It has been interested in its own security, which is characteristic of the competition which marks the conflict for power between sovereign states. But one cannot know in advance what would be the effect on Russian fears if the American people forced their leaders to pursue a policy of substituting law for the present anarchy of international relations. In a world of law, Russian security would be equal to our own, and for the American people to espouse this wholeheartedly, something that should be possible under the workings of democracy, might work a kind of miracle in Russian thinking.

At present the Russians have no evidence to convince them that the American people are not contentedly supporting a policy of military preparedness which they regard as a policy of deliberate intimidation. If they had evidences of a passionate desire by Americans to preserve peace in the one way it can be maintained, by a supranational regime of law, this would upset Russian calculations about the peril to Russian security in current trends of American thought. Not until a genuine, convincing offer is made to the Soviet Union, backed by an aroused American public, will one be entitled to say what the Russian response would be.

It may be that the first response would be to reject the world of law. But if from that moment it began to be clear to the Russians that such a world was coming into existence without them, and that their own security was being increased, their ideas necessarily would change.

I am in favor of inviting the Russians to join a world government authorized to provide security, and if they are unwilling to join, to proceed to establish supranational security without them. Let me admit quickly that I see great peril in such a course. If it is adopted it must be done in a way to make it utterly clear that the new regime is not a combination of power against Russia. It must be a combination that by its composite nature will greatly reduce the chances of war. It will be more diverse in its interests than any single state, thus less likely to resort to aggressive or preventive war. It will be larger, hence stronger than any single nation. It will be geographically much more extensive, and thus more difficult to defeat by military means. It will be dedicated to supranational security, and thus escape the emphasis on national supremacy which is so strong a factor in war.

If a supranational regime is set up without Russia, its service to peace will depend on the skill and sincerity with which it is done. Emphasis should always be apparent on the desire to have Russia take part. It must be clear to Russia, and no less so to the nations comprising the organization, that no penalty is incurred or implied because a nation declines to join. If the Russians do not join at the outset, they must be sure of a welcome when they do decide to join. Those who create the organization must understand that they are building with the final objective of obtaining Russian adherence.

These are abstractions, and it is not easy to outline the specific lines a partial world government must follow to induce the Russians to join. But two conditions are clear to me: the new organization must have no military secrets; and the Russians must be free to have observers at every session of the organization, where its new laws are drafted, discussed, and adopted, and where its policies are decided. That would destroy the great factory of secrecy where so many of the world's suspicions are manufactured.

It may affront the military-minded person to suggest a regime that does not maintain any military secrets. He has been taught to believe that secrets thus divulged would enable a war-minded nation to seek to conquer the earth. (As to the so-called secret of the atomic bomb, I am assuming the Russians will have this through their own efforts within a short time.) I grant there is a risk in not maintaining military secrets. If a sufficient number of nations have pooled their strength they can take this risk, for their security will be greatly increased. And it can be done with greater assurance because of the decrease of fear, suspicion, and distrust that will result. The tensions of the increasing likelihood of war in a world based on sovereignty would be replaced by the relaxation of the growing confidence in peace. In time this might so allure the Russian people that their leaders would mellow in their attitude toward the West.

Membership in a supranational security system should not, in my opinion, be based on any arbitrary democratic standards. The one requirement from all should be that the representatives to supranational organization—assembly and council—must be elected by the people in each member country through a secret ballot. These representatives must represent the people rather than any government—which would enhance the pacific nature of the organization.

To require that other democratic criteria be met is, I believe, inadvisable. Democratic institutions and standards are the result of historic developments to an extent not always appreciated in the lands which enjoy them. Setting arbitrary standards sharpens the ideological differences between the Western and Soviet systems.

But it is not the ideological differences which now are pushing the world in the direction of war. Indeed, if all the Western nations were to adopt socialism, while maintaining their national sovereignty, it is quite likely that the conflict for power between East and West would continue. The passion expressed over the economic systems of the present seems to me quite irrational. Whether the economic life of America should be dominated by relatively few individuals, as it is, or these individuals should be controlled by the state, may be important, but it is not important enough to justify all the feelings that are stirred up over it.

I should wish to see all the nations forming the supranational state pool all their military forces, keeping for themselves only local police. Then I should like to see these forces commingled and distributed as were the regiments of the former Austro-Hungarian Empire. There it was appreciated that the men and officers of one region would serve the purposes of empire better by not being stationed exclusively in their own provinces, subject to local and racial pulls.

I should like to see the authority of the supranational regime restricted altogether to the field of security. Whether this would be possible I am not sure. Experience may point to the desirability of adding some authority over economic matters, since under modern conditions these are capable of causing national upsets that have in them the seeds of violent conflict. But I should prefer to see the function of the organization altogether limited to the tasks of security. I also should like to see this regime established through the strengthening of the United Nations, so as not to sacrifice continuity in the search for peace.

I do not hide from myself the great difficulties of establishing a world government, either a beginning without Russia or one with Russia. I am aware of the risks. Since I should not wish it to be permissible for any country that has joined the supranational organization to secede, one of these risks is a possible civil war. But I also believe that world government is certain to come in time, and that the question is how much it is to be permitted to cost. It will come, I believe, even if there is another world war, though after such a war, if it is won, it would be world government established by the victor, resting on the victor's military power, and thus to be maintained permanently only through the permanent militarization of the human race.

But I also believe it can come through agreement and through the force of persuasion alone, hence at low cost. But if it is to come in this way it will not be enough to appeal to reason. One strength of the communist system of the East is that it has some of the character of a religion and inspires the emotions of a religion. Unless the cause of peace based on law gathers behind it the force and zeal of a religion, it hardly can hope to succeed. Those to whom the moral teaching of the human race is entrusted surely have a great duty and a great opportunity. The atomic scientists, I think, have become convinced that they cannot arouse the American people to the truths of the atomic era by logic alone. There must be added that deep power of emotion which is a basic ingredient of religion. It is to be hoped that not only the churches but the schools, the colleges, and the leading organs of opinion will acquit themselves well of their unique responsibility in this regard.

32

THE WAR IS WON BUT
PEACE IS NOT

Pʜʏsɪcɪsᴛs ꜰɪɴᴅ ᴛʜᴇᴍsᴇʟᴠᴇs in a position not unlike that of Alfred Nobel. Alfred Nobel invented the most powerful explosive ever known up to his time, a means of destruction par excellence. In order to atone for this, in order to relieve his human conscience he instituted his awards for the promotion of peace and for achievements of peace. Today, the physicists who participated in forging the most formidable and dangerous weapon of all times are harassed by an equal feeling of responsibility, not to say guilt. And we cannot desist from warning, and warning again, we cannot and should not slacken in our efforts to make the nations of the world, and especially their governments, aware of the unspeakable disaster they are certain to provoke unless they change their attitude toward each other and toward the task of shaping the future. We helped in creating this new weapon in order to prevent the enemies of mankind from achieving it ahead of us, which, given the mentality of the Nazis, would have meant inconceivable destruction and the enslavement of the rest of the world. We delivered this weapon into the hands of the American and the British people as trustees of the whole of mankind, as fighters for peace and liberty. But so far we fail to see any guarantee of peace, we do not see any guarantee of the freedoms that were promised to the nations in the Atlantic Charter. The war is won, but the peace is not. The great powers, united in fighting, are now divided over the peace settlements. The world was promised freedom from fear, but in fact fear has increased tremendously since the termination of the war. The world was promised freedom from want, but large parts of the world are faced with starvation while others are living in abundance. The nations were promised liberation and justice. But we have witnessed, and are witnessing even now, the sad spectacle of "liberating" armies firing into populations who want their independence and social equality, and supporting in those countries, by force of arms, such parties and personalities as appear to be most suited to serve vested interests. Territorial questions and arguments of power, obsolete though they are, still prevail over the essential demands of common welfare and justice. Allow me to be more specific about just one case, which is but a symptom of the general situation: the case of my own people, the Jewish people.

As long as Nazi violence was unleashed only, or mainly, against the Jews the rest of the world looked on passively, and even treaties and agreements were made with the patently criminal government of the Third Reich. Later, when Hitler was on the point of taking over Rumania and Hungary, at the time when Maidanek and Oswiecim were in Allied hands, and the methods of the gas chambers were well known all over the world, all attempts to rescue the Rumanian and Hungarian Jews came to naught because the doors of Palestine were closed to Jewish immigrants by the British government, and no country could be found that would admit those forsaken people. They were left to perish like their brothers and sisters in the occupied countries.

We shall never forget the heroic efforts of the small countries, of the Scandinavian, the Dutch, the Swiss nations, and of individuals in the occupied parts of Europe who did all in their power to protect Jewish lives. We do not forget the humane attitude of the Soviet Union who was the only one among the big powers to open her doors to hundreds of thousands of Jews when the Nazi armies were advancing in Poland. But after all that has happened, and was not prevented from happening, how is it today? While in Europe territories are being distributed without any qualms about the wishes of the people concerned, the remainders of European Jewry, one fifth of its pre-war population, are again denied access to their haven in Palestine and left to hunger and cold and persisting hostility. There is no country, even today, that would be willing or able to offer them a place where they could live in peace and security. And the fact that many of them are still kept in the degrading conditions of concentration camps by the Allies gives sufficient evidence of the shamefulness and hopelessness of the situation. These people are forbidden to enter Palestine with reference to the principle of democracy, but actually the Western powers, in upholding the ban of the White Paper, are yielding to the threats and the external pressure of five vast and underpopulated Arab States. It is sheer irony when the British Foreign Minister tells the poor lot of European Jews they should remain in Europe because their genius is needed there, and, on the other hand, advises them not to try to get at the head of the queue lest they might incur new hatred and persecution. Well, I am afraid, they cannot help it; with their six million dead they have been pushed at the head of the queue, of the queue of Nazi victims, much against their will.

The picture of our postwar world is not bright. As far as we, the physicists, are concerned, we are no politicians and it has never been our wish to meddle in politics. But we know a few things that the politicians do not know. And we feel the duty to speak up and to remind those responsible that there is no escape into easy comforts, there is no distance ahead for proceeding little by little and delaying the necessary changes into an indefinite future, there is no time left for petty bargaining. The situation calls for a courageous effort, for a radical change in our whole attitude, in the entire political concept. May the spirit that prompted Alfred Nobel to create his great institution, the spirit of trust and confidence, of generosity and brotherhood among men, prevail in the minds of those upon whose decisions our destiny rests. Otherwise human civilization will be doomed.

33

THE MENACE OF MASS
DESTRUCTION

E VERYONE IS AWARE OF the difficult and menacing situation
in which human society—shrunk into one community with a
common fate—finds itself, but only a few act accordingly.
Most people go on living their every-day life: half frightened,
half indifferent, they behold the ghostly tragi-comedy that is
being performed on the international stage before the eyes
and ears of the world. But on that stage, on which the actors
under the floodlights play their ordained parts, our fate of
tomorrow, life or death of the nations, is being decided.

It would be different if the problem were not one of things
made by Man himself, such as the atomic bomb and other
means of mass destruction equally menacing all peoples. It
would be different, for instance, if an epidemic of bubonic
plague were threatening the entire world. In such a case conscientious and expert persons would be brought together and
they would work out an intelligent plan to combat the plague.
After having reached agreement upon the right ways and
means, they would submit their plan to the governments.
Those would hardly raise serious objections but rather agree
speedily on the measures to be taken. They certainly would
never think of trying to handle the matter in such a way that
their own nation would be spared whereas the next one
would be decimated.

But could not our situation be compared to one of a

menacing epidemic? People are unable to view this situation
in its true light, for their eyes are blinded by passion. General fear and anxiety create hatred and aggressiveness. The
adaptation to warlike aims and activities has corrupted the
mentality of man; as a result, intelligent, objective and humane thinking has hardly any effect and is even suspected
and persecuted as unpatriotic.

There are, no doubt, in the opposite camps enough people
of sound judgment and sense of justice who would be capable
and eager to work out together a solution for the factual
difficulties. But the efforts of such people are hampered by
the fact that it is made impossible for them to come together
for informal discussions. I am thinking of persons who are
accustomed to the objective approach to a problem and who
will not be confused by exaggerated nationalism or other
passions. This forced separation of the people of both camps
I consider one of the major obstacles to the achievement of
an acceptable solution of the burning problem of international security.

As long as contact between the two camps is limited to the
official negotiations I can see little prospect for an intelligent
agreement being reached, especially since considerations of
national prestige as well as the attempt to talk out of the
window for the benefit of the masses are bound to make
reasonable progress almost impossible. What one party suggests officially is for that reason alone suspected and even
made unacceptable to the other. Also behind all official negotiations stands—though veiled—the threat of naked power.
The official method can lead to success only after spade-work
of an informal nature has prepared the ground; the conviction that a mutually satisfactory solution can be reached
must be gained first; then the actual negotiations can get
under way with a fair promise of success.

We scientists believe that what we and our fellow-men do
or fail to do within the next few years will determine the fate

of our civilization. And we consider it our task untiringly to explain this truth, to help people realize all that is at stake, and to work, not for appeasement, but for understanding and ultimate agreement between peoples and nations of different views.

34

THE SCHOOLS AND THE
PROBLEM OF PEACE

BY VIRTUE OF ITS GEOGRAPHIC situation the United States is
in the fortunate position of being able to teach a rational
pacifism in its schools, without having to fear for its security.
For there is no serious danger of a military attack from the
outside, and as a result no compulsion to educate youth in a
military spirit. On the other hand there is the danger of treating this problem purely from the emotional point of view. Yet
little is gained by mere wishful thinking, without a clear
grasp of the essential difficulties of the problem.

In the first place it ought to be made clear to youth that
the United States may be at any time drawn into military
involvements, even though a direct attack on the country
need scarcely be feared. Mere reference to America's participation in the last World War is sufficient proof of this. Even
Americans can hope for true security against being drawn
into military involvements only from a satisfactory solution
of the problem of peace in general. It is necessary to warn
against the view that political isolation of the United States
from the outside can result in adequate security for Americans. Instead a serious interest in an international solution
of the problem of peace must be awakened among young
people. In particular must youth be given a clear understanding of the grave responsibility which American politicians
have assumed by failing to support Wilson's grandly con-

ceived plans after peace was concluded, thus impairing the effectiveness of the League of Nations.

It must be pointed out that the mere demand for disarmament is futile, so long as there are great nations who are prepared to attain their future position in the world by means of military expansion. The reasonableness of the position represented by France, for example—namely that the security of the individual countries must be insured by international institutions—must be set forth. To achieve such security international treaties for common defense against those who break the peace are necessary but not sufficient. Instead, military defense resources must become internationalized by amalgamation and exchange of forces on a grand scale to such an extent that the military forces stationed in any one country cannot possibly be used exclusively for the purpose of pursuing the goals of that country.

To prepare the nations for such effective insurance of the peace, this vital problem should be clearly and sharply brought to the attention of young people. The spirit of international solidarity too should be strengthened and national chauvinism combatted as a harmful force impeding progress.

Schools ought to be intent on presenting history from the point of view of progress and the growth of human civilization, rather than using it as a means for fostering in the minds of the growing generation the ideals of outward power and military successes. In my opinion the use of H. G. Wells' *World History* should be highly recommended from this aspect.

It is of indirect yet nevertheless considerable importance, finally, that in the teaching of geography and history a sympathetic understanding be fostered for the characteristics of the different peoples of the world, especially for those whom we are in the habit of describing as "primitive."

35

ON MILITARY SERVICE

I STAND FIRMLY BY THE PRINCIPLE that a real solution of the problem of pacifism can be achieved only by the organization of a supranational court of arbitration, which, differing from the present League of Nations in Geneva, would have at its disposal the means of enforcing its decisions. In short, an international court of justice with a permanent military establishment, or better, police force. An excellent expression of this conviction of mine is contained in Lord Davies' book, *Force* (London, Ernst Benn, Ltd., 1934), the reading of which I strongly recommend to everyone who is seriously concerned with this fundamental problem of mankind.

Taking as starting point this fundamental conviction, I stand for every measure which appears to me capable of bringing mankind nearer to this goal. Up to a few years ago, the refusal to bear arms by courageous and self-sacrificing persons *was* such a measure; it is no longer—especially in Europe—a means to be recommended. When the great Powers had nearly equally democratic governments, and when none of these Powers founded its future plans on military aggression, the refusal to do military service on the part of a fairly large number of citizens might have induced the governments of these Powers to look favorably on international legal arbitration. Moreover, such refusals were apt to educate public opinion to real pacifism. The public came to consider as oppression any pressure brought by the State upon its citizens to force them to fulfil their military obligations, besides considering such pressure unethical from the moral standpoint.

Under these circumstances, such refusals worked for the highest good.

Today, however, we are brought face to face with the fact that powerful States make independent opinions in politics impossible for their citizens, and lead their own people into error through the systematic diffusion of false information. At the same time, these States become a menace to the rest of the world by creating military organizations which encompass their entire population. This false information is spread by a muzzled press, a centralized radio service, and school education ruled by an aggressive foreign policy. In States of that description, refusal to perform military service means martyrdom and death for those courageous enough to object. In those States in which citizens still cling to some of their political rights, refusal to do military service means weakening the power of resistance of the remaining sane portions of the civilized world.

Because of this, no reasonable human being would today favor the refusal to do military service, at least not in Europe, which is at present particularly beset with dangers.

I do not believe that under present circumstances passive resistance is an effective method, even if carried out in the most heroic manner. Other times, other means, even if the final aim remains the same.

The confirmed pacifist must therefore at present seek a plan of action different from that of former, more peaceful times. He must try to work for this aim: That those States which favor peaceful progress may come as close together as possible in order to diminish the likelihood that the warlike programs of political adventurers whose States are founded on violence and brigandage will be realized. I have in mind, in the first place, well-considered and permanent concerted action on the part of the United States and the British Empire, together with France and Russia when possible.

Perhaps the present danger will facilitate this *rapproche-*

ment and thus bring about a pacifistic solution of international problems. This would be the hopeful side to the present dark situation; here consistent action can contribute much toward influencing public opinion in the right direction.

36

MILITARY INTRUSION IN SCIENCE

THE MILITARY MENTALITY

It seems to me that the decisive point in the situation lies in the fact that the problem before us cannot be viewed as an isolated one. First of all, one may pose the following question: From now on institutions for learning and research will more and more have to be supported by grants from the state, since, for various reasons, private sources will not suffice. Is it at all reasonable that the distribution of the funds raised for these purposes from the taxpayer should be entrusted to the military? To this question every prudent person will certainly answer: "No!" For it is evident that the difficult task of the most beneficent distribution should be placed in the hands of people whose training and life's work give proof that they know something about science and scholarship.

If reasonable people, nevertheless, favor military agencies for the distribution of a major part of the available funds, the reason for this lies in the fact that they subordinate cultural concerns to their general political outlook. We must then focus our attention on these practical political viewpoints, their origins and their implications. In doing so we shall soon recognize that the problem here under discussion is but one of many, and can only be fully estimated and properly adjudged when placed in a broader framework.

The tendencies we have mentioned are something new for

OUT OF MY LATER YEARS

America. They arose when, under the influence of the two World Wars and the consequent concentration of all forces on a military goal, a predominantly military mentality developed, which with the almost sudden victory became even more accentuated. The characteristic feature of this mentality is that people place the importance of what Bertrand Russell so tellingly terms "naked power" far above all other factors which affect the relations between peoples. The Germans, misled by Bismarck's successes in particular, underwent just such a transformation of their mentality—in consequence of which they were entirely ruined in less than a hundred years.

I must frankly confess that the foreign policy of the United States since the termination of hostilities has reminded me, sometimes irresistibly, of the attitude of Germany under Kaiser Wilhelm II, and I know that, independent of me, this analogy has most painfully occurred to others as well. It is characteristic of the military mentality that non-human factors (atom bombs, strategic bases, weapons of all sorts, the possession of raw materials, etc.) are held essential, while the human being, his desires and thoughts—in short, the psychological factors—are considered as unimportant and secondary. Herein lies a certain resemblance to Marxism, at least insofar as its theoretical side alone is kept in view. The individual is degraded to a mere instrument; he becomes "human materiel." The normal ends of human aspiration vanish with such a viewpoint. Instead, the military mentality raises "naked power" as a goal in itself—one of the strangest illusions to which men can succumb.

In our time the military mentality is still more dangerous than formerly because the offensive weapons have become much more powerful than the defensive ones. Therefore it leads, by necessity, to preventive war. The general insecurity that goes hand in hand with this results in the sacrifice of the citizen's civil rights to the supposed welfare of the state.

Political witch-hunting, controls of all sorts (e.g., control of teaching and research, of the press, and so forth) appear inevitable, and for this reason do not encounter that popular resistance, which, were it not for the military mentality, would provide a protection. A reappraisal of all values gradually takes place insofar as everything that does not clearly serve the utopian ends is regarded and treated as inferior.

I see no other way out of prevailing conditions than a far-seeing, honest and courageous policy with the aim of establishing security on supranational foundations. Let us hope that men will be found, sufficient in number and moral force, to guide the nation on this path so long as a leading role is imposed on her by external circumstances. Then problems such as have been discussed here will cease to exist.

37

INTERNATIONAL SECURITY

GEOGRAPHICALLY THE AMERICANS are without doubt in an especially favorable position, and menace to this country through military attack need not necessarily be given serious consideration. Nevertheless they manifest a real interest in the building up an international court of arbitration for the purpose of settling peaceably all international disputes or disagreements and with power to guarantee indemnities. The World War has shown the fate of the nations to be closely interwoven, and the world-wide economic crisis teaches us all the same.

Therefore it is essential that the American youth direct their energies to the end that the United States shall take active part in all efforts toward making international order a reality. It is obvious that the war and the post-war period have been a source of great concern to many Americans. It also follows that the continued policy of aloofness would not only injure all mankind, but harm the United States as well.

Personalities

38

ISAAC NEWTON

Reason, of course, is weak, when measured against its never-ending task. Weak, indeed, compared with the follies and passions of mankind, which, we must admit, almost entirely control our human destinies, in great things and small. Yet the works of the understanding outlast the noisy bustling generations and spread light and warmth across the centuries. Consoled by this thought let us turn, in these unquiet days, to the memory of Newton, who three hundred years ago was given to mankind.

To think of him is to think of his work. For such a man can be understood only by thinking of him as a scene on which the struggle for eternal truth took place. Long before Newton there had been virile minds who conceived that it ought to be possible, by purely logical deduction from simple physical hypotheses, to make cogent explanations of phenomena perceptible to the senses. But Newton was the first to succeed in finding a clearly formulated basis from which he could deduce a wide field of phenomena by means of mathematical thinking, logically, quantitatively and in harmony with experience. Indeed, he might well hope that the fundamental basis of his mechanics would come in time to furnish the key to the understanding of all phenomena. So thought his pupils—with more assurance than he himself—and so his successors, up till the end of the eighteenth century. How did this miracle come to birth in his brain? Forgive me, reader, the illogical question. For if by reason we could deal with the problem of the "how," then there could be no question of a miracle in the proper sense of the word. It is the goal of every activity of the intellect to convert a "miracle" into something which it has grasped. If in this case the miracle permits itself to be converted, our admiration for the mind of Newton becomes only the greater thereby.

Galileo, by ingenious interpretation of the simplest facts of experience, had established the proposition: a body upon which no external force is at work permanently maintains its original velocity (and direction); if it alters its velocity (or the direction of its movement) the change must be referred to an external cause.

To utilize this knowledge quantitatively the conceptions velocity and rate of change of velocity—that is, acceleration in the case of any given motion of a body conceived as dimensionless (material point)—must first be interpreted with mathematical exactness. The task led Newton to invent the basis of differential and integral calculus.

This in itself was a creative achievement of the first order. But for Newton, as a physicist, it was simply the invention of a new kind of conceptual language which he needed in order to formulate the general laws of motion. For a given body he had now to put forward the hypothesis that his precisely formulated acceleration both in magnitude and direction was proportional to the force directed upon it. The coefficient of proportionality which characterizes the body with reference to its power of acceleration completely describes the (dimensionless) body with reference to its mechanical quality; thus was discovered the fundamental conception of mass.

All the foregoing might be described—though in the extremely modest manner of speaking—as an exact formulation of something the essence of which had already been recognized by Galileo. But it by no means succeeded in solving the main problem. In other words, the law of motion yields the movement of a body, only when the direction and magnitude of the force exerted upon it are known for all times.

Thus the problem reduced itself to another problem: how to find out the operative forces. To a mind any less bold than Newton's it must have seemed hopeless, considering the immeasurable multifarity of the effects which the bodies of a universe seem to produce upon each other. Moreover, the bodies whose motions we perceive are by no means dimensionless points—that is to say, perceptible as material points. How was Newton to deal with such chaos?

If we push a cart moving without friction on a horizontal plane it follows that the force we exert upon it is given directly. That is the ideal case from which the law of motion is derived. That we are not here dealing with a dimensionless point appears unessential.

How does it stand then with a falling body in space? A freely falling body behaves almost as simply as the dimensionless point, if one regards its movement as a whole. It is accelerated downwards. The acceleration, according to Galileo, is independent of its nature and its velocity. The earth, of course, must be decisive for the existence of this acceleration. It seemed, then, that the earth by its mere presence exerted a force upon the body. The earth consists of many parts. The idea seemed inevitable that each of these parts affects the falling body and that all these effects are combined. There seems then to be a force which bodies by their very presence exert upon each other through space. These forces seem to be independent of velocities, dependent only upon the relative position and quantitative property of the various bodies exerting them. This quantitative property might be conditioned by its mass, for the mass seems to characterize the body from the mechanical point of view. This strange effect of things at a distance may be called gravitation.

Now to gain precise knowledge of this effect, one has only to find out how strong is the force exerted upon each other by two bodies of given mass from a given distance. As for their direction, it would probably be no other than the line connecting them. Finally then, what remains unknown is only the dependence of this force upon the distance between the two bodies. But this one cannot know *a priori*. Here, only experience could be of use.

Such experience, however, was available to Newton. The acceleration of the moon was known from its orbit and could be compared with the acceleration of the freely falling body on the surface of the earth. Furthermore, the movements of the planets about the sun had been determined by Kepler with great exactness and comprehended in simple empirical laws. So it was possible to ascertain how the effects of gravitation coming from the earth and those coming from the sun depended on the factor of distance. Newton found that everything was explainable by a force which was inversely proportional to the square of the distance. And with that the goal was reached, the science of celestial mechanics was born, confirmed a thousand times over by Newton himself and those who came after him. But how about the rest of physics? Gravitation and the law of motion could not explain everything. What determined the equilibrium of the parts of a solid body? How was light to be explained, how electrical phenomena? By introducing material points and forces of various kinds acting at a distance, everything seemed in a fair way to be derivable from the law of motion.

That hope has not been fulfilled, and no one any longer believes in the solution of all our problems on this basis. Nevertheless, the thinking of physicists today is conditioned to a high degree by Newton's fundamental conceptions. It has so far not been possible to substitute for the Newtonian unified conception of the universe a similarly unified comprehensive conception. But what we have gained up till now would have been impossible without Newton's clear system.

From observation of the stars have chiefly come the intellectual tools indispensable to the development of modern

technique. For the abuse of the latter in our time creative
intellects like Newton's are as little responsible as the stars
themselves, contemplating which their thoughts took wing. It
is necessary to say this, because in our time esteem for intellectual values for their own sake is no longer so lively as it
was in the centuries of the intellectual renascence.

39

JOHANNES KEPLER

IN KEPLER'S LETTERS we find ourselves confronted with a sensitive personality, passionately devoted to the quest for deeper insight into the character of natural processes—a man who reached the exalted goal he set himself in spite of all internal and external difficulties. Kepler's life was devoted to the solution of a dual problem. The sun and the planets change their apparent position with reference to their background of fixed stars in a complex manner open to immediate observation. In other words, all the observations and records compiled with such care dealt not actually with the movements of the planets in space but with temporal shifts undergone by the direction earth-planet in the course of time.

Once Copernicus had convinced the small group capable of grasping it that in this process the sun must be regarded as being at rest, with the planets, including the earth, revolving about the sun, the first great problem proved to be this: to determine the true motions of the planets, including the earth, as they might be visible to an observer on the nearest fixed star who was equipped with a perfect stereoscopic double-telescope. This was Kepler's first great problem. The second problem was embodied in this question: What are the mathematical laws under which these motions proceed? It is plain that the solution of the second problem, if at all within reach of the human mind, was predicated on the solution of the first. Before a theory explaining a certain process can be tested, that process must first be known.

Kepler's solution of the first problem is based on a truly

inspired notion that made possible the determination of the true orbit of the earth. To construct that orbit, a second fixed point in planetary space, in addition to the sun, is required. When such a second point is available, it and the sun may both be used as points of reference for angular measurements, and the earth's true orbit can be determined by the same methods of triangulation that customarily serve in surveying and cartography.

But where was such a second fixed point to be found, since all visible objects, except the sun, themselves execute motions that are not known in detail? This was Kepler's answer: The apparent motions of the planet Mars are known with great accuracy, including the time of its revolution about the sun (the "Martian year"). It is probable that at the end of each Martian year Mars is at the same spot in (planetary) space. If we limit ourselves for the time being to these points in time, then the planet Mars represents for them a fixed point in planetary space, a point that may be used in triangulation.

Employing this principle, Kepler first of all determined the true motion of the earth in planetary space. Since the earth itself may be used as a point for triangulation at any time, he was also able to determine the true motions of the other planets from his observations.

This is how Kepler gained the basis for formulating the three fundamental laws with which his name will remain associated for all time to come. Today, after the fact, no one can fully appreciate how much ingenuity, how much hard and tireless work was required to discover these laws and ascertain them with such precision.

The reader ought to know this as he learns from the letters under what hardships Kepler accomplished this gigantic work. He refused to be paralyzed or discouraged either by poverty or by the lack of comprehension among those of his contemporaries who had the power to shape his life and

work. Yet he was dealing with a subject that offered immediate danger to him who professed the truth. But Kepler was
one of the few who are simply incapable of doing anything
but stand up openly for their convictions in every field. At
the same time he was not one who took undiluted pleasure in
personal controversy, as was plainly the case with Galileo,
whose inspired barbs delight the informed reader even today.
Kepler was a devout Protestant, but he made no secret of the
fact that he did not approve of all decisions by the Church.
He was, accordingly, regarded as a kind of moderate heretic
and treated as such.

This brings me to the inner difficulties Kepler had to overcome—difficulties at which I have already hinted. They are
not as readily perceived as the outward difficulties. Kepler's
lifework was possible only once he succeeded in freeing himself to a great extent of the intellectual traditions into which
he was born. This meant not merely the religious tradition,
based on the authority of the Church, but general concepts
on the nature and limitations of action within the universe
and the human sphere, as well as notions of the relative importance of thought and experience in science.

He had to rid himself of the animist approach in research,
a mode of thought oriented toward ulterior ends. He first had
to recognize that even the most lucidly logical mathematical
theory was of itself no guarantee of truth, becoming meaningless unless it was checked against the most exacting
observations in natural science. But for this philosophical
orientation Kepler's work would not have been possible. He
does not speak of it, but the inner struggle is reflected in his
letters. Let the reader watch out for remarks concerning
astrology. They show that the vanquished inner foe had been
rendered harmless, even though he was not yet altogether
dead.

40

MARIE CURIE IN MEMORIAM

AT A TIME WHEN a towering personality like Mme. Curie
has come to the end of her life, let us not merely rest content
with recalling what she has given to mankind in the fruits of
her work. It is the moral qualities of its leading personalities
that are perhaps of even greater significance for a generation
and for the course of history than purely intellectual accomplishments. Even these latter are, to a far greater degree than
is commonly credited, dependent on the stature of character.

It was my good fortune to be linked with Mme. Curie
through twenty years of sublime and unclouded friendship.
I came to admire her human grandeur to an ever growing
degree. Her strength, her purity of will, her austerity toward
herself, her objectivity, her incorruptible judgment—all these
were of a kind seldom found joined in a single individual.
She felt herself at every moment to be a servant of society
and her profound modesty never left any room for compla-
cency. She was oppressed by an abiding sense for the asper-
ities and inequities of society. This is what gave her that
severe outward aspect, so easily misinterpreted by those who
were not close to her—a curious severity unrelieved by any
artistic strain. Once she had recognized a certain way as the
right one, she pursued it without compromise and with extreme tenacity.

The greatest scientific deed of her life—proving the existence of radioactive elements and isolating them—owes its
accomplishment not merely to bold intuition but to a devotion and tenacity in execution under the most extreme hard-

415

ships imaginable, such as the history of experimental science has not often witnessed.

If but a small part of Mme. Curie's strength of character and devotion were alive in Europe's intellectuals, Europe would face a brighter future.

41

MAX PLANCK IN MEMORIAM

A MAN TO WHOM IT HAS been given to bless the world with a great creative idea has no need for the praise of posterity. His very achievement has already conferred a higher boon upon him.

Yet it is good—indeed, it is indispensable—that representatives of all who strive for truth and knowledge should be gathered here today from the four corners of the globe. They are here to bear witness that even in these times of ours, when political passion and brute force hang like swords over the anguished and fearful heads of men, the standard of our ideal search for truth is being held aloft undimmed. This ideal, a bond forever uniting scientists of all times and in all places, was embodied with rare completeness in Max Planck.

Even the Greeks had already conceived the atomistic nature of matter and the concept was raised to a high degree of probability by the scientists of the nineteenth century. But it was Planck's law of radiation that yielded the first exact determination—independent of other assumptions—of the absolute magnitudes of atoms. More than that, he showed convincingly that in addition to the atomistic structure of matter there is a kind of atomistic structure to energy, governed by the universal constant h, which was introduced by Planck.

This discovery became the basis of all twentieth-century research in physics and has almost entirely conditioned its development ever since. Without this discovery it would not have been possible to establish a workable theory of molecules and atoms and the energy processes that govern their transformations. Moreover, it has shattered the whole framework of classical mechanics and electrodynamics and set science a fresh task: that of finding a new conceptual basis for all physics. Despite remarkable partial gains, the problem is still far from a satisfactory solution.

In paying homage to this man the American National Academy of Sciences expresses its hope that free research, for the sake of pure knowledge, may remain unhampered and unimpaired.

42
PAUL LANGEVIN IN MEMORIAM

THE NEWS OF PAUL LANGEVIN'S DEATH dealt me a greater blow than most of the events of these fateful years, so fraught with disappointment. Why should this have been the case? Was his not a long life, crowded with fruitful creative work—the life of a man in harmony with himself? Was he not widely revered for his keen insight into intellectual problems, universally beloved for his devotion to every good cause, for his understanding kindness toward all creatures? Is there not a certain satisfaction in the fact that natural limits are set to the life of the individual, so that at its conclusion it may appear as a work of art?

The sorrow brought on by Paul Langevin's passing has been so particularly poignant because it has given me a feeling of being left utterly alone and desolate. There are so very few in any one generation, in whom clear insight into the nature of things is joined with an intense feeling for the challenge of true humanity and the capacity for militant action. When such a man departs, he leaves a gap that seems unbearable to his survivors.

Langevin was endowed with unusual clarity and agility in scientific thought, together with a sure intuitive vision for the essential points. It was as a result of these qualities that his lectures exerted a crucial influence on more than one generation of French theoretical physicists. But Langevin also knew a great deal about experimental technique and his criticism and constructive suggestions always carried a fruitful effect. His own original researches, moreover, decisively influenced the development of science, mainly in the fields of magnetism and ion theory. Yet the burden of responsibility which he was always ready to assume circumscribed his own research work, so that the fruits of his labors emerge in the publications of other scientists to a greater extent than in his own.

It appears to me as a foregone conclusion that he would have developed the Special Theory of Relativity, had that not been done elsewhere; for he had clearly perceived its essential aspects. Another admirable thing is that he fully appreciated the significance of De Broglie's ideas—from which Schrödinger subsequently developed the methods of wave mechanics—even before these ideas had become consolidated into a consistent theory. I vividly recall the pleasure and warmth with which he told me about it—and I also remember that I followed his remarks but hesitantly and doubtfully.

All his life Langevin suffered from an awareness of the deficiencies and inequities of our social and economic institutions. Yet he believed firmly in the power of reason and knowledge. So pure in heart was he that he was convinced all men should be ready for complete personal renunciation, once they had seen the light of reason and justice. Reason was his creed—a creed that was to bring not only light but also salvation. His desire to promote the happier life for all men was perhaps even stronger than his craving for pure intellectual enlightenment. Thus it was that he devoted much of his time and vital energy to political enlightenment. No one who appealed to his social conscience ever went away from him empty-handed. Thus it was too that the very moral grandeur of his personality earned him the bitter enmity of many of the more humdrum intellectuals. He in turn understood them all and in his kindness never harbored resentment against anyone.

I can only give expression to my gratitude for having personally known this man of purity and illumination.

43
WALTHER NERNST IN MEMORIAM

W<small>ALTHER</small> <small>NERNST</small>, who died recently, was one of the most characteristic and most interesting scholars with whom I have been closely connected during my life. He did not miss any of the conferences on physics in Berlin, and his brief remarks gave evidence of a truly amazing scientific instinct combined both with a sovereign knowledge of an enormous volume of factual materials, which was always at his command, and with a rare mastery of the experimental methods and tricks in which he excelled. Although sometimes good-naturedly smiling at his childlike vanity and self-complacency, we all had for him not only a sincere admiration, but also a personal affection. So long as his egocentric weakness did not enter the picture, he exhibited an objectivity very rarely found, an infallible sense for the essential, and a genuine passion for knowledge of the deep interrelations of nature. But for such a passion his singularly creative productivity and his important influence on the scientific life of the first third of this century would not have been possible.

He ascended from Arrhenius, Ostwald and Van't Hoff, as the last of a dynasty which based their investigations on thermodynamics, osmotic pressure and ionic theory. Up to 1905 his work was essentially restricted to that range of ideas. His theoretical equipment was somewhat elementary, but he mastered it with a rare ingenuity. I refer, for instance, to the theory of electromotive powers in solutions of locally variable concentration, the theory of diminution of the solubility by adding a dissolved substance. During this period he invented the witty null-method of determining the dielectric constant of electrically conducting bodies by means of Wheatstone's Bridge (alternating current, telephone as indicator, compensating capacity in comparison-bridge branches).

This first productive period is largely concerned with improving the methodology and completing the exploration of a field the principles of which had already been known before Nernst. This work led him gradually to a general problem which is characterized by the question: Is it possible to compute from the known energy of the conditions of a system, the useful work which is to be gained by its transition from one state into another? Nernst realized that a theoretical determination of the transition work A from the energy-difference U by means of equations of thermodynamics alone is not possible. There could be inferred from thermodynamics that, at absolute zero, the temperature of the quantities A and U must be equal. But one could not derive A from U for any arbitrary temperatures, even if the energy-values or differences in U were known for all conditions. This computation was not possible until there was introduced, with regard to the reaction of these quantities under low temperatures, an assumption which appeared obvious because of its simplicity. This assumption is simply that A becomes temperature-independent under low temperatures. The introduction of this assumption as a hypothesis (third main principle of the theory of heat) is Nernst's greatest contribution to theoretical science. Planck found later a solution which is theoretically more satisfactory; namely, the entropy disappears at absolute zero temperature.

From the standpoint of the older ideas on heat, this third main principle required very strange reactions of bodies under low temperatures. To pass upon the correctness of this principle, the methods of calorimetry under low temperatures had to be greatly improved. The calorimetry of high temperatures also owes to Nernst considerable progress. Through all these investigations, as well as through many stimulating suggestions with which his untiring inventive genius supplied experimenters in his field, he promoted the research work of his generation most effectively. The beginnings of the quantum theory were assisted by the important results of those caloric investigations, and this especially before Bohr's theory of the atom made spectroscopy the most important experimental field. Nernst's standard work, "Theoretical Chemistry," offers, not only to the student but also to the scholar, an abundance of stimulating ideas; it is theoretically elementary, but clever, vivid and full of intimations of manifold interrelations. It truly reflects his intellectual characteristics.

Nernst was not a one-sided scholar. His sound common sense engaged successfully in all fields of practical life, and every conversation with him brought something interesting to light. What distinguished him from almost all his fellow-countrymen was his remarkable freedom from prejudices. He was neither a nationalist nor a militarist. He judged things and people almost exclusively by their direct success, not by a social or ethical ideal. This was a consequence of his freedom from prejudices. At the same time he was interested in literature and had such a sense of humor as is very seldom found with men who carry so heavy a load of work. He was an original personality; I have never met any one who resembled him in any essential way.

44

PAUL EHRENFEST IN
MEMORIAM

IT HAPPENS SO OFTEN NOWADAYS that men of high qualities depart this life of their own free will that we no longer feel such a conclusion to be unusual. Yet the decision to take leave generally stems from an incapacity—or at least an unwillingness—to resign oneself to new and more difficult *outward* conditions of life. To refuse to live out one's natural life because of *inner* conflicts that are felt to be intolerable—that is even today in persons of sound mind a rare occurrence, possible only in the case of the noblest and morally most exalted personalities. It is to such a tragic inner conflict that our friend Paul Ehrenfest has succumbed. Those who knew him well, as was vouchsafed to me, know that this unblemished personality in the main fell victim to a conflict of conscience that in some form or other is spared no university teacher who has passed, say, his fiftieth year.

I came to know him twenty-two years ago. He visited me in Prague, coming straight from Russia where he as a Jew was debarred from teaching at institutions of higher learning. He was looking for a sphere of work in central or western Europe. But we talked little of that, for it was the state of science at the time that took up almost all of our interest. Both of us realized that classical mechanics and the theory of the electric field had failed in the face of the phenomena of heat radiation and molecular processes (the statistical theory of heat), but there seemed to be no feasible way out of this dilemma. The logical gap in Planck's Theory of Radiation—which we both, nevertheless, greatly admired—was apparent to us. We also discussed the Theory of Relativity, to which he responded with a certain skepticism but with the critical judgment peculiar to him. Within a few hours we were true friends—as though our dreams and aspirations were meant for each other. We remained joined in close friendship until he departed this life.

His stature lay in his unusually well developed faculty to grasp the essence of a theoretical notion, to strip a theory of its mathematical accouterments until the simple basic idea emerged with clarity. This capacity made him a peerless teacher. It was on its account that he was invited to scientific congresses; for he always brought clarity and acuteness into any discussion. He fought against fuzziness and circumlocution, when necessary employing his sharp wit and even downright discourtesy. Some of his utterances could have been interpreted almost as arrogant, yet his tragedy lay precisely in an almost morbid lack of self-confidence. He suffered incessantly from the fact that his critical faculties transcended his constructive capacities. In a manner of speaking, his critical sense robbed him of his love for the offspring of his own mind even before they were born.

Shortly after our first encounter there occurred the great turning-point in Ehrenfest's outward career. Our revered master, Lorentz, anxious to retire from regular university teaching, had recognized Ehrenfest for the inspired teacher that he was and recommended him as his successor. A marvelous sphere of activity opened up to the still youthful man. He was not merely the best teacher in our profession whom I have ever known; he was also passionately preoccupied with the development and destiny of men, especially his students. To understand others, to gain their friendship and trust, to aid anyone embroiled in outer or inner struggles, to encourage youthful talent—all this was his real element, almost more than immersion in scientific problems. His students and colleagues in Leyden loved and esteemed him. They knew his utter devotion, his nature so wholly attuned to service and help. Should he not have been a happy man?

In truth he felt unhappier than anyone else who was close to me. The reason was that he did not feel equal to the lofty task that confronted him. Of what use was it that everyone held him in esteem? His sense of inadequacy, objectively unjustified, plagued him incessantly, often robbing him of the peace of mind necessary for tranquil research. So greatly did he suffer that he was compelled to seek solace in distraction. His frequent aimless travels, his preoccupation with the radio, and many other features of his restless life stemmed not from a need for composure and harmless hobbies but rather from a curious urge for escape caused by the psychic conflict at which I have hinted.

In the last few years this situation was aggravated by the strangely turbulent development which theoretical physics has recently undergone. To learn and to teach things that one cannot fully accept in one's heart is always a difficult matter, doubly difficult for a mind of fanatical honesty, a mind to which clarity means everything. Added to this was the increasing difficulty of adaptation to new thoughts which always confronts the man past fifty. I do not know how many readers of these lines will be capable of fully grasping that tragedy. Yet it was this that primarily occasioned his escape from life.

It seems to me that the tendency toward exaggerated self-criticism is associated with experiences in boyhood. Humiliation and mental oppression by ignorant and selfish teachers wreak havoc in the youthful mind that can never be undone and often exert a baleful influence in later life. The intensity of such experiences in Ehrenfest's case may be judged from the fact that he refused to entrust his dearly beloved children to any school.

His relations with his friends played a far greater role in Ehrenfest's life than is the case with most men. He was virtually dominated by his sympathies and also by antipathies based on moral judgments. The strongest relationship in his life was that to his wife and fellow worker, an unusually strong and steadfast personality and his intellectual equal. Perhaps her mind was not quite as agile, versatile, and sensitive as his own, but her poise, her independence of others, her steadfastness in the face of all hardships, her integrity in thought, feeling, and action—all these were a blessing to him and he repaid her with a veneration and love such as I have not often witnessed in my life. A fateful partial estrangement from her was a frightful experience for him, one with which his already wounded soul was unable to cope.

We whose lives have been enriched by the power and integrity of his spirit, the kindness and warmth of his rich mind, and not least his irrepressible humor and trenchant wit—we know how much his departure has impoverished us. He will live on in his students and in all whose aspirations were guided by his personality.

45

MAHATMA GANDHI

A LEADER OF HIS PEOPLE, unsupported by any outward authority: a politician whose success rests not upon craft nor the mastery of technical devices, but simply on the convincing power of his personality; a victorious fighter who has always scorned the use of force; a man of wisdom and humility, armed with resolve and inflexible consistency, who has devoted all his strength to the uplifting of his people and the betterment of their lot; a man who has confronted the brutality of Europe with the dignity of the simple human being, and thus at all times risen superior.

Generations to come, it may be, will scarce believe that such a one as this ever in flesh and blood walked upon this earth.

46

CARL VON OSSIETZKY

ONLY ONE WHO SPENT the years following the First World War in Germany can fully understand how hard a battle it was that a man like Ossietzky had to fight. He knew that the tradition of his countrymen, bent on violence and war, had not lost its power. He knew how difficult, thankless and dangerous a task it was, to preach sanity and justice to his countrymen who had been hardened by a rough fate and the demoralizing influence of a long war. In their blindness they repaid him in hatred, persecution and slow destruction; to heed him and to act accordingly would have meant their salvation and would have been a true relief for the whole world.

It will be to the eternal fame of the Nobel Foundation that it bestowed its high honor on this humble martyr, and that it is resolved to keep alive his memory and the memory of his work. It is also wholesome for mankind today, since the fatal illusion against which he fought has not been removed by the outcome of the last war. The abstention from the solution of human problems by brute force—is the task today as it was then.

My People

47

WHY DO THEY HATE THE JEWS?

I SHOULD LIKE TO BEGIN by telling you an ancient fable, with a few minor changes—a fable that will serve to throw into bold relief the mainsprings of political anti-Semitism:

The shepherd boy said to the horse: "You are the noblest beast that treads the earth. You deserve to live in untroubled bliss; and indeed your happiness would be complete were it not for the treacherous stag. But he practiced from youth to excel you in fleetness of foot. His faster pace allows him to reach the water holes before you do. He and his tribe drink up the water far and wide, while you and your foal are left to thirst. Stay with me! My wisdom and guidance shall deliver you and your kind from a dismal and ignominious state."

Blinded by envy and hatred of the stag, the horse agreed. He yielded to the shepherd lad's bridle. He lost his freedom and became the shepherd's slave.

The horse in this fable represents a people, and the shepherd lad a class or clique aspiring to absolute rule over the people; the stag, on the other hand, represents the Jews.

I can hear you say: "A most unlikely tale! No creature would be as foolish as the horse in your fable." But let us give it a little more thought. The horse had been suffering the pangs of thirst, and his vanity was often pricked when he saw the nimble stag outrunning him. You, who have known no such pain and vexation, may find it difficult to understand that hatred and blindness should have driven the horse to act

433

with such ill-advised, gullible haste. The horse, however, fell an easy victim to temptation because his earlier tribulations had prepared him for such a blunder. For there is much truth in the saying that it is easy to give just and wise counsel—to others!—but hard to act justly and wisely for oneself. I say to you with full conviction: We all have often played the tragic role of the horse and we are in constant danger of yielding to temptation again.

The situation illustrated in this fable happens again and again in the life of individuals and nations. In brief, we may call it the process by which dislike and hatred of a given person or group are diverted to another person or group incapable of effective defense. But why did the role of the stag in the fable so often fall to the Jews? Why did the Jews so often happen to draw the hatred of the masses? Primarily because there are Jews among almost all nations and because they are everywhere too thinly scattered to defend themselves against violent attack.

A few examples from the recent past will prove the point: Toward the end of the nineteenth century the Russian people were chafing under the tyranny of their government. Stupid blunders in foreign policy further strained their temper until it reached the breaking point. In this extremity the rulers of Russia sought to divert unrest by inciting the masses to hatred and violence toward the Jews. These tactics were repeated after the Russian government had drowned the dangerous revolution of 1905 in blood—and this maneuver may well have helped to keep the hated regime in power until near the end of the World War.

When the Germans had lost the World War hatched by their ruling class, immediate attempts were made to blame the Jews, first for instigating the war and then for losing it. In the course of time, success attended these efforts. The hatred engendered against the Jews not only protected the privileged classes, but enabled a small, unscrupulous and insolent group to place the German people in a state of complete bondage.

The crimes with which the Jews have been charged in the course of history—crimes which were to justify the atrocities perpetrated against them—have changed in rapid succession. They were supposed to have poisoned wells. They were said to have murdered children for ritual purposes. They were falsely charged with a systematic attempt at the economic domination and exploitation of all mankind. Pseudo-scientific books were written to brand them an inferior, dangerous race. They were reputed to foment wars and revolutions for their own selfish purposes. They were presented at once as dangerous innovators and as enemies of true progress. They were charged with falsifying the culture of nations by penetrating the national life under the guise of becoming assimilated. In the same breath they were accused of being so stubbornly inflexible that it was impossible for them to fit into any society.

Almost beyond imagination were the charges brought against them, charges known to their instigators to be untrue all the while, but which time and again influenced the masses. In times of unrest and turmoil the masses are inclined to hatred and cruelty, whereas in times of peace these traits of human nature emerge but stealthily.

Up to this point I have spoken only of violence and oppression against the Jews—not of anti-Semitism itself as a psychological and social phenomenon existing even in times and circumstances when no special action against the Jews is under way. In this sense, one may speak of latent anti-Semitism. What is its basis? I believe that in a certain sense one may actually regard it as a normal manifestation in the life of a people.

The members of any group existing in a nation are more closely bound to one another than they are to the remaining population. Hence a nation will never be free of friction while such groups continue to be distinguishable. In my belief, uniformity in a population would not be desirable, even if it were attainable. Common convictions and aims, similar interests, will in every society produce groups that, in a certain sense, act as units. There will always be friction between such groups—the same sort of aversion and rivalry that exists between individuals.

The need for such groupings is perhaps most easily seen in the field of politics, in the formation of political parties. Without parties the political interests of the citizens of any state are bound to languish. There would be no forum for the free exchange of opinions. The individual would be isolated and unable to assert his convictions. Political convictions, moreover, ripen and grow only through mutual stimulation and criticism offered by individuals of similar disposition and purpose; and politics is no different from any other field of our cultural existence. Thus it is recognized, for example, that in times of intense religious fervor different sects are likely to spring up whose rivalry stimulates religious life in general. It is well known, on the other hand, that centralization—that is, elimination of independent groups—leads to one-sidedness and barrenness in science and art because such centralization checks and even suppresses any rivalry of opinions and research trends.

Just What Is a Jew?

The formation of groups has an invigorating effect in all spheres of human striving, perhaps mostly due to the struggle between the convictions and aims represented by the different groups. The Jews too form such a group with a definite character of its own, and anti-Semitism is nothing but the antagonistic attitude produced in the non-Jews by the Jewish group. This is a normal social reaction. But for the political abuse resulting from it, it might never have been designated by a special name.

What are the characteristics of the Jewish group? What, in

the first place, is a Jew? There are no quick answers to this question. The most obvious answer would be the following: A Jew is a person professing the Jewish faith. The superficial character of this answer is easily recognized by means of a simple parallel. Let us ask the question: What is a snail? An answer similar in kind to the one given above might be: A snail is an animal inhabiting a snail shell. This answer is not altogether incorrect; nor, to be sure, is it exhaustive; for the snail shell happens to be but one of the material products of the snail. Similarly, the Jewish faith is but one of the characteristic products of the Jewish community. It is, furthermore, known that a snail can shed its shell without thereby ceasing to be a snail. The Jew who abandons his faith (in the formal sense of the word) is in a similar position. He remains a Jew.

Difficulties of this kind appear whenever one seeks to explain the essential character of a group.

The bond that has united the Jews for thousands of years and that unites them today is, above all, the democratic ideal of social justice, coupled with the ideal of mutual aid and tolerance among all men. Even the most ancient religious scriptures of the Jews are steeped in these social ideals, which have powerfully affected Christianity and Mohammedanism and have had a benign influence upon the social structure of a great part of mankind. The introduction of a weekly day of rest should be remembered here—a profound blessing to all mankind. Personalities such as Moses, Spinoza and Karl Marx, dissimilar as they may be, all lived and sacrificed themselves for the ideal of social justice; and it was the tradition of their forefathers that led them on this thorny path. The unique accomplishments of the Jews in the field of philanthropy spring from the same source.

The second characteristic trait of Jewish tradition is the high regard in which it holds every form of intellectual aspiration and spiritual effort. I am convinced that this great respect for intellectual striving is solely responsible for the contributions that the Jews have made toward the progress of knowledge, in the broadest sense of the term. In view of their relatively small number and the considerable external obstacles constantly placed in their way on all sides, the extent of those contributions deserves the admiration of all sincere men. I am convinced that this is not due to any special wealth of endowment, but to the fact that the esteem in which intellectual accomplishment is held among the Jews creates an atmosphere particularly favorable to the development of any talents that may exist. At the same time a strong critical spirit prevents blind obeisance to any mortal authority.

I have confined myself here to these two traditional traits, which seem to me the most basic. These standards and ideals find expression in small things as in large. They are transmitted from parents to children; they color conversation and judgment among friends; they fill the religious scriptures; and they give to the community life of the group its characteristic stamp. It is in these distinctive ideals that I see the essence of Jewish nature. That these ideals are but imperfectly realized in the group—in its actual everyday life—is only natural. However, if one seeks to give brief expression to the essential character of a group, the approach must always be by the way of the ideal.

Where Oppression Is a Stimulus

In the foregoing I have conceived of Judaism as a community of tradition. Both friend and foe, on the other hand, have often asserted that the Jews represent a race; that their characteristic behavior is the result of innate qualities transmitted by *heredity* from one generation to the next. This opinion gains weight from the fact that the Jews for thousands of years have predominantly married within their own group. Such a custom may indeed *preserve* a homogeneous

race—if it existed originally; it cannot *produce* uniformity of
the race—if there was originally a racial intermixture. The
Jews, however, are beyond doubt a mixed race, just as are all
other groups of our civilization. Sincere anthropologists are
agreed on this point; assertions to the contrary all belong
to the field of political propaganda and must be rated accordingly.

Perhaps even more than on its own tradition, the Jewish
group has thrived on oppression and on the antagonism it has
forever met in the world. Here undoubtedly lies one of the
main reasons for its continued existence through so many
thousands of years.

The Jewish group, which we have briefly characterized in
the foregoing, embraces about sixteen million people—less
than one per cent of mankind, or about half as many as the
population of present-day Poland. Their significance as a
political factor is negligible. They are scattered over almost
the entire earth and are in no way organized as a whole—
which means that they are incapable of concerted action of
any kind.

Were anyone to form a picture of the Jews solely from the
utterances of their enemies, he would have to reach the conclusion that they represent a world power. At first sight that
seems downright absurd; and yet, in my view, there is a
certain meaning behind it. The Jews as a group may be
powerless, but the sum of the achievements of their individual members is everywhere considerable and telling, even
though these achievements were made in the face of obstacles. The forces dormant in the individual are mobilized,
and the individual himself is stimulated to self-sacrificing
effort, by the spirit that is alive in the group.

Hence the hatred of the Jews by those who have reason to
shun popular enlightenment. More than anything else in the
world, they fear the influence of men of intellectual independence. I see in this the essential cause for the savage

hatred of Jews raging in present-day Germany. To the Nazi group the Jews are not merely a means for turning the resentment of the people away from themselves, the oppressors; they see the Jews as a nonassimilable element that cannot be driven into uncritical acceptance of dogma, and that, therefore—as long as it exists at all—threatens their authority because of its insistence on popular enlightenment of the masses.

Proof that this conception goes to the heart of the matter is convincingly furnished by the solemn ceremony of the burning of the books staged by the Nazi regime shortly after its seizure of power. This act, senseless from a political point of view, can only be understood as a spontaneous emotional outburst. For that reason it seems to me more revealing than many acts of greater purpose and practical importance.

In the field of politics and social science there has grown up a justified distrust of generalizations pushed too far. When thought is too greatly dominated by such generalizations, misinterpretations of specific sequences of cause and effect readily occur, doing injustice to the actual multiplicity of events. Abandonment of generalization, on the other hand, means to relinquish understanding altogether. For that reason I believe one may and must risk generalization, as long as one remains aware of its uncertainty. It is in this spirit that I wish to present in all modesty my conception of anti-Semitism, considered from a general point of view.

In political life I see two opposed tendencies at work, locked in constant struggle with each other. The first, optimistic, trend proceeds from the belief that the free unfolding of the productive forces of individuals and groups essentially leads to a satisfactory state of society. It recognizes the need for a central power, placed above groups and individuals, but concedes to such power only organizational and regulatory functions. The second, pessimistic, trend assumes that free interplay of individuals and groups leads to the destruction of society; it thus seeks to base society exclusively upon authority, blind obedience and coercion. Actually this trend is pessimistic only to a limited extent: for it is optimistic in regard to those who are, and desire to be, the bearers of power and authority. The adherents of this second trend are the enemies of the free groups and of education for independent thought. They are, moreover, the carriers of political anti-Semitism.

Here in America all pay lip service to the first, optimistic, tendency. Nevertheless, the second group is strongly represented. It appears on the scene everywhere, though for the most part it hides its true nature. Its aim is political and spiritual dominion over the people by a minority, by the circuitous route of control over the means of production. Its proponents have already tried to utilize the weapon of anti-Semitism as well as of hostility to various other groups. They will repeat the attempt in times to come. So far all such tendencies have failed because of the people's sound political instinct.

And so it will remain in the future, if we cling to the rule: Beware of flatterers, especially when they come preaching hatred.

48

THE DISPERSAL OF EUROPEAN
JEWRY

THE HISTORY OF THE PERSECUTIONS which the Jewish people
have had to suffer is almost inconceivably long. Yet the war
that is being waged against us in Central Europe today [1] falls
into a special category of its own. In the past we were persecuted *despite* the fact that we were the people of the Bible;
today, however, it is just *because* we are the people of the
Book that we are persecuted. The aim is to exterminate not
only ourselves but to destroy, together with us, that spirit
expressed in the Bible and in Christianity which made possible the rise of civilization in Central and Northern Europe.
If this aim is achieved Europe will become a barren waste.
For human community life cannot long endure on a basis of
crude force, brutality, terror, and hate.

Only understanding for our neighbors, justice in our deal-
ings, and willingness to help our fellow men can give human
society permanence and assure security for the individual.
Neither intelligence nor inventions nor institutions can serve
as substitutes for these most vital parts of education.

Many Jewish communities have been uprooted in the wake
of the present upheaval in Europe. Hundreds of thousands of
men, women, and children have been driven from their homes
and made to wander in despair over the highways of the
world. The tragedy of the Jewish people today is a tragedy

[1] Spoken in 1939.

which reflects a challenge to the fundamental structure of modern civilization.

One of the most tragic aspects of the oppression of Jews and other groups has been the creation of a refugee class. Many distinguished men in science, art, and literature have been driven from the lands which they enriched with their talents. In a period of economic decline these exiles have within them the possibilities for reviving economic and cultural effort; many of these refugees are highly skilled experts in industry and science. They have a valuable contribution to make to the progress of the world. They are in a position to repay hospitality with new economic development and the opening up of new opportunities of employment for native populations. I am told that in England the admission of refugees was directly responsible for giving jobs to 15,000 unemployed.

As one of the former citizens of Germany who have been fortunate enough to leave that country, I know I can speak for my fellow refugees, both here and in other countries, when I give thanks to the democracies of the world for the splendid manner in which they have received us. We, all of us, owe a debt of gratitude to our new countries, and each and every one of us is doing the utmost to show our gratitude by the quality of our contributions to the economic, social, and cultural work of the countries in which we reside.

It is, however, a source of gravest concern that the ranks of the refugees are being constantly increased. The developments of the past week have added several hundred thousand potential refugees from Czechoslovakia. Again we are confronted with a major tragedy for a Jewish community which had a noble tradition of democracy and communal service.

The power of resistance which has enabled the Jewish people to survive for thousands of years is a direct outgrowth of Jewish adherence to the Biblical doctrines on the relationships among men. In these years of affliction our readiness to help one another is being put to an especially severe test. Each of us must personally face this test, that we may stand it as well as our fathers did before us. We have no other means of self-defense than our solidarity and our knowledge that the cause for which we are suffering is a momentous and sacred cause.

49

LET'S NOT FORGET

IF WE AS JEWS CAN LEARN anything from these politically sad times, it is the fact that destiny has bound us together, a fact which in times of quiet and security, we often so easily and gladly forget. We are accustomed to lay too much emphasis on the differences that divide the Jews of different lands and different religious views. And we forget often that it is the concern of every Jew, when anywhere the Jew is hated and treated unjustly, when politicians with flexible consciences set into motion against us the old prejudices, originally religious, in order to concoct political schemes at our expense. It concerns every one of us because such diseases and psychotic disturbances of the folk-soul are not estopped by oceans and national borders, but act precisely like economic crises and epidemics.

50

UNPUBLISHED PREFACE
TO A BLACKBOOK

THIS BOOK IS A COLLECTION of documentary material on the systematic work of destruction by which the German Government murdered a great proportion of the Jewish people. Responsibility for the truth of the facts set forth is borne by the Jewish organizations that have joined to create the present work and present it to the public.

The purpose of this publication is manifest. It is to convince the reader that an international organization for safeguarding the sanctity of life can effectively fulfill its purpose only if it does not limit itself to protecting countries against military attack but also extends its protection to national minorities within the individual countries. For in the last reckoning it is the individual who must be protected against annihilation and inhuman treatment.

It is true that this goal can be attained only if the principle of non-intervention, which has played such a fateful role in the last decades, is cast overboard. Yet today no one can doubt the need for this far-reaching step any longer. For even those who envision only the attainment of protection against military attack from the outside must today realize that the disasters of war are preceded by certain internal developments in the various countries, and not merely by military and armaments preparations.

Not until the creation and maintenance of decent conditions of life for all men are recognized and accepted as a common obligation of all men and all countries—not until then shall we, with a certain degree of justification, be able to speak of mankind as civilized.

Percentagewise the Jewish people have lost more than any other people affected by the disasters of recent years. If a truly just settlement is to be striven for, the Jewish people must be given special consideration in the organization of the peace. The fact that the Jews, in the formal political sense, cannot be regarded as a nation, insofar as they possess no country and no government, ought to be no impediment. For the Jews have been treated as a uniform group, as though they were a nation. Their status as a uniform political group is proved to be a fact by the behavior of their enemies. Hence in striving toward a stabilization of the international situation they should be considered as though they were a nation in the customary sense of the word.

Another factor must be emphasized in this connection. In parts of Europe Jewish life will probably be impossible for years to come. In decades of hard work and voluntary financial aid the Jews have restored the soil of Palestine to fertility. All these sacrifices were made because of trust in the officially sanctioned promise given by the governments in question after the last war, namely that the Jewish people were to be given a secure home in their ancient Palestinian country. To put it mildly, the fulfillment of this promise has been but hesitant and partial. Now that the Jews—especially the Jews in Palestine—have in this war too rendered a valuable contribution, the promise must be forcibly called to mind. The demand must be put forward that Palestine, within the limits of its economic capacity, be thrown open to Jewish immigration. If supranational institutions are to win that confidence that must form the most important buttress for their endurance, then it must be shown above all that those who, trusting to these institutions, have made the heaviest sacrifices are not defrauded.

51

THE GOAL OF
HUMAN EXISTENCE

Our age is proud of the progress it has made in man's intellectual development. The search and striving for truth and knowledge is one of the highest of man's qualities— though often the pride is most loudly voiced by those who strive the least. And certainly we should take care not to make the intellect our god; it has, of course, powerful muscles, but no personality. It cannot lead, it can only serve; and it is not fastidious in its choice of a leader. This characteristic is reflected in the qualities of its priests, the intellectuals. The intellect has a sharp eye for methods and tools, but is blind to ends and values. So it is no wonder that this fatal blindness is handed on from old to young and today involves a whole generation.

Our Jewish forbears, the prophets and the old Chinese sages understood and proclaimed that the most important factor in giving shape to our human existence is the setting up and establishment of a goal; the goal being a community of free and happy human beings who by constant inward endeavor strive to liberate themselves from the inheritance of anti-social and destructive instincts. In this effort the intellect can be the most powerful aid. The fruits of intellectual effort, together with the striving itself, in cooperation with the creative activity of the artist, lend content and meaning to life.

But today the rude passions of man reign in our world,

more unrestrained than ever before. Our Jewish people, a small minority everywhere, with no means of defending themselves by force, are exposed to the cruelest suffering, even to complete annihilation, to a far greater degree than any other people in the world. The hatred raging against us is grounded in the fact that we have upheld the ideal of harmonious partnership and given it expression in word and deed among the best of our people.

52

OUR DEBT TO ZIONISM

Rarely since the conquest of Jerusalem by Titus has the Jewish community experienced a period of greater oppression than prevails at the present time. In some respects, indeed, our own time is even more troubled, for man's possibilities of emigration are more limited today than they were then.

Yet we shall survive this period too, no matter how much sorrow, no matter how heavy a loss in life it may bring. A community like ours, which is a community purely by reason of tradition, can only be strengthened by pressure from without. For today every Jew feels that to be a Jew means to bear a serious responsibility not only to his own community, but also toward humanity. To be a Jew, after all, means first of all, to acknowledge and follow in practice those fundamentals in humaneness laid down in the Bible—fundamentals without which no sound and happy community of men can exist.

We meet today because of our concern for the development of Palestine. In this hour one thing, above all, must be emphasized: Judaism owes a great debt of gratitude to Zionism. The Zionist movement has revived among Jews the sense of community. It has performed productive work surpassing all the expectations any one could entertain. This productive work in Palestine, to which self-sacrificing Jews throughout the world have contributed, has saved a large number of our brethren from direst need. In particular, it has been possible to lead a not inconsiderable part of our youth toward a life of joyous and creative work.

Now the fateful disease of our time—exaggerated national-ism, borne up by blind hatred—has brought our work in Palestine to a most difficult stage. Fields cultivated by day must have armed protection at night against fanatical Arab outlaws. All economic life suffers from insecurity. The spirit of enterprise languishes and a certain measure of unemploy-ment (modest when measured by American standards) has made its appearance.

The solidarity and confidence with which our brethren in Palestine face these difficulties deserve our admiration. Vol-untary contributions by those still employed keep the unem-ployed above water. Spirits remain high, in the conviction that reason and calm will ultimately reassert themselves. Everyone knows that the riots are artificially fomented by those directly interested in embarrassing not only ourselves but especially England. Everyone knows that banditry would cease if foreign subsidies were withdrawn.

Our brethren in other countries, however, are in no way behind those in Palestine. They, too, will not lose heart but will resolutely and firmly stand behind the common work. This goes without saying.

Just one more personal word on the question of parti-tion. I should much rather see reasonable agreement with the Arabs on the basis of living together in peace than the creation of a Jewish state. Apart from practical consideration, my awareness of the essential nature of Judaism resists the idea of a Jewish state with borders, an army, and a measure of temporal power no matter how modest. I am afraid of the inner damage Judaism will sustain—especially from the de-velopment of a narrow nationalism within our own ranks, against which we have already had to fight strongly, even without a Jewish state. We are no longer the Jews of the Maccabee period. A return to a nation in the political sense of the word would be equivalent to turning away from the spiritualization of our community which we owe to the genius of our prophets. If external necessity should after all compel us to assume this burden, let us bear it with tact and patience.

One more word on the present psychological attitude of the world at large, upon which our Jewish destiny also depends. Anti-Semitism has always been the cheapest means employed by selfish minorities for deceiving the people. A tyranny based on such deception and maintained by terror must inevitably perish from the poison it generates within itself. For the pressure of accumulated injustice strengthens those moral forces in man which lead to a liberation and purification of public life. May our community through its suffering and its work contribute toward the release of those liberating forces.

53

TO THE HEROES OF THE BATTLE OF THE WARSAW GHETTO

THEY FOUGHT AND DIED as members of the Jewish nation, in the struggle against organized bands of German murderers. To us these sacrifices are a strengthening of the bond between us, the Jews of all the countries. We strive to be one in suffering and in the effort to achieve a better human society, that society which our prophets have so clearly and forcibly set before us as a goal.

The Germans as an entire people are responsible for these mass murders and must be punished as a people if there is justice in the world and if the consciousness of collective responsibility in the nations is not to perish from the earth entirely. Behind the Nazi party stands the German people, who elected Hitler after he had in his book and in his speeches made his shameful intentions clear beyond the possibility of misunderstanding. The Germans are the only people who have not made any serious attempt of counter-action leading to the protection of the innocently persecuted. When they are entirely defeated and begin to lament over their fate, we must not let ourselves be deceived again, but keep in mind that they deliberately used the humanity of others to make preparation for their last and most grievous crime against humanity.

54

BEFORE THE MONUMENT TO THE MARTYRED JEWS OF THE WARSAW GHETTO

THE MONUMENT BEFORE WHICH you have gathered today was built to stand as a concrete symbol of our grief over the irreparable loss our martyred Jewish nation has suffered. It shall also serve as a reminder for us who have survived to remain loyal to our people and to the moral principles cherished by our fathers. Only through such loyalty may we hope to survive this age of moral decay.

The more cruel the wrong that men commit against an individual or a people, the deeper their hatred and contempt for their victim. Conceit and false pride on the part of a nation prevent the rise of remorse for its crime. Those who have had no part in the crime, however, have no sympathy for the sufferings of the innocent victims of persecution and no awareness of human solidarity. That is why the remnants of European Jewry are languishing in concentration camps and the sparsely populated lands of this earth close their gates against them. Even our right, so solemnly pledged, to a national homeland in Palestine is being betrayed. In this era of moral degradation in which we live the voice of justice no longer has any power over men.

Let us clearly recognize and never forget this: That mutual cooperation and the furtherance of living ties between the Jews of all lands is our sole physical and moral protection in the present situation. But for the future our hope lies in over-

454

coming the general moral abasement which today gravely menaces the very existence of mankind. Let us labor with all our powers, however feeble, to the end that mankind recover from its present moral degradation and gain a new vitality and a new strength in its striving for right and justice as well as for a harmonious society.

THE CALLING OF THE JEWS

This is a time when there seems to be a particular need for men of philosophical persuasion—that is to say, friends of wisdom and truth—to join together. For while it is true that our time has accumulated more knowledge than any earlier age, that love of truth and insight which lent wings to the spirit of the Renaissance has grown cold, giving way to sober specialization rooted in the material spheres of society rather than in the spiritual. But groups such as this one are devoted solely to spiritual aims.

In centuries past Judaism clung exclusively to its moral and spiritual tradition. Its teachers were its only leaders. But with adaptation to a larger social whole this spiritual orientation has receded into the background, though even today the Jewish people owe to it their apparently indestructible vigor. If we are to preserve that vigor for the benefit of mankind, we must hold to that spiritual orientation toward life.

The Dance about the Golden Calf was not merely a legendary episode in the history of our forefathers—an episode that seems to me in its simplicity more innocent than that total adherence to material and selfish goals threatening Judaism in our own days. At this time a union of those who rally to the spiritual heritage of our people has supreme justification. This is all the more true for a group that is free of all historical and national narrowness. We Jews should be and remain the carriers and patrons of spiritual values. But we should also always be aware of the fact that these spiritual values are and always have been the common goal of all mankind.

MOSES MAIMONIDES

THERE IS SOMETHING SUBLIME in the spectacle of men joining together in a spirit of harmony to honor the memory of a man whose life and work lie seven centuries in the past. This feeling is accentuated all the more sharply at a time in which passion and strife tend more than usually to obscure the influence of reasoned thought and balanced justice. In the bustle of everyday life our view grows clouded with desire and passion, and the voice of reason and justice is almost inaudible in the hubbub of the struggle of all against all. But the ferment of those times long past has long since been stilled, and scarcely more is left of it than the memory of those few who exerted a crucial and fruitful influence on their contemporaries and thus on later generations as well. Such a man was Maimonides.

Once the Teutonic barbarians had destroyed Europe's ancient culture, a new and finer cultural life slowly began to flow from two sources that had somehow escaped being altogether buried in the general havoc—the Jewish Bible and Greek philosophy and art. The union of these two sources, so different one from the other, marks the beginning of our present cultural epoch, and from that union, directly or indirectly, has sprung all that makes up the true values of our present-day life.

Maimonides was one of those strong personalities who by their writings and their human endeavors helped to bring about that synthesis, thus paving the way for later developments. Just how this happened will be related to us tonight by friends whose studies have come closer than I to the heart of Maimonides' lifework and the history of the European mind.

May this hour of grateful remembrance serve to strengthen within us the love and esteem in which we hold the treasures of our culture, gained in such bitter struggle. Our fight to preserve those treasures against the present powers of darkness and barbarism cannot then but carry the day.

57

STEPHEN WISE

Among all those whom I have personally met who have labored in the cause of justice and in the interest of the hard-pressed Jewish people, only a few were at all times selfless—but there was no one who gave his love and energy with such consuming devotion as Stephen Wise. All his life he has been a fighter for the cause of Zionism to which the memory of his ceaseless activities will be bound for ever. He has walked the thorny paths of the true prophet, at all times disdaining sordid compromise and never bending the knee to those in power. By relentlessly exposing the weakness and imperfections both in our own ranks and in the larger political arena of the non-Jewish world, he has made great and lasting contributions wherever he has gone. There are those who do not love him, but there is no one who has ever denied him recognition and respect, for everybody knows that behind the enormous labors of this man there has always been the passionate desire to make mankind better and happier.

58

TO THE UNIVERSITY OF JERUSALEM

THE LITTLE THAT I COULD DO, in a long life favored by external circumstances to deepen our physical knowledge, has brought me so much praise that for a long time I have felt rather more embarrassed than elated. But from you there comes a token of esteem that fills me with pure joy—joy about the great deeds that our Jewish people have accomplished within a few generations, under exceptionally difficult conditions, by itself alone, through boundless courage and immeasurable sacrifices. The University which twenty-seven years ago was nothing but a dream and a faint hope, this University is today a living thing, a home of free learning and teaching and happy brotherly work. There it is, on the soil that our people have liberated under great hardships; there it is, a spiritual center of a flourishing and buoyant community whose accomplishments have finally met with the universal recognition they deserved.

In this last period of the fulfilment of our dreams there was but one thing that weighed heavily upon me: the fact that we were compelled by the adversities of our situation to assert our rights through force of arms; it was the only way to avert complete annihilation. The wisdom and moderation the leaders of the new state have shown gives me confidence, however, that gradually relations will be established with the Arab people which are based on fruitful cooperation and mutual respect and trust. For this is the only means through which both peoples can attain true independence from the outside world.

59

THE AMERICAN COUNCIL
FOR JUDAISM

I AM VERY HAPPY INDEED to hear that the platform for which the American Council for Judaism stands is meeting with strong opposition. This organization appears to me to be nothing more than a pitiable attempt to obtain favor and toleration from our enemies by betraying true Jewish ideals and by mimicking those who claim to stand for 100 per cent Americanism. I believe this method to be both undignified and ineffective. Our opponents are bound to view it with disdain and even with contempt, and in my opinion justly. He who is untrue to his own cause cannot command the respect of others. Apart from these considerations, the movement in question is a fairly exact copy of the Zentralverein Deutscher Staatsbürger Jüdischen Glaubens ("Central Association of German Citizens of Jewish Faith") of unhappy memory, which in the days of our crucial need showed itself utterly impotent and corroded the Jewish group by undermining that inner certitude by which alone our Jewish people could have overcome the trials of this difficult age.

60

THE JEWS OF ISRAEL

There is no problem of such overwhelming importance to
us Jews as consolidating that which has been accomplished
in Israel with amazing energy and an unequalled willingness
for sacrifice. May the joy and admiration that fill us when we
think of all that this small group of energetic and thoughtful
people has achieved give us the strength to accept the great
responsibility which the present situation has placed upon us.

When appraising the achievement, however, let us not lose
sight of the cause to be served by this achievement: rescue of
our endangered brethren, dispersed in many lands, by uniting
them in Israel; creation of a community which conforms as
closely as possible to the ethical ideals of our people as they
have been formed in the course of a long history.

One of these ideals is peace, based on understanding and
self-restraint, and not on violence. If we are imbued with this
ideal, our joy becomes somewhat mingled with sadness, because our relations with the Arabs are far from this ideal at
the present time. It may well be that we would have reached
this ideal, had we been permitted to work out, undisturbed
by others, our relations with our neighbors, for we *want* peace
and we realize that our future development depends on
peace.

It was much less our own fault or that of our neighbors
than of the Mandatory Power, that we did not achieve an un-
divided Palestine in which Jews and Arabs would live as
equals, free, in peace. If one nation dominates other nations,
as was the case in the British Mandate over Palestine, she can

hardly avoid following the notorious device of Divide et Impera. In plain language this means: create discord among the governed people so they will not unite in order to shake off the yoke imposed upon them. Well, the yoke has been removed, but the seed of dissension has borne fruit and may still do harm for some time to come—let us hope not for too long.

The Jews of Palestine did not fight for political independence for its own sake, but they fought to achieve free immigration for the Jews of many countries where their very existence was in danger; free immigration also for all those who were longing for a life among their own. It is no exaggeration to say that they fought to make possible a sacrifice perhaps unique in history.

I do not speak of the loss in lives and property fighting an opponent who was numerically far superior, nor do I mean the exhausting toil which is the pioneer's lot in a neglected arid country. I am thinking of the additional sacrifice that a population living under such conditions has to make in order to receive, in the course of eighteen months, an influx of immigrants which comprise more than one third of the total Jewish population of the country. In order to realize what this means you have only to visualize a comparable feat of the American Jews. Let us assume there were no laws limiting the immigration into the United States; imagine that the Jews of this country volunteered to receive more than one million Jews from other countries in the course of one year and a half, to take care of them, and to integrate them into the economy of this country. This would be a tremendous achievement, but still very far from the achievement of our brethren in Israel. For the United States is a big, fertile country, sparsely populated with a high living standard and a highly developed productive capacity, not to compare with small Jewish Palestine whose inhabitants, even without the additional burden of mass immigration, lead a hard and frugal life, still threatened by enemy attacks. Think of the privations and personal sacrifices which this voluntary act of brotherly love means for the Jews of Israel.

The economic means of the Jewish Community in Israel do not suffice to bring this tremendous enterprise to a successful end. For a hundred thousand out of more than three hundred thousand persons who immigrated to Israel since May 1948 no homes or work could be made available. They had to be concentrated in improvised camps under conditions which are a disgrace to all of us.

It must not happen that this magnificent work breaks down because the Jews of this country do not help sufficiently or quickly enough. Here, to my mind, is a precious gift with which all Jews have been presented: the opportunity to take an active part in this wonderful task.

ACKNOWLEDGMENTS

ARTICLE

2. From *Portraits and Self-Portraits* by George Schreiber; Houghton, Mifflin Co., Boston, 1936.
3. From *I Believe*, edited by Clifton Fadiman; copyright by Simon & Schuster, Inc., New York, 1939.
4. From a message on Founder's Day of the Young Men's Christian Association, October 11, 1937.
5. From the Time Capsule statement at the New York World's Fair, dated August 10, 1938.
6. From *Freedom, Its Meaning*, edited by Ruth Nanda Anshen; Harcourt Brace and Co., New York, 1940. (Translation prepared by James Gutmann, Professor of Philosophy, Columbia University.)
7. From an address at the commencement exercises of Swarthmore College, 1938.
8. I. From an address at Princeton Theological Seminary before the Northeastern Regional Conference of the American Association of Theological Schools, May 19, 1939.
   II. From *Science, Philosophy and Religion*, a Symposium; published by the Conference on Science, Philosophy and Religion in Their Relation to the Democratic Way of Life, Inc., New York, 1941.
9. From an address at the Seventy-second Convocation of the University of the State of New York in Chancellors Hall of the State Education Building at Albany, New York, in celebration of the Tercentenary of Higher Education in America, October 15, 1936. (Translation prepared by Lina Arronet.)
10. From *The American People's Encyclopedia*, copyright by the Spencer Press, Inc., Chicago, 1949.
11. From *Science Illustrated*; New York, April, 1946.
12. Originally published in the *London Times*, November 28, 1919.
13. From *The Journal of the Franklin Institute*, Vol. 221, No. 3; March, 1936.
14. From *Science*; Washington, D. C., May 24, 1940.
15. A broadcast recording for the Science Conference; London, September 28, 1941, and published in *Advancement of Science*; London, Vol. 2, no. 5.

465

16. From *Relativity—A Richer Truth* by Philipp Frank; published by the Beacon Press, Boston, 1950.
17. From *Technion Journal*; New York, 1946.
18. From *Monthly Review*; New York, May, 1949.
19. From *Pageant*; New York, January, 1946.
20. From *Science*; Washington, D. C., Winter issue, 1935–36. (Translation prepared by Heinz and Ruth Norden.)
21. From a broadcast over ABC to the Rally of Students for Federal World Government; Chicago, May 24, 1946.

22. From *One World or None*, edited by Katherine Way and Dexter Masters; Whittlesey House, New York, 1946.
23. From the address delivered at Carnegie Hall, New York, upon receiving the One World Award, April 27, 1948.

24. From a speech delivered in Albert Hall, London, October, 1933.

25. From the message to the Peace Congress of Intellectuals in Wroclav. (This message was never delivered, but was released to the press on August 29, 1948.)
26. From *United Nations World*; New York, October, 1947.
27. From Moscow *New Times*, November 26, 1947; and from *Bulletin of the Atomic Scientists*; Chicago, February, 1948.
28. From a statement to the National Wartime Conference, 1944.

29. From *The Nation*; New York, October 3, 1934.
30. Written in 1936 for a gathering of university teachers which never took place.
31. From *Atlantic Monthly*; Boston, November, 1945 and November, 1947. As told to Raymond Swing.
32. From an address at the Fifth Nobel Anniversary Dinner at the Hotel Astor, New York, December 10, 1945.

33. From an address at the second annual dinner given by the Foreign Press Association to the General Assembly and Security Council of the United Nations, at the Waldorf-Astoria Hotel, New York, November 11, 1947.
34. From an address delivered at the Conference of the Progressive Education Association, November 23, 1934.

35. From *Policy*; Chicago, November 27, 1934.
36. From *The American Scholar*; New York, Summer, 1947.
37. From an address to the students of the California Institute of Technology, January 22, 1933.
38. From *The Manchester Guardian*; Manchester, England, Christmas, 1942.

39. Preface to *Johannes Kepler's Letters* edited by Mrs. David Baum-gardt.

40. Statement on the occasion of the Curie Memorial Celebration at the Roerich Museum, New York, November 23, 1935.

41. Statement read at the Memorial Services for Max Planck, April, 1948.

42. From *La Pensee*; Paris, February–March, 1947.

43. From *The Scientific Monthly*; Washington, D. C., Vol. LIV, February, 1942.

44. From *Almanak van het Leidsche Studentencorps* published by S. C. Doesburg Verlag, Leiden, Holland; 1934.

45. Statement on the occasion of Mahatma Gandhi's 75th birthday, 1944.

46. Statement read at the Nobel Foundation Dinner, December 10, 1946.

47. From *Collier's*; New York, November 26, 1938.

48. From an address over the Columbia Broadcasting System for the United Jewish Appeal, March 22, 1939.

49. Written in 1934.

50. Unpublished preface to a Black Book. Written in 1945.

51. From a broadcast for the United Jewish Appeal, April 11, 1943.

52. From an address delivered at the "Third Seder" celebration of the National Labor Committee for Palestine, at the Commodore Hotel, New York, April 17, 1938, and published in *New Palestine*; Washington, D. C., April 29, 1938.

53. From *Bulletin of the Society of Polish Jews*; New York, 1944.

54. From a statement read at the unveiling of the Memorial for the Battle of the Warsaw Ghetto; Warsaw, April 19, 1948.

55. From an address to the Jewish Academy of Sciences and Arts; March 22, 1936.

56. From a statement read at the Maimonides Jubilee Celebration, New York, April, 1935. (Translation prepared by Heinz and Ruth Norden.)

57. From *Opinion*; New York, March, 1949.

58. Statement to the Hebrew University in Jerusalem, Israel, on March 15, 1949.

59. From a letter to the Committee on Unity for Palestine, New York, 1945.

60. From a broadcast for the United Jewish Appeal, over the National Broadcasting Company, November 27, 1949.

Index

Mercury
orbit of, 115, 143-145
perihelion of, 143-145
Mercury barometer, 157
Michelson, A.A., 58-59, 60
Michelson-Morley experiment, 58,
167-168
Mill, J. St., 266
Minkowski, H., 61-63, 101-102, 140
Minkowski-space, 171, 174, 177
Morley, E.W., 59, 60 (see Michelson-
Morley experiment)
Moses, 196, 437
Motion
of co-ordinate systems, 13-14
curvilinear, 83
definition of, 10-12
of earth, 18, 57-58
of heavenly bodies, 13,16-17
law of, 44, 57
of liquids, 165
Newton's law of, 73, 155
non-uniform, 70, 79
relative, 11, 67-68
uniform translation, 15-16

N

Nernst, Walther, 421, 422, 423
Newcomb, S., 144
Newton, Isaac, 81, 230, 233, 242, 243,
244, 245, 258, 259, 260, 261, 262,
263, 264, 265, 268, 270, 288, 290,
291, 292, 293, 294, 337, 407, 408,
409, 410
Newtonian mechanics, 13-14, 114,
119-121, 142-145
law of gravitation, 53
law of motion, 73, 155
space and time in, 164-165
Nobel, Alfred, 388
Non-Euclidean continuum, 94, 95,
99-100
Non-Euclidean geometry, 122
Nuclear transformation processes, 54

O

Optics, 16, 23, 49
Orbits, elliptical, 115, 143-145
Ossietzky, 429
Ostwald, 421

P

Parabola, 10, 11
Pasteur, 337
Path-curve, 11
Pauli, 272
Perihelion of Mercury, 143-145
Physics, 162, 163, 165-166
system of co-ordinates in, 9
and time, 27-28, 31, 62, 169-170
Place specifications, 7
Planck, Max, 273, 294, 295, 417, 422,
425
Planets, orbits of, 114-115, 143-145
Plato, 340
Poincare, H., 122, 253
Points
co-ordinates of, 105-106
in three dimensions, 61
Position, concept of, 7-8, 10
Principle of equivalence, 172, 175
Principle of relativity (see General
theory of relativity; Special theory
of relativity)
Pythagorean theorem, 174

Q

Quantum theory, 178
Quasi-Euclidean universe, 129
Quasi-spherical universe, 129

R

Radiation, 51-52
Radioactive substances, 54, 55
Recollections, 159-160
Red shift (spectral), 56, 116, 149-151,
153
Reference-bodies, 6-8, 9
equivalence of, 68
Galileian, 68-69, 109